MIXED FEELINGS

Mixed Feelings

Feminism, Mass Culture,
and Victorian Sensationalism

ANN CVETKOVICH

 RUTGERS UNIVERSITY PRESS

New Brunswick, New Jersey

An earlier version of chapter four, "Ghostlier Determinations: The Economy of Sensa-tion and The Woman in White," *appeared in* Novel *23 (Fall 1989): 24–43.*

Library of Congress Cataloging-in-Publication Data
Cvetkovich, Ann, 1957–
    Mixed feelings: feminism, mass culture, and Victorian
sensationalism / Ann Cvetkovich.
        p.   cm.
    Includes bibliographical references and index.
    ISBN 0-8135-1856-3 (cloth).—ISBN 0-8135-1857-1 (pbk.)
    1. English fiction—19th century—History and criticism.
    2. Feminism and literature—Great Britain—History—19th   century.
    3. Women and literature—Great Britain—History—19th century.
    4. Great Britain—Popular culture—History—19th century.
    5. Sensationalism in literature. I. Title.
PR878.F45C85 1992
823'.809352042—dc20   92–4457
                                                                              CIP

British Cataloging-in-Publication information available.

*In memory
of Ann Elmore Haig-Brown*

CONTENTS

ACKNOWLEDGMENTS

This book began as a dissertation under the guidance of Harry Shaw, Jonathan Culler, and Dorothy Mermin, for whose contributions in the early stages of this project I remain grateful. A Charlotte Newcombe Fellowship from the Woodrow Wilson Foundation helped me finish my dissertation. As a graduate student at Cornell, I was able to immerse myself in the theoretical discourses—poststructuralist, Foucauldian, psychoanalytic, feminist, and Marxist—that underlie the book's more specific concerns, and I am grateful for the inspiration provided by Cynthia Chase, Walter Cohen, Neil Hertz, Mark Seltzer, Jim Siegel, and Gayatri Spivak. Financial support for the crucial year during which my dissertation metamorphosed into a book came from the Andrew W. Mellon Foundation and the University of Texas Research Institute. I would like to thank my colleagues at Wesleyan University's Center for the Humanities, especially Dick Ohmann, the director, for providing such a pleasurable intellectual community. I was particularly fortunate during that year to work with Nancy Armstrong and Christina Crosby, to whom I am indebted for making Victorian culture important to me. Another source of institutional support, although a less formal one, has been the Marxist Literary Group's annual Institute on Culture and Society, which has given me an ideal forum for intellectual exchange and a network of valued friends. I especially want to thank Mark Driscoll, Patrick Hagopian, Tres Pyle, Hilary Radner, and Paul Smith. Among my colleagues at the University of Texas, Ramon Saldivar, Lisa Moore, and especially Barbara Harlow, have been dedicated comrades and friends. I owe special thanks to Leslie Mitchner at Rutgers University Press, whose early interest in my project and ongoing enthusiasm and insight have been invaluable.

I have consistently been struck by the apparent contradiction between this book's critical interrogation of the discourse of affect and the very real psychic pain that writing it so often produced. Without the emotional support of many friends, I would not have survived, much less written anything. Especially important were those who made academic work something other than the center of my life. I want to thank Radhika Balakrishnan, Joseph Fratesi, Sean Eve, David Gillcrist, Pat McKearn, Erin Obodiac, Kate Aurthur, Helen Knode, Chris Newfield, Rafael Allen, Kay Turner, and Ella Gant. Jeff Nunokawa's insights about the Victorian novel were matched by his insights about me. Vijay Balakrishnan catalyzed the emotional and creative energies without which my work would be of little consequence to me. And to my family, especially my mother, Valerie Haig-Brown, my grandmother, Ann Haig-Brown, and my aunt, Celia Haig-Brown, I owe thanks for unfailing faith.

In the final stages of writing, my work was often interrupted by the illness of my friends John Hernandez and Skip Fulton, both of whom died of AIDS in 1991. The day I sent off the final manuscript is also the last day I saw Skip alive; barely able to talk or move, but fully appreciating the significance of my accomplishment, he insisted that I describe the book to another friend. What I learned from him about emotion and politics, whether at ACT UP demonstrations or in hospital rooms, is incalculable and, if that work delayed this work, it also explained why it matters to think about the politics of affect. I also want to thank Gretchen Phillips for making closure imaginable by offering other passions.

I would not have finished this book without a group of women whose emotional support has been indistinguishable from their intellectual support. For listening sympathetically and responding critically, and for teaching me how to make intellectual work a part of everyday life, I thank Zofia Burr, Avery Gordon, Wahneema Lubiano, Adela Pinch, and Lora Romero.

MIXED FEELINGS

Introduction

The Politics of Affect

This book is the product of my own mixed feelings about a feminist politics of affect. The claim that the personal is political has been used to authorize the expression of feeling as the inspiration for or first step toward a social movement. The process of consciousness raising central to the feminist movement two decades ago was a response to the sense that an absence of outlets for the expression of rage and sadness not only prevented political action but constituted a form of oppression. Feminist cultural studies within the academy have been influenced by this strategy in its emphasis on personal narrative and individual voice, seeking to enable the articulation of female experience. Implicit in a feminist politics of affect is the assumption that the association of femininity with affect has led to the simultaneous devalorization of both.

There is a difference, however, between claiming that affect has a historical and political significance and claiming that affective expression is transgressive. The absence of a mass feminist movement suggests that the links between personal and social transformation are by no means guaranteed. At least as important as the potentially liberating effects of affective expression are the ways in which, within middle-class American culture in particular, a discourse about affect serves to contain resistance, especially from women. Rather than leading to social change, the expression of feeling can become an end in itself or an individualist solution to systemic problems. This containment strategy is particularly evident in the discourse of

popular psychology, which recommends the expression of feeling as therapeutic or blames the repression of anger and pain for women's psychic distress and social disempowerment. Often therapy becomes a substitute for
political action, a privatized and personalized solution to problems that are
ultimately social and collective. Furthermore, by pathologizing women's
suffering, pop psychology risks holding women themselves responsible for
their situations. The discourse of addiction, which has been extended to
include not just food and drugs but love, constructs desire and affective
bonds as personal rather than social diseases and seeks a cure in twelve-
step groups rather than restructured social relations. If most families are
dysfunctional, however, trying to cure the family through therapy may be
futile, although very effective for enforcing political docility. What needs to
be questioned is the very definition of normalcy. If the family by its very
nature produces suffering, then the problems pathologized as neurotic are
in fact social. Family troubles which are so often the subject of melodrama
and sensationalism, would be solved by social transformation, not therapy.
The intimate relation between the family and capitalism would have to be
examined, not in order to save or fix the family, but in order to change it
radically or eliminate it entirely. If the transformation of capitalism requires
the redistribution of property, then the transformation of the family might
involve a redistribution of affect, so that desire and affective relations would
not be so narrowly confined to the individual bonds between family
members.

The representation of social problems as affective dilemmas can be
traced to its origins in eighteenth- and nineteenth-century culture. This
book focuses more particularly on the 1860s and 1870s, the period in that
broader cultural history during which a discourse about "sensationalism"
became the vehicle for the politics of affect. In the sensation novels to be
considered in this book, the representation of the sensationalized woman
establishes the relation between femininity and affect crucial to the middle-
class domestic ideology that both grants and denies power to women.[1] A
feminist politics of affect that does not take into account the mutual dependence of female affect and middle-class hegemony runs the risk of too readily celebrating the subversive powers of affective expression. Whether she
expresses her feelings or must restrain them, the middle-class woman is in
any case constructed as a feeling individual. The ideological purposes
served by linking femininity and affect and by constructing individual subjectivity in terms of affective life need to be more adequately understood if
contemporary political agendas are to avoid merely replicating the social

structures they seek to alter. If nineteenth-century culture *constructed* the distinction between the personal and the political, then the contemporary claim that the personal is political does not mean that the personal as it currently exists is political. Rather, the political agenda must consist in re-aligning the relations between the private and public spheres, or in transforming the institutions that construct private life or personal experience as separate from public life. Often the personal is political precisely because it is constructed as not being political, and that separation cannot be wished away by an act of consciousness or analysis; it can only be altered by material and social transformation. Otherwise, practices designed to repoliticize the personal, such as consciousness-raising groups, remain only a symptom of the separation of public and private spheres, not a cure.

If the feminist movement of the last two decades has introduced affect to the political process, more recently AIDS activism has also made the claim that personal affective expression can lead to public political action. Whenever this project has made me skeptical about the progressive potential of affect, I have drawn inspiration and encouragement from the contemporary example of the political activism that has emerged to address the AIDS crisis. ACT UP (the AIDS Coalition to Unleash Power) represents the possibility that private experiences of grief and death can be transformed into collective action. ACT UP's mission statement declares the group to be "united in anger and committed to direct action to end the AIDS crisis," thus suggesting that feelings can form the basis for a political movement. AIDS activism assumes that the person with AIDS suffers from more than just a physical disease. It turns the personal grief and distress of those who are HIV positive or have AIDS, and those who have lost friends, lovers, and family members, into a collective grief and transforms collective grief into anger and action. For example, the Names Project Quilt literally joins the deaths of individuals into a collective death and the public display of the quilt makes possible a ritual of collective mourning.

In order for the battle against AIDS to become an organized collective struggle, however, the target of anger must shift from the biological fact of the disease to the social institutions and ideologies that hasten its course. Hence, ACT UP has directed its attention to the medical and governmental bureaucracies that have failed to provide treatment and funding, as well as to the ideologies of racism, sexism, and homophobia that underlie responses to the disease. Political activism is thus predicated on reconceptualizing individual deaths as the result of social processes. For example,

"Silence = Death," one of the slogans popularized by ACT UP, redefines death as a social rather than a literal fact, as an effect of being unable to speak rather than an effect of being literally unable to live. It is homophobia as much as AIDS that kills people, when those who are dying are morally condemned for their sexuality or when the already difficult process of being openly gay is exacerbated by illness. For the white middle-class gay men who are the majority of ACT UP's membership, the problem of AIDS has been inextricably tied to a gay liberation politics that fights against the silencing of sexual identity. The group thus links death from AIDS to the more subtle and indirect ways in which homophobia threatens the existence of gays and lesbians. The person with AIDS provides only one particularly tangible instance of the suffering created by a network of social relations whose effects may often be more difficult to perceive. ACT UP's ability to move from the medical to the social dimensions of AIDS has also made it attentive to the importance of coalition politics. The group has attempted to form coalitions across race, gender, and class lines and to attend to the particular problems confronted by groups such as women, lesbians, intravenous drug users, and people of color. In other words, ACT UP addresses the specific impact of AIDS on different social groups and analyzes how AIDS is a symptom of social problems for groups other than white middle-class gay men.

This linkage has not been without its controversies. In an article in *The Nation,* for example, Darrell Yates Rist argues that the gay community's investment in AIDS activism is evidence of a melancholy death wish that takes money and energy away from other political causes and issues that the gay community needs to consider. His views were contested by numerous respondents who argued that, far from shifting attention away from other kinds of gay and lesbian activism, AIDS activism had enabled both new forms of gay and lesbian politics and a refusal to submit to a deadly disease.[2] Even within ACT UP, there are constant debates about whether the group's attention to issues such as racism, reproductive rights, immigration laws, and even gay and lesbian politics detracts from its ability to focus on AIDS. The question often raised is what do these other issues have to do with AIDS ? The reply is that AIDS cannot be tackled simply by focusing on treatment and research, but that all of these struggles are connected.

AIDS activism analyzes the person with AIDS as a symptom of social problems. The texts that form the basis of this book construct the sensational spectacle of figures such as the female criminal, the silenced woman, or the suffering factory worker in order to call attention to problems such as women's inequality or capitalist exploitation. The battle against AIDS must direct itself not just at the immediate physical symptoms of illness but at the social structures that determine the reception and treatment of the disease. AIDS activism depends on the assumption that death from AIDS is a particularly extreme and poignant instance of the effects of socially produced inequities; the grief and anger provoked by death must also be aimed at the frequently less visible presence of structural violence. By the same token, if the sensational figures that Victorian texts render so compelling affectively are to be effective politically, those figures must be read as local symptoms of more general problems.

It is no easy task, however, to transform personal and emotional responses to concrete instances of suffering into political action. In the context of AIDS activism, the grief and anger generated by the life-and-death melodrama of AIDS must be focused on social problems that are both more and less intransigent than the health crisis—more intransigent because AIDS is the symptom of more widespread social problems. And less intransigent because those social problems may be amenable to transformation in a way that the disease itself is not. The tangible effects of AIDS provide a vehicle for addressing homophobia, racism, and attitudes towards sexuality and drug use, problems that not only aggravate the effects of AIDS but produce other forms of suffering as well. In reading how affect is represented in and produced by Victorian texts, it is important to attend to how the representation of local instances of suffering can both call attention to and obscure complex social relations, and can both inspire and displace social action. If AIDS is a symptom of other social problems, then curing AIDS alone is not sufficient to resolve those problems. At the same time, recognizing that AIDS is a social and not just a medical problem makes it possible to avoid the sentimental fatalism of declaring that nothing can be done. The politics of affect is double-edged; the representation of complex social relations in the form of affectively compelling local instances of suffering can make social problems seem both manageable and unsolvable.

ACT UP is also an instructive example of a political project that must direct itself not just toward generating affect, but also toward desensationalizing representations of AIDS. Representing AIDS as caused by promiscuity or sexual deviance provides society a convenient and sensationalized scapegoat.[3] AIDS activists have had to counteract these representations, challenging the attitudes toward homosexuality and drug use that lead to the depiction of people with AIDS as morally suspect individuals whose transgressive vices make them responsible for their own illnesses and dangerously capable of spreading it to other, "innocent" victims. AIDS activism thus has a double strategy, at once dramatically calling attention to the AIDS crisis and to those who have exacerbated it and shifting blame away from those whom a sensationalizing press would target.

One of the claims of this book is that the assumptions that affective expression forms the basis for political action and itself constitutes a political act derive from a nineteenth-century discourse that made affect meaningful. Central to the construction of middle-class hegemony in the nineteenth century was the gendered division between the private and public spheres and the assignment of women to the affective tasks of the household. A discourse about affect represented marriage and the family as the product of natural affective bonds and individual self-expression. The construction of affect as natural, however, also meant that it might be uncontrollable; the discourse of affect thus includes the apparently contradictory construction of affect as the source of both social stability and social instability. This contradiction is embodied in the figure of the middle-class woman, whose capacity for emotional expression at once exemplifies the domestic ideal and represents the threat of transgression.

In order to examine nineteenth-century discourses of affect, I have chosen to focus on the nineteenth-century sensation novel because of the important role of mass and popular culture in constructing the discourse of affect. I seek to explain how the sensational force of melodramatic narrative organizes affective life and to explore the politics of sensational representations and sensational response to those representations. Nineteenth-century constructions of the relations between affect and mass culture have left their mark on contemporary discourses.[4] It is still the case that popular culture is often dismissed as sensationalist, on the assumption that representations that exaggerate reality or create extreme, and hence false, emotional responses are aesthetically inferior, morally suspect, or politically retrograde. Such complaints come from both the left and the right, with the left tending to emphasize the political effects of mass culture and the right tending to emphasize its moral or aesthetic lapses. They are particularly likely to emerge in response to women's popular culture, where melodrama, sentimentality, sensationalism, and other forms of emotional excess are viewed with added suspicion because they are associated with femininity as well as popularity. At the same time, more favorable assessments of mass culture, whether from Marxists or feminists, often simply reverse the relation between affective intensity and political value, seeing the emotions produced by mass culture as evidence of transgressive impulses, as the germ of desire for social transformation, or as signs of dissatisfaction with oppressive social structures. Feminists in particular are inclined to question the link between mass culture's supposed sensationalism and its feminization, arguing that what seem like sensational representations might merely be a reality that cannot be acknowledged by the dominant culture or a fantasy necessitated by the impossibility of constructing realistic solutions to social problems.

The novels under consideration in this book participate in the discourse of affect by constructing the household and the women who occupy it as mysterious and compelling. The readers who are excited by the sensational lure of their mysteries are provided with experiences of affect that are ultimately regulated and controlled. The solution to the mysteries rationalizes intense affect and makes it safe. In the process of explaining the affective dilemmas of private life, the sensation novel performs the cultural work of representing social problems as affective problems and hence confirming the importance of emotional expression to middle-class life. The middle-class subject, and especially the middle-class woman, is constructed as a feeling subject.

How affect is generated and fixed, particularly in the figures of the mysterious woman and the suffering woman, is a major focus of this book, which contains readings of three of the most important sensation novels, Mary Elizabeth Braddon's *Lady Audley's Secret,* Wilkie Collins's *The Woman in White,* and Mrs. Henry Wood's *East Lynne,* and a high-culture novel that shows the influence of the sensation novel, George Eliot's *Daniel Deronda.* My aim is not to describe the social function of the sensation novel in terms of how it represents a history that takes place outside the text. Rather, the work of the novels is itself a part of Victorian history, and I trace the importance of the social construction of affect to nineteenth-century social formations. I am less interested in establishing historical truths about the nineteenth century than in uncovering nineteenth-century paradigms within contemporary theoretical and political frameworks. Twentieth-century theory makes it possible to historicize nineteenth-century ideology, and nineteenth-century ideology makes it possible to historicize twentieth-century theory. Theory and history thus exist in a necessary and productive tension with one another. In order to trace their mutual dependence, I shall explore the politics of affect in the nineteenth century, as manifest in the sensation novel and discussions about it in Chapter 1 and examine the politics of affect in the twentieth century as manifest in theories of mass culture in Chapter 2, in which I not only outline the theoretical paradigms that underlie the readings of the novels, but suggest how such theories are implicated in, and not just descriptive of, the politics and history of affect.

Following this theoretical opening, I shall explore, through readings of the novels, the specific mechanisms of the narrative construction of affect. In the chapters on *Lady Audley's Secret* and *the Woman in White* I focus on the figure of the mysterious woman and on the affective power of secrets. The affect generated by the mysterious woman incites the process of investigation that reveals secrets and hidden crimes. In the unraveling of these mysteries, less tangible secrets and crimes can be forgotten in the thrill that comes with discovering a real secret. At issue is the question of whether the figure of the mystery woman, especially when she is represented as criminal or transgressive, provides the terms for resistance.

The possibility of reading the mad, criminal, or mysterious woman as a figure for resistance must be qualified by an analysis of the functions served by the affect she produces, particularly for the men who investigate her mystery. The sensationalized female figures of *Lady Audley's Secret* and *The Woman in White* are accompanied by their counterparts, the male detectives who seek to explore their secrets. Tracing the affective attraction of these male characters to the women who so powerfully lure them on reveals a different version of the politics of affect; through their investigation of female secrets, both Robert Audley and Walter Hartright assume positions of power. The feminized or sensitive man consolidates his position all the more firmly because of the invisibility of his aspirations, which appear in the guise of a nervous reluctance to assert control. In these narratives of masculine affect, it is evident that the discourse of affect enables a covert form of domination. To follow Michel Foucault, it is power as discipline rather than power as punishment, a power all the more effective because it appears as a feminized susceptibility to affect rather than as overt control.

In chapters on *East Lynne* and *Daniel Deronda,* I focus on the sensational figure of the suffering woman, the politics of melodrama, and the relations between visible physical pain and invisible psychic or emotional pain. Whereas the sensation narratives about the mystery woman are problematic because they also introduce the male figures who expose and contain these woman, the narratives about suffering women are problematic in so far as they invent rather than discover psychic pain. In *East Lynne* and in *Daniel Deronda,* which borrows from the sensation novel in order to make a melodrama of interiority, the sensationalizing of the silenced woman is at its most powerful. The drama in these novels turns on the spectacle of the middle-class woman who not only cannot act to relieve her misery but cannot articulate her feelings of pain. This scenario enables the fantasy that the expression of affect alone would constitute a solution to her dilemma. In George Eliot's novel, the silencing of Gwendolen Harleth by her husband Grandcourt provides the groundwork for a politics of sympathy, represented by Daniel Deronda's role as the recipient of Gwendolen's confessions of guilt and anguish. Yet, like the investigations by the sensitive men of *Lady Audley's Secret* and *The Woman in White,* Daniel's scrutiny of Gwendolen's hidden life constitutes a form of power that replicates, rather than alters, the structures that confined her in the first place.

One of the central questions raised by this book is the political significance of psychic pain, particularly as a means of diagnosing the status of the middle-class woman. It can be argued that the middle-class woman's oppression takes the form of psychic disturbance rather than material deprivation, manifesting itself as anxiety, hysteria, depression, or madness. As both Foucault's work and feminist critiques of psychoanalysis suggest, such diagnoses are often not "real" but produced as a means of both containing women and managing other social problems through the scapegoating of women's sexuality and affect. At the same time, to the extent that psychic pain is a real problem for middle-class women, it may be a problem that cannot be alleviated by private or individual solutions such as the expression of feeling or the work of therapy. Psychic pain is thus at once real and not real, and it is also peculiar because it is not visible in the way that physical pain is. Psychic pain provides evidence of the effects of disciplinary rather than overt power; the middle-class woman provides a central example of how power operates in covert ways by producing particular kinds of subjectivity. A political agenda that would address or transform this application of power would be difficult to formulate.

The relation between *East Lynne* and *Daniel Deronda* is also important because it suggests the ties between the sensation novel and the high-culture novel. The links between Eliot's ethics of sympathy and the sensation novel suggest that what has often been called her psychological realism might more accurately be called her psychological melodrama or sensationalism. Eliot appropriates the emotional power of popular novels (despite her avowed disdain for silly novels by lady novelists) in order to turn affect into moral sentiment rather than pleasure or entertainment. She sensationalizes the interior self, however, rather than external events; Gwendolen, for example, only fantasizes about killing her husband rather than actually doing it. In highlighting the drama of the inner life, she seeks to render the invisible visible, to make the middle-class woman's psychic pain as "real" as more overt forms of suffering. Eliot's appropriation of popular culture's affective power for high culture resembles the efforts of Marxist and feminist critics of mass culture to see in popular culture the "raw material of social change." The same difficulty that contemporary critics face, the problem of how to turn private or personal emotions into political action, is one that Eliot confronts in constructing an ideology of sympathy. That Eliot's ethical project is suspect, that in it affect is a means by which women are dominated, as well as that which underwrites the nationalist and colonialist impulses of Daniel's Zionist mission, suggests that nineteenth-century culture might contain important lessons for contemporary cultural critics.

What a reading of the politics of affect in these Victorian novels reveals is that the expression of affect is as much a way to dominate as it is a way to resist domination. The production of scenarios of repressed or silenced affect gives rise to strategies of containment that do not appear as such because they operate within a discursive field in which affect is constructed as natural and indubitable. Furthermore, by formulating the middle-class woman's suffering as a function of her silenced affects, these novels propose individualist solutions to what are in fact intransigent social problems. The structures of bourgeois social life, which create a private domestic sphere, are reinforced rather than challenged by the intimate scrutiny of the internal landscape of women's lives. George Eliot's claims for the importance of the invisible drama of female interiority lead her to sensationalize what might otherwise appear to be the mundane details of everyday life, but this strategy remains symptomatic of the social divisions it purports to address.

If the sensation novel can only focus on the emotional symptoms of capitalist culture, what other forms of narrative might provide a more comprehensive account of the social structures that create those symptoms? It is with this question in mind that, in the final chapter, I turn to Karl Marx's *Capital,* a text of the same milieu as the sensation novel but one that turns its attention to the plight of the male laborer rather than the middle-class woman.

Just as Eliot uses sensationalism to produce high-culture fiction and a self-conscious political and ethical agenda, so too Marx uses sensationalism to unveil the exploitation of the worker and the logic of capital. *Capital* is a sensational melodrama, in which the worker is the victim and the capitalist is the villain. *Capital* provides a particularly good instance of how sensationalism might be used for progressive purposes, and of how it might be applied to masculine subjects and domains.

Because of the centrality of Marxist methods to my analysis of the sensation novel, it seems especially important to return to the text that generated those methods, especially since Marx is describing the same industrial capitalist culture that gave rise to the sensation novel. In light of Foucauldian and feminist critiques of Marx, which are also at issue in this book, it is important not to consider *Capital* a master text. It is necessary to question Marx's privileging of the factory and the worker over the home and the middle-class woman and to question the extent to which he focuses on overt exploitation to the exclusion of disciplinary power. Marx's text provides an opportunity to consider the political economy of affect, to determine how the emotional and domestic conflicts of the sensation novel are related to the mechanisms of capitalist production and industrialization. Juxtaposing the two narratives makes it possible to consider how the figure of the middle-class woman and her suffering serves not simply as a drama about women, but as a vehicle for the representation of more pervasive forms of social suffering. The gendering of that pain as female and the sensation novel's emphasis on psychic pain stands in contrast to Marx's emphasis on the physical exploitation of workers in the factory and the construction of the relation between capital and labor as the explanatory narrative for capitalist culture.

Despite their differences, however, both Marx and the Victorian novelists use sensationalism. Marx's narrative is itself sensational, emphasizing the fetishistic appeal of the commodity and slowly unveiling the secret of the worker's labor and the extraction of surplus value. Understood as a representational strategy, Marx's sensationalism is not necessarily any more effective in revealing the truth about capitalism than the sensation novel. The worker's physical exploitation is only one sensational symptom of the effects of a system of social relations that turns surplus value into capitalist profit. Just as the commodity's meaning or value must not be fetishized as intrinsic to it, so too must the effects of industrial production on the worker's body be understood as the embodiment of a system of relations of which it remains only one materially visible or sensational site. Reading the sensation novel within the context of Marx's framework for analyzing the material symptoms of social processes, we could say that the sensationalized figure of the woman, no less than the fetishized commodity, has a secret. That secret is not a tangible or sensational entity, however; rather, it consists of an analysis of the social relations that connect the suffering or sensational middle-class woman to the suffering worker. That story is told as much by the sensation novel as by *Capital*.

One

Marketing Affect: The Nineteenth-Century Sensation Novel

The appearance of the Victorian sensation novel in the 1860s marks the moment at which sensations became sensational. Whereas the use of the term "sensation" to refer to perceptions originates in the 1600s as part of the ideology of empiricism, the sensation novel prompted a less neutral use of the term to refer to literature whose aim was to produce "an excited or violent feeling" (OED). The "sensational" became an aesthetically, morally, and politically loaded term used to dismiss both particular kinds of representations and the affective responses they produce.

In exploring the politics of sensationalism and affect, I presume that the process of naming and assigning social and cultural meanings to bodily responses, such as "sensations," has a history. My project is thus part of the larger enterprise of producing a history of the body and of physiological experiences such as affect and sexuality. Recent scholarship in this area has been profoundly revisionist because it has provided histories of phenomena that had previously been considered natural or outside the work of culture. The importance of Foucault's work on the history of sexuality, for example, resides not just in its specific details, but in its claim that sexuality *has* a history and is not a natural or prediscursive entity.[1] Tracing the cultural construction of the body or sexuality has revealed how ideologies are naturalized by the often invisible work of attaching meanings to physical processes. I have studied the sensation novel and the politics of sensation in order to participate in this broader project of exploring the political consequences of constructing the body, sexuality, and affect as "natural." Thus, I am less interested in offering a descriptive history of the sensation novel than in considering how a discourse about the "sensational" or affective serves as a vehicle for the promulgation of ideologies of gender and mass culture. And I have found in Victorian criticism of the sensation novel an opportunity to examine how and why "sensationalism" acquired its new meaning and a bad reputation. What I have uncovered points to a more general theory of the politics of sensationalism.

The Advent of the Sensation Novel

The sensation novel, the fad genre of the 1860s, was primarily characterized in terms of its capacity to shock, excite, and move audiences. Victorian critics decried the genre with a discourse about affect and sensationalism that is perhaps unequaled in its vehemence. Deemed by one reviewer "a virus spreading in all directions," the sensation novel acquires its name not only because of its melodramatic focus on crime and sex or because of its capacity to "preach to the nerves," but because of its enormous popularity.[2] "A novel comes out which 'makes a sensation,' and 'has a run'; that is to say, it goes through a number of editions—large and small—and serves as a fertile topic of conversation for the whole novel-reading population of Great Britain and Ireland for some weeks at a time."[3] Regardless of whether they liked them or not, the Victorian critics were forced to speak about this new literary phenomenon because sensation novels were everywhere, produced and consumed in such vast numbers that their appeal demanded explanation. The genre that depends so heavily on secrets and suspense itself becomes something of a mystery: why is literature that seems to have no redeeming aesthetic qualities so successful? Describing himself as "haunted" by "mysterious publications," Wilkie Collins postulates the existence of an "unknown public" eagerly consuming reading material whose attraction is to him incomprehensible.[4] Another puzzled critic describes *East Lynne* as the book "which some inscrutable breath of popular liking has blown into momentary celebrity."[5] No longer able to confine themselves to questions of aesthetic value, the reviewers had to explain public tastes that threatened to render their own opinions irrelevant.

Aside from having been dubbed with a name that gives it notoriety, the sensation novel is not really a distinct genre. Rather it resembles other popular and mass-produced subgenres of the novel that appeared during the rise of capitalism. A popular literature, whose respectability was continually a subject of debate, began to flourish in the eighteenth century, once the technology and reading public was available to create a mass publishing industry. Despite their differences, genres such as the Gothic novel, the sentimental novel, the novel of sensibility, the Newgate novel, the domestic novel, and the detective novel are similar to the sensation novel in their ability to produce affect, and it was often their affective power that attracted critical attention. From the moment of its appearance in England in the eighteenth century, the novel had to struggle to achieve respectability as a form of high culture, a process which was the subject of intense debate by the middle of the nineteenth century, and which ultimately culminated by the end of the century in the splitting of the novel into a high-culture form and a series of popular or mass-produced subgenres that continue to exist today.[6] It is difficult to chronicle an accurate history of this process because much of the contemporary scholarship takes for granted the aesthetic distinction between high and low culture made by the Victorians. Many critics of the novel have implicitly or explicitly separated canonical authors, such as Richardson, Austen, Dickens, and Eliot, from the popular novels that influenced them and along side of which their work was read, in the interest of constructing a high-culture novel tradition. Popular genres, such as the sensation novel, are consigned to second-rate status through a process that often replicates nineteenth-century discourses suspicious of working-class readers, female audiences, and affectively powerful or nonrealist literature.

The Critical Response to the Sensation Novel

The Victorian critical response to the sensation novel is a useful index to the ideologies that construct and are constructed by the distinction between high and mass culture, and it provides an important case history of the mechanisms by which aesthetic distinctions mask moral and political ones. As defined by the Victorian critics, the term "sensation novel" refers more to the genre's status as mass culture than to its particular narrative style or content. Thus, histories of the sensation novel that assume it to be a distinct subgenre and attempt to explain or define it in terms of its plot are limited in scope.[7] The sensation novel was specifically the target of attack because it represented the entry into middle-class publishing institutions of the sensationalism that characterized the working-class literature of the preceding decades, such as G. W. M. Reynolds's *Mysteries of London,* and the stage melodrama.[8] The popular entertainment of the 1840s was received within the context of class tensions, specifically the Chartist movement, produced by the industrial revolution, and the moral denigration of such literature was often a thinly disguised attack on its potential political subversiveness. The hostility that critics of the sensation novel directed toward the genre is part of a longer history of attacks on popular culture, attacks in which a discourse about affect and gender figures prominently.

Rather that directly attacking mass culture's political effects, however, nineteenth-century critics often focused instead on its aesthetic flaws, which they attributed to mass production and commodification. Concerns about the novel's popularity among audiences who, prior to the eighteenth century, might not have had access to the printed word at all (either because they couldn't afford books or because they couldn't read them) became even more pronounced in the wake of the industrial revolution's impact on cultural production. The sensation novel's popularity was in part made possible by changes in the conditions of publishing that consolidated the genre's status as a form of mass culture: "One of the chief causes of this perverted and vitiated taste may be traced to the fact, that nearly every novel is first brought out in the pages of some periodical magazine."[9] Although circulating libraries and serial publication were already prevalent in the eighteenth century, between 1820 and 1860 there was a massive rise in the number of periodicals that published novels in serial form. The price of these publications, as well as the price of novels issued in book form, dropped considerably, making it possible for the reading material aimed at various different classes to sell in far greater numbers.[10] The spectacular success of Dickens's novels, beginning with the serial publication of *The Pickwick Papers* in 1836, demonstrated that cultural production could be a profitable endeavor; however, the critics worried about the effects of mass publication on literary quality. Sensationalism had flourished among publications for the lower classes, which included cheap reprints of Gothic fiction, crime reports, and melodrama. A taste for such literature now seemed to have invaded more respectable spheres, and the extraordinary success of the sensation novel compelled the critics to distinguish between popularity and literary value. As one critic put it, in remarks concerning the author of *Lady Audley's Secret*: "If the test of genius were success, we should rank Miss Braddon very high in the list of our great novelists. . . . By the unthinking crowd she is regarding as a woman of genius. The magazine to which she contributes is almost certain to have a large circulation, and to enrich its fortunate proprietors. She has bewitched so many persons that those who have the misfortune to be blind to her charms have had small chance of being listened to when pronouncing an adverse judgment.[11] Braddon is here figured as though she were one of the unscrupulous heroines of her novels, capable of "bewitching" the public into admiring her clever, but morally suspect, productions. Faced with her success, the critic had to declare genius to be measured in other terms than the judgment of the "unthinking crowd."

The term "sensation novel" thus functioned as a label for literature perceived to be aesthetically inferior, and by implication morally questionable, and whose popularity thus caused concern about the status of both culture and society. Fear that sensation novels were destroying the market for novels of greater aesthetic merit pervades the reviews:

> Sensationalism must be left to be dealt with by time, and the improvement of the public taste. But it is worthwhile stopping to note, amidst all the boasted improvement of the nineteenth century, that whilst Miss Braddon's and Mr. Wilkie Collins' productions sell by thousands of copies, "Romola" with difficulty reaches a second edition.[12]

> Mr. Trollope's charming girls do not . . . call forth half so much notice from the press as do the Aurora Floyds of contemporary fiction. . . . Though they seem to flourish side by side, and though the public, according to such evidence as can be obtained on the subject, seems to throw itself with more apparent eagerness upon the hectic than upon the wholesome, still we cannot but hope that Mr. Anthony Trollope has in reality a larger mass of readers than Miss Braddon.[13]

Trollope and Eliot are placed in a different class from Collins, Braddon, and Wood, and the sensation novel is presented as a direct challenge to the success of the novel as a form of high culture. Rather than accepting that different novels might serve different audiences and purposes, the critics hoped to see the works they deemed to have aesthetic merit achieve the sensation novel's popularity. In defining the sensation novel as inferior or second-rate fiction, the critics constructed the category of a high-culture novel whose moral mission was to displace the popular forms that were entertaining and corrupting the mass reading public.

Victorian responses to the sensation novel's popularity also indicated concern about literature's status as a commodity. Wilkie Collins described the ubiquity of popular novels as follows:

> Day after day, and week after week, the mysterious publications haunted my walks, go where I might.... There they were in every town, large or small. I saw them in fruit-shops, in oyster-shops, in cigar-shops, in lozenge-shops.... Wherever the speculative daring of one man could open a shop, and the human appetites and necessities of his fellow-mortals could keep it from shutting up again— there, as it appeared to me, the unbound picture-quarto instantly entered, set itself up obtrusively in the window, and insisted on being looked at by everybody. "Buy me, borrow me, stare at me, steal me. Oh, inattentive stranger, do anything but pass me by!"[14]

Sold in the company of fruit, oysters, cigars, and lozenges, the book that says, "Buy me, borrow me, stare at me, steal me," is not asking to be read but to be acquired. Collins's description of how the popular novel was displayed to appeal to the consumer's gaze also suggests that the sensation novel's success owed much to the rise of consumer culture in the Victorian period. Its mid-century appearance coincided with the introduction of the department store and other marketing tactics designed to make consumption easier and more attractive.[15] The sensation novel also made its mark at about the same time as W. H. Smith and Sons and other companies introduced railway bookstalls and cheap editions designed for light travel reading. The sensation novel's lack of artistic value was attributed to its production by an industry concerned only with economic value: "No divine influence can be imagined as presiding over the birth of his [the sensation novelist's] work, beyond the market-law of demand and supply; no more immortality is dreamed of for it than for the fashions of the current season. A commercial atmosphere floats around works of this class, redolent of the manufactory and the shop. The public wants novels, and novels must be made—so many yards of printed stuff, sensation-pattern, to be ready by the beginning of the season."[16]

Literary production should be free of the "commercial atmosphere" of the "manufactory and the shop," a special sphere in which the "market-law of supply and demand" should not be what determines the substance or distribution of the object. When produced as commodities, novels become "yards of printed stuff" churned out according to a single pattern that deprives them of any individual specificity. Aesthetic value and market value are at odds, because the cycle of production and consumption requires new fads and fashions each season in order to ensure constant sales, whereas culture should aim for "immortality." One concerned critic even suggested that only novels that are at least twenty years old and have thus stood the test of time should be allowed in the circulating libraries.[17] With the rise of mass culture comes a form of consumption antithetical to traditional aesthetic values; works are to be read and then discarded, replaced by the next season's fad. The progress represented by the expansion of the publishing industry marks a decline in the history of culture. The success of the novel has to be told as a counternarrative to the Victorian belief in perpetual progress:

> At no age, so far as we are aware, has there yet existed anything resembling the extraordinary flood of novels which is now pouring over this land—certainly with fertilising results, so far as the manufacture itself is concerned. There were days, halcyon days—as one still may ascertain from the gossip of the seniors of society—when an author was a natural curiosity, recognized and stared at as became the rarity of the phenomenon. No such thing is possible nowadays, when most people have been in print one way or other—when stains of ink linger on the prettiest of fingers, and to write novels is the normal condition of a large section of society.[18]

The "halcyon days" in which the author was a privileged member of society are gone. The phrase "prettiest of fingers" suggests that cultural production is no longer the domain of an elite minority because large numbers of women have taken up writing. The critic, Mrs. Oliphant, herself a novelist, was perhaps anxious that the sensation novel not be taken as representative of what women writers are capable of producing, and furthermore that the presence of women authors not be seen as simply the result of marketplace demand.

Victorian Critics and the Discourse of Affect

Prominent in the Victorian critics' attempts to explain the appeal of the sensation novel were their fears about the dangerous affects that such literature produces. Explaining why sensational fiction sold so well, one critic claimed: "Excitement, and excitement alone, seems to be the great end at which they [sensation novels] aim—an end which must be accomplished at any cost."[19] Not only was a discourse about affect crucial to Victorian constructions of the differences between good and bad literature, but these judgments of aesthetic value were often the covert means by which high culture was distinguished from an increasingly visible mass culture. The critics repeatedly emphasized the emotional state produced by the sensation novel, the form that "preaches to the nerves," rather than the content of the novels themselves.[20] Sensational content was simply the vehicle for sensational affect: "Sensational stories were tales aimed at this effect simply—of exciting in the mind some deep feeling of overwrought interest by the means of some terrible passion or crime."[21] Even when critics emphasized the immorality of the events, such as murder or adultery, that moved sensation novel readers, they seemed especially concerned about the immorality of feeling itself, taking it as a sign of an absence of control or rationality. As the term "sensation" novel itself suggests, the critics feared the prospect of a reader reduced to a body reacting instinctively to a text. The attraction to sensation was constantly referred to as an "appetite" or "craving," and the critics were concerned that cultural experience had descended to the level of base natural functions: "There is something unspeakably disgusting in this ravenous appetite for carrion, this vulture-like instinct which smells out the newest mass of social corruption, and hurries to devour the loathsome dainty before the scent has evaporated."[22] According to this discourse, the sensation novel is deplorable because it reduces its readers to the condition of animals who are driven by instincts. The publishing industry stimulates demand by creating a need that resembles an "appetite," but the inappropriateness of the model of eating to describe cultural consumption means that satisfying that appetite is a form of addiction or perversion.

The Victorian critics explained the attractions of reading sensation fiction in terms that resemble those of twentieth-century explanations of mass culture's appeal. H. L. Mansel, for example, suggested the functional relation between life in an industrial and urbanized society and leisure reading: "The exigencies of railway travelling do not allow much time for examining the merits of a book before purchasing it; and keepers of bookstalls, as well as of refreshment rooms, find an advantage in offering their customers something hot and strong, something that may catch the eye of the hurried passenger, and promise temporary excitement to relieve the dullness of a journey."[23] Here we are given what amounts to a materialist analysis of the role of culture; in an era of rapid travel, quick-fix amusements are necessary, and the "hot and strong" content of the novels acts as an advertising come-on to "catch the eye" of the consumer. In a similar account, the sensation novel was likened to a drug that soothed the mind, an argument reminiscent of more recent theories about mass culture's capacity to relieve anxieties: "They are recommended, moreover, as good stimulants in these days of toil and worry, and as well fitted for relieving overtaxed brains by diverting our thoughts from the absorbing occupations of daily life."[24] Capitalism and the body are connected in so far as stimulating the nerves is a way of stimulating exchange. The reader's body becomes a machine hooked into the circuit of production and consumption, rather than a disinterested entity floating above economic exigencies in search of aesthetic or moral truth. In the following passage, the word "stimulant" is also used to describe the process of production rather than the action on the body: "The violent stimulant of serial publication—of *weekly* publication, with its necessity for frequent and rapid recurrence of piquant situation and startling incident—is the thing of all others most likely to develop the germ, and bring it to fuller and darker bearing." [25] The reader's body reproduces the logic of capital, responding obligingly to the "frequent and rapid recurrence" of sensational episodes in order to keep the wheels of production rolling. As George Henry Lewes says of the "exciting" situations and "breathless rapidity of movement" that mark the sensation novel: "Whether the movement be absurd or not matters little, the essential thing is to keep moving." [26] There is a slippage here between what is in the novels and what they produce; the content has the effect of "exciting" the reader, and what keeps moving is as much the reader's nerves as the novel's plot. Thus, a similar slippage is possible between bodily and economic activity, as indicated by how the term "sensation" was used to describe the content of the novels, the affects they produced, *and* the sales they achieved.

The plots of sensation novels were declared to be merely vehicles to sustain the reader's interest so that constant and rapid consumption would be guaranteed. Grappling with the problem of describing the fascination of the "page-turner," the critics assumed that there is something cheap about a novel whose content is subsumed to the task of producing a constant level of interest, and vulgar about an audience that values the emotional state reading produces, rather than the object that produces it. The reader becomes passive in the face of the violent mechanics of the novel, "compelled to go on to the end, whether he likes it or not." [27] Although the reviews contain moralizing objections to the fact that sex and crime seem most easily to arouse attention, the real target of criticism seemed to be an experience of reading that is purely affective. "Violent and illegitimate means," in the opinions of the critics, were used to create "arbitrary sensations"; realism was invoked as a value in order to decry the incidents that create sensation as false. Characters such as Lady Audley or Isabel Vane were declared untrue to life; authors were accused of making bigamy, adultery, murder, and vice seem rampant.

The critics' discourse also demonstrates the connections between sensation and gender that lead twentieth-century feminist critics, such as

Elaine Showalter and Nina Auerbach, to emphasize the importance of the genre as a forum for women authors to depict the condition of women. Lurking behind the descriptions of the biological nature of the response to sensational fiction is the suggestion that this form of arousal is closely akin to sexual excitement. As D. A. Miller has pointed out, descriptions of the body's reaction to sensation fiction resemble descriptions of the hysterical woman;[28] one way to disavow or scapegoat sensation is to deem it the province of the feminine. For the critics, one of the most distressing aspects of the sensation novel's focus on sexuality was its depiction of women who transgress social conventions. Lady Audley, for example, "is at once the heroine and the monstrosity" of *Lady Audley's Secret*. The following critic deplored how the sensation novel represented women as sexual beings:

> What is held up to us as the story of the feminine soul as it really exists underneath its conventional coverings, is a very fleshly and unlovely record. Women driven wild with love . . . in fits of sensual passion . . . who give and receive burning kisses and frantic embraces. . . . She waits now for flesh and muscles, for strong arms that seize her, and warm breath that thrills her through, and a host of other physical attractions. . . . The peculiarity of it in England is that it is oftenest made from the woman's side—that it is women who describe those sensuous raptures—that this intense appreciation of flesh and blood, this eagerness of physical sensation, is represented as the natural sentiment of English girls.[29]

The bodily sensations the critics deplored in the sensation novel received additional censure when they were connected to female sexuality.

Underlying the critics' discourse about sensation fiction are the assumptions that body and emotion are distinct from and inferior to mind and reason and that culture should make its appeal to the "higher" faculties. The construction of mass culture as primarily appealing to feeling rather than reason underwrites the dismissal of it as aesthetically inferior. Affect also figures prominently in the moral panic that pervades such aesthetic pronouncements. Feelings and emotions, like sexuality, are construed as "natural" and, hence, uncivilized and irrational. Bad art appeals to the emotions, and aroused emotions are dangerous because they prompt people to behave immorally. This ethical discourse also frequently masks a political discourse, enabling the disparagement of cultural forms that appealed to marginalized groups, such as the working-class or women. The subtext of dismissals of the sensation novel as bad art is the fear that it encourages those who enjoy it to rebel against social restrictions.

From the perspective of the twentieth century, the Victorian critics' outraged reactions to the sensation novel might seem to have exaggerated the threat the genre represented and to be at least as emotionally excessive as their target. Still, their discourse established a relation between affective states and their social meanings that remains with us. The language of bodily sensation and addiction that the Victorian critics invoked continues to be prevalent in dismissals of mass culture that construct the desire for mass culture as analogous to a bodily need symptomatic of moral or social corruption. Even the more sympathetic accounts of the sensation novel or of contemporary mass culture endorse its potential subversiveness by means of a discourse about its affective power. Rather than being cause for alarm, the dangerous sentiments produced by mass culture can be celebrated as signs of resistance or transgression. Whether, as the equivalent of a drug, mass culture deadens or stimulates affective responses, the consumer is constructed as a reading body, and affective experience, conceived in physical terms, is assigned moral or political value.

Sensationalism and the Construction of Affect

In order to understand the politics of affect, then, we must trace how affective experience is made meaningful. How "sensations" become "sensational" is one instance in a larger history of the discourse of affect. The ambiguity of the term "sensation" novel, which can refer either to the sensational events in the texts or to the responses they produce is not accidental. The sensation novel, and sensationalism more generally, makes events emotionally vivid by representing in tangible and specific terms social and historical structures that would otherwise remain abstract. Sensationalism works by virtue of the link that is constructed between the concreteness of the "sensation-al" event and the tangibility of the "sensational" feelings it produces. Emotionally charged representations produce bodily responses that, because they are physically felt, seem to be natural and thus to confirm the naturalness or reality of the event. The tangibility (and hence "realness" or "naturalness") of feeling or nervous response is invested with significance as a sign of the concreteness or reality of the representation.

I also contend that this connection between sensational events and bodily sensation or affect has a political dimension. What are the political consequences, for example, of the frequent dismissal of sensationalism as the product of exaggerated or unrealistic representations and correspondingly false or exaggerated responses? What political or cultural work is performed by this gesture, which often seems to be no more than an aesthetic evaluation? If, as the example of ACT UP suggests, sensationalism can also be endorsed as a useful tactic for goading people into an awareness of social problems, what political possibilities are overlooked when sensationalism is condemned?

Not only do I assume that the link between sensational events and bodily sensations is constructed rather than natural, I also assume that the apparent naturalness of bodily sensation or affect is itself a construction. Like sexuality and other physical processes, affect is not a pre-discursive entity, a fact that is often obscured by the construction of affects or bodily sensations as natural. To study the politics of affect, then, is more broadly to study the politics of cathexis and to explore how meanings are given to the energy attached to particular events and representations.

The link between the "sensational-al" and the "sensational," or between the apparent tangibility of feelings and the apparent reality of events, is often accompanied by a link between affective power and visibility. Sensationalism renders social structures not just tangible or concrete, but visible. Borrowing from the theatrical melodrama, the sensation novel achieved its effects through spectacle. Sensational events often turn on the rendering visible of what remains hidden or mysterious, and their affecting power arises from the satisfaction or thrill of seeing. Sensationalism's use of the visual, of the relation between the hidden and the seen, contributes to its capacity to make the abstract seem concrete. It rests on the assumption that the immediately perceptible, because it can be seen or felt, is real and true and natural because perception itself is natural. The apparent naturalness of these connections between the visible, the real, and the affectively powerful can be called into question at moments when the meaning of a visible event is not as natural or self-evident as the emotions it produces seem to be.

Sensationalism thus produces the *embodiment,* in both the literal and figurative senses, of social structures. It not only renders them concrete, by embodying them in a single and powerful representation, but the responses it produces are bodily or physical experiences that seem immediate and natural. The capacity of sensationalism to make both representations and their meanings seem as natural as bodily responses raises a number of questions about its political consequences. It suggests, for example, why sensationalism might work in a conservative way as a means of naturalizing ideology. Furthermore, if affective responses are not as natural as they seem to be, then the construction of affect as natural might well be part of a discursive apparatus that performs the work of what Foucault has described as the disciplining of the body. Discipline is powerful precisely because it functions as though it were natural rather than imposed. A disciplinary apparatus that functions by means of the individual subject's feelings is quite literally embodied in the self. I will explore how the reading body whose nervous responses are engaged and regulated by popular texts learns to cope with emotional shock and excess.

The Victorian critics' responses to the sensation novel also suggest that the relations between sensation and ideologies of gender and femininity need to be explored. The sensation novel's sensational representations are very often literally bodies, particularly women's bodies, whose erotic appeal is part of their sensational appeal. The apparent naturalness of sensational responses is closely tied to the apparently natural capacity of women's bodies to produce sensations. It also emerges from the apparently natural capacity of women's bodies to *experience* sensation. The association of femininity with emotional excess underwrites, for example, the nineteenth-century production of ideologies of domesticity, which depended on the construction of the middle-class woman as responsible for and ideally suited to the affective labors to be performed in the home.

Because recent feminist theory has challenged the naturalness of ideologies of gender, it is possible to question Victorian constructions of the relation between femininity and affect. If femininity is falsely naturalized, then affect has also been falsely naturalized. The point, however, is not to correct the "error" of assuming that affect is natural, but to examine the effects of constructing it as such. Central to examining the politics of affect is the exploration of how ideologies of gender and ideologies of affect are mutually dependent. Furthermore, the construction of a non-essentialist feminist agenda would have to include the project of constructing a politics of affect that does not rest on an essentialist conception of affect. This book seeks to contribute to that project by tracing how the nineteenth-century sensation novel and its Victorian critics constructed affect and constructed the connection between affect and gender.

TWO

Theorizing Affect: Twentieth-Century Mass Culture Criticism

It is difficult to analyze the politics of affect and sensationalism in Victorian culture because contemporary cultural criticism remains installed within nineteenth-century discourses about affect. Thus, the critical methods used to analyze Victorian sensationalism must themselves be scrutinized in order to clarify the assumptions underlying theories of affect and affect's place in theory. To that end, I shall explore in this chapter the discourse of affect implicit in Marxist and feminist theories of mass culture, and its connections to contemporary theories of affect provided by Foucauldian and psychoanalytic cultural criticism.

Marxist Cultural Theory and the Management of Affect

Even when contemporary Marxist critics of mass culture are sometimes more enthusiastic than the Victorians about its subversive potential, they are equally dependent on assumptions about its affective powers in order to make claims for its political significance. Marxist theories have been crucial to legitimating mass culture as an object of studies that explain the social significance of the pleasures derived from cultural activities. Popularity and affective power are linked; a genre such as the sensation novel is worth studying precisely because it is popular, that is, because it generates enthusiasm, cathexis, pleasure, fear, excitement, tears, terror—in short, affect. The pleasure afforded by mass forms is assumed to be neither meaningless nor harmless; in fact, it might be one of the more insidious mechanisms by which capitalism makes it possible for people to love their subjection, providing them with leisure activities that allow them to forget their exploitation and to imbibe the ideology that keeps the system afloat. In a more optimistic vein, it has been argued that mass culture provides fantasies of a different or better life and thus encourages critical impulses. For women confined to the home, for example, reading trashy romances or watching soap operas might be the only form that freedom takes.

The double agenda of recent Marxist criticism—to critique mass culture and to locate its progressive potential—depends on assessing how culture mobilizes affect. On the one hand, this work seeks to show how culture serves capitalism, not simply as a profit-making venture, but also by fostering conservative ideologies and providing diversions that absorb subversive energies. On the other hand, it sees culture as a domain for the expression of resistance and looks to the enormous appeal of mass forms as a power to be appropriated for progressive political purposes.

The project of not only taking mass culture seriously, but also exploring its active role in producing social transformation, has depended on revisionist accounts of ideology that challenge Marxist economism and its tendency to describe ideology as a "superstructure" that reflects the economic "base." Although criticisms of economism are as old as Marxist theory itself, new accounts of ideology have been consolidated by the influence of poststructuralism on Marxist cultural theory. Work on mass culture has, for example, been influenced by Louis Althusser's theory of the "relative autonomy" of ideology, which grants to ideology, and thus to culture, the power to influence material and social conditions. The rejection of "reflection theory" and the claim that ideology is not merely "false consciousness" have underwritten studies of mass culture that focus on how the psychic processes it engages construct "the imaginary relations of individuals to their real conditions of existence."[1] If the production and reproduction of ideology is an important agent in the maintenance of capitalism, rather than its passive adjunct, then mass culture, a crucial vehicle for the dissemination of ideology and the formation of subjectivity, cannot be easily dismissed.

Positive assessments of mass culture have also been influenced by Gramscian notions of hegemony. Work by Stuart Hall and the Birmingham Center for Contemporary Cultural Studies stresses that hegemony is secured by popular consent rather than through coercion. Hegemony is thus not the result of the ruling class's imposition of ideology on the passive or mystified masses. As one of the means by which hegemony is secured, mass culture "is viewed neither as the site of the people's cultural deformation nor as that of their cultural self-affirmation . . . rather, it is viewed as a force field of relations shaped, precisely, by these contradictory pressures and tendencies."[2] In this model, social transformation does not entail the disappearance of hegemony; and, if the dominant culture articulates rather than represses the desires of oppositional cultures, then power relations can shift through a rearticulation, rather than replacement, of hegemonic discourse.

Although I share the desire of Marxist critics to explain and appropriate mass culture's power, I want to argue that contemporary theories of mass culture often depend on the problematic assumption that culture merely reroutes affect rather than actively constructing it. The claim that mass culture displaces or transforms affect rests on the assumption that affect is a natural or prediscursive entity, which exists independently of the cultural forms that structure and produce it. Furthermore, this model does not account for the fact that mass culture actually *creates* affect, by representing complex social issues in simpler and emotionally engaging terms, that is, by sensationalizing them. To put it another way, attempts to grant mass culture a positive or transformative potential depend on a version of what Foucault calls the repressive hypothesis. By assuming that mass culture thwarts the fulfillment of desires and affects that exist independently of it, theorists can propose that mass culture is liberatory because it enables repressed or forbidden impulses to be unleashed or expressed.

The problems created by the presence of the repressive hypothesis in Marxist mass-culture theory can be observed in Fredric Jameson's account of the utopian dimensions of mass culture. Like many other critics, Jameson challenges Adorno and Horkheimer's claim that the "culture industry" manipulates and dehumanizes its audiences.[3] Jameson insists on the dialectical relation between reactionary and utopian dimensions of culture in order to avoid a narrowly instrumentalist position. He argues that "we cannot fully do justice to the ideological function of works like these unless we are willing to concede the presence within them of a more positive function as well: of what I will call, following the Frankfurt School, their Utopian or transcendent potential—that dimension of even the most degraded type of mass culture which remains implicitly, and no matter how faintly, negative and critical of the social order from which, as a product and a commodity, it springs."[4] Jameson's Hegelian faith in the immanence of negative or critical elements is significant as a counterresponse to the dismissal of mass culture. Its drawback is that it guarantees in advance that every text will contain subversive elements without providing any substantive account of the specific nature of subversion. Characteristic of this theoretical position is its dialectical relation to earlier theories of mass culture; mass culture must have subversive elements because it would be politically suspect to assume otherwise. The task of criticism is the search for positive value.[5] Often the specific textual form that utopian fantasies take is erased in the process of reading these forms as a vehicle for the expression of subversive desires. By failing to historicize the utopian moment, Jameson comes close to removing the very historicism that is fundamental to his Marxism.

Part of the problem with Jameson's theory of the utopian is that he fails to articulate clearly the theory of affect upon which it depends. He wavers between recognizing that mass culture constructs affective responses and implying that it taps into raw or natural libidinal energies that are the potential source of resistance. In Jameson's Freudian model of how culture interacts with the psyche's libidinal economy, the affective charge generated by a text is as important as the text itself: "If the ideological function of mass culture is understood as a process whereby otherwise dangerous and protopolitical impulses are 'managed' and defused, rechanneled and offered spurious objects, then some preliminary step must also be theorized in which these same impulses—the raw material upon which the process works—are initially awakened within the very text that seeks to still them.[6] Jameson here valorizes affect as the source of political change. Culture has a utopian dimension in so far as it "awakens" the "dangerous and protopolitical impulses" that are "the raw material" for social action. A critique of mass culture consists of showing how it displaces this energy, by offering it "spurious objects," or causes it to disappear by "defusing" it. Because the "raw material" of impulse is potentially separable from the process that manages it, Jameson can find cause for political hope. But by calling for a theory of some "preliminary first step," he posits a first principle that is suspiciously essentialist in its conception of affect. Phrases such as "raw material" suggest that affect is an intrinsically subversive energy whose natural potential is held in check by the repressive force of cultural constructions.

Even as he stresses the positive potential of mass culture's capacity to generate affect, however, Jameson describes this production of affect as how mass culture *manages* affect: "To rewrite the concept of a management of desire in social terms now allows us to think repression and wish-fulfillment together within the unity of a single mechanism, which gives and takes alike in a kind of psychic compromise or horse-trading, which strategically arouses fantasy content within careful symbolic containment structures which defuse it, gratifying intolerable, unrealizable, properly imperishable desires only to the degree to which they can again be laid to rest."[7] If desire is not only "defused" but "aroused" by a text, it does not exist independently of or prior to the symbolic structures that give it expression. There is a more intimate relation between representation and affect than is implied by the utopian prospect that the quantum of libidinal energy bound to a fantasy could simply transfer to another, more suitable object. Instead, the containment strategy that displaces or lays to rest affect works by virtue of its capacity to arouse affect. Thus, mass-cultural texts are not simply a conduit for emotions; they actively construct affective experience.

Michel Foucault and the Construction of Affect

Although Jameson's model for mass culture sometimes seems to assume the repressive hypothesis, his description of how mass culture "manages" affect is closer to Foucault's critique of how the construction of sexuality as repressed sets in place a discursive apparatus that controls and regulates sexuality. The parallel between Jameson's and Foucault's projects suggests why both the history and theory of mass culture and the history and theory of sexuality, or more generally, affect, are related endeavors. Mass culture is a discursive apparatus by means of which affective experience is constructed. To borrow further from Foucault's model, theories of mass culture, like psychoanalysis, should not expect liberation to result from the expression of the desires that mass culture represses, since mass culture functions precisely by constructing those affects as repressed in the first place.

Theories of mass culture might benefit from the extension of Foucault's account of the history of sexuality to include affect. Like sexuality, affect should be understood as discursively constructed; furthermore, the centrality of sexuality in the construction of the modern self is accompanied by an emphasis on sentiment, feeling, and emotion. Foucault has suggested that sex becomes the truth of the self, a truth which is produced rather than naturally given; by the same token, within modern culture, feelings or emotions become the locus for psychological self-excavation.[8] The sensation novel is part of a longer history of the construction of affect as meaningful, one evident in the cultural domain in the eighteenth-century novels of sensibility and sentimentality and in the emphasis on feelings in

Romantic poetry and representations of the sublime. The construction of the distinction between high and mass culture is also intimately bound up with the production of a discourse about affect, since high culture is often celebrated as that which produces good affects and mass culture is often dismissed on grounds that it produces bad affects.

This cultural discourse about affect also links the construction of gender relations and the household with the construction of mass culture. Feelings are constructed as part of a private life that lies outside the marketplace and are a sign of the natural and authentic self. The domestic sphere, where affect has free rein, is constructed as the domain of both feminine control and leisure. The rise of consumer culture and domestic culture under modern capitalism structures gender relations and institutions of mass culture in tightly connected ways. Like Marxist cultural theorists, Foucault emphasizes the political importance of the cultural domain; he also suggests the political significance of domains that have traditionally been designated as both feminine and nonpolitical, such as sexuality, the household, the body, and private life.

If affect is historically constructed, it can then become, as Foucault suggests of sexuality under the rule of the repressive hypothesis, not the mechanism for the liberation of the self but instead the mechanism for the containment and discipline of the self. The study of mass culture might include then the project of elaborating how mass culture enables the regulation of subjectivity through the management of affect. What, then, of possibilities for resistance or social transformation? Foucauldian analysis has suggested that there is no pure term of resistance; sexuality, for example, is not outside the cultural domain, or that which is repressed by it, and thus its expression is not intrinsically liberating. By the same token, mass culture's production of affect cannot be seen as inherently transgressive or liberatory. However, Foucault's understanding of the relation between power and resistance, his claim that "where there is power there is resistance" (and thus that resistance is not exterior to power) might be taken as another way of explaining the dialectic between mass culture's ideological and utopian functions that Jameson attempts to formulate. Both models suggest that the political consequences of mass culture's production of affect are not certain, that it can operate both for and against dominant social structures. But the questioning of the repressive hypothesis requires a theory of mass culture that attends more closely to the construction and regulation of affect, as well as to the consequences of constructing affect as natural or pre-discursive. A theory of mass culture that itself subscribes to the repressive hypothesis cannot adequately historicize the nineteenth-century construction of affect or theorize the politics of affect.

Psychoanalysis and the Cultural Production of Affect

Although Marxist accounts of mass culture and a Foucauldian account of affect can be fruitfully combined, the role of psychoanalysis in both Jameson's model of mass culture and Foucault's discussion of sexuality suggests a possible tension between the two theories. Marxist analyses of mass culture depend on a psychoanalytic model, thus assuming the very apparatus that Foucault attempts to historicize. The argument that mass culture manages or releases affect presumes the existence of affect prior to the work of culture and thus establishes a repressive hypothesis. The Marxist claims that mass culture's dream-like fantasies and its production of pleasure are the symptoms of underlying social problems or dissatisfaction also invoke psychoanalytic models of symptom formation and displacement. Advocates of this position assume that affect is displaced from the social to the cultural realm and that a more direct expression of social contradictions might produce change. Even if culture is granted a more active role, these critics assume that it enables the expression of tensions that arise elsewhere. All of these theoretical formulations borrow the language of psychoanalysis in order to explain the psychic and social functions of mass culture.

Suspicious of the repressive hypothesis and of psychoanalysis in general, the Foucauldian critic might remain skeptical of Marxist claims for the subversive powers of mass culture. Foucault analyzes disciplinary models of power and forms of domination that are less overt than economic exploitation because they involve consent rather than coercion. Psychoanalytic institutions and models are central to the formation of modern disciplinary power, which enables the control and production of subjectivity through claims to liberate the psyche. The conflict between Marxist and Foucauldian models does not, however, mean that Foucauldian work displaces or supersedes Marxist work. Rather, the apparent tensions between Foucault and Marxism can also be located as a tension *within* Marxism, since the work of Marxist cultural theorists has also stressed the complex and contradictory ways in which culture, ideology, and hegemony sustain power relations.

Rather than dismiss psychoanalytic theory, I have found it useful to retain a psychoanalytic model, but one that, inflected by poststructuralism, is already attentive to the work of the repressive hypothesis. Such models make it possible to see how the repressive hypothesis is installed in order to naturalize affect as the hidden source of the true self. Neil Hertz's discussion of the politics of cathexis, for example, resembles both Marxian and Foucauldian accounts of how resistance and affect are managed. Discussing conservative accounts of revolutionary violence in France in the nineteenth century, Hertz traces the mechanics of the production and management of affect in "the representation of what would seem to be a political threat as if it were a sexual threat." He explains that the Medusa-like figure of "a hideous and fierce but not exactly sexless woman" serves as a reassuring emblem of social conflict because it transforms political anxiety into castration anxiety. This displacement from the political to the sexual realm allows for both the expression of anxiety and the management of anxiety because the threat of castration is warded off by the apparent naturalness of gender difference evident from perceptions of the body. Confronted by a woman, who has no penis, the male spectator both confronts the possibility of castration and then, by invoking a natural gender difference, reassures himself that he need not fear such loss. The management of castration anxiety enables the management of political anxiety; the subtext of these scenarios is that revolutionary violence is the product of those who challenge not only class distinctions but gender distinctions. If the latter is natural, then so too is the former.

Like critics of mass culture, Hertz argues that representations enable social anxiety to be at once expressed and defused. He argues that the affective power of the Medusa-figure rests not solely in its displacement of the political onto the sexual but also in the pleasure that comes from the very work of representation. The revolutionary violence that might otherwise be too complex to describe is condensed in the figure of the Medusa-like woman. Hertz suggests that representing an anxiety in the affectively charged terms of a dramatic encounter between clearly differentiated entities is reassuring: "The field is narrowed to the point where a complex of historical factors can be ignored in favor of a thrilling encounter in which intimations of sheer weakness and sheer power are exchanged. I would grant that this way of thinking about women's sexuality is illusory; but I would argue that the texts we've been considering work to create that illusion, to transform one set of anxieties into another, more manageable one, and that the all-or-nothing logic of castration scenarios is what makes that transformation possible."[9] Hertz links the heightening of affect to representations that reduce a complex set of factors to a single legible difference.

This claim reflects the influence of poststructuralist theory on his model, for he is implying that binary differences are always constructions, even when they pass themselves off as natural. Such binary oppositions manage anxiety because they render intelligible that which is anxiety-producing precisely because it is not susceptible to such ordering.

Hertz's model undoes the repressive hypothesis. If affect cannot be separated from its containment, and if the same affect can both represent and ward off anxiety, it cannot be counted on to guarantee a text's subversive tendencies. Using Foucault's terms, we could say that melodrama, sensationalism, or the sublime tend to represent power as negative and repressive, and resistance as exterior to monolithic power. The belief, for example, that revolution can be achieved by cutting off the head of a king or seizing state power, assumes a single transformative moment. Countering this melodramatic model, Foucault suggests that power is dispersed and that sites of resistance are multiple, a fact that both expands the domain of politics but also makes revolution less possible (or to some readers denies the possibility of resistance altogether). Sensationalism might be problematic as a means of coping with the positive or disciplinary model of power.

Hertz's discussion of affectively charged representations helps show how affect is *produced* by representations rather than preceding them. Reading his analysis also shows how psychoanalysis, far from presuming the reality of the castration complex or of gender difference, shows how it is produced. For the fact that castration scenarios work to manage anxiety would have to be historically specific to cultures in which gender difference, signified by being castrated or not castrated, is likely to be read as a natural fact. Hertz implicitly deconstructs conservative representations of revolution by suggesting that the scapegoating made possible by the naturalness of gender difference is in fact the work of ideology. Citing Laplanche's analysis of the castration complex, Hertz suggests that the reassurance implicit in any scenario that structures anxiety stems from its ability to link a theory with a perception. According to Laplanche, "It goes without saying, that castration is precisely not a reality, but a thematization of reality. A certain theorization of reality, which, for Freud, is so anchored in perception that to deny castration is finally the same thing as denying perceptual experience itself." Laplanche's formulation is very close to an analysis of the politics of sensation: sensationalism functions by transferring the apparent naturalness of feeling to its representation in order to consolidate the naturalness of the representation that produces that feeling. In the case of castration anxiety, gender difference seems as natural as the horrifying but also reassuring spectacle of a woman's genitals. But, as Laplanche points out, this spectacle is not a self-evident reality, nor is the sensation itself; rather it is a "theorization of reality."

This analysis suggests that we trace historically, as part of the history and politics of affect, what figures get charged with the weight of the natural. Castration anxiety would thus become not a universal phenomenon, but a scenario that functions as if natural in certain societies. Hertz's discussion of how political threats come to be represented as sexual threats presumes historical conditions in which sexual narratives are more clearly legible and affectively powerful than political ones. Part of my project, for example, will be to explore why figures such as the beautiful but insane woman or the suffering but silent woman can do the cultural work of representing social anxieties. It is important to consider how the ideologies of gender and affect that these figures represent and produce provide a reassuring structure or explanation for anxiety.

It is also significant that Hertz's analysis is a discussion of the sublime, the high-culture version of affect. I would suggest that melodrama, sentimentality, and sensation display the same structure, but are dismissed as inferior, feminized, and trashy genres. The basic melodramatic structure, in which either the hero and villain are easily identified and dramatically opposed or the suffering heroine is victimized and persecuted, follows the same pattern of rendering anxiety coherent. One of my aims is to trace the underlying similarity between mass culture and high culture, which can be revealed by the similarities in their politics of affect.

It is possible to conceive of Foucauldian, Marxist, and psychoanalytic theories as all providing the terms for describing mass culture as contradictory in its politics, neither totally liberatory nor totally reactionary. Yet juxtaposing any two of these theories often highlights the tendency of one or the other to stress either mass culture's liberatory possibilities or its conservative tendencies. Foucauldian work, for example, seems more skeptical about resistance than Marxist work. Psychoanalysis seems to propose forms of resistance and liberation that Foucault would challenge. And Marxism seems at times skeptical of psychoanalysis's emphasis on the family and private life. Some versions of psychoanalytic theory question Marxist assumptions that psychic pain can be alleviated by social transformation. Both Marxist and Foucauldian work tends to historicize psychoanalysis, but psychoanalysis challenges this historicizing work by invoking the prospect of inevitable psychic structures.

Feminist Criticism and Mass Culture

The tensions between Marxist, Foucauldian, and psychoanalytic theories of mass culture grow still more complicated in the context of feminist criticism. The claim that mass culture simultaneously expresses and defuses resisting sentiments has been enormously productive for feminist analysis, which has in turn provided a new rationale for the study of popular forms as the voice of the disenfranchised. Less inclined than traditional critics to separate high and mass culture, since both are the source of ideologies of sexual difference, feminists have also argued that the distinction itself is a function of assumptions about gender. They have been eager to reject the idea that mass culture merely manipulates its audience, since to assume that its female consumers are unenlightened or passive is to consign them to the marginal position that they have traditionally been forced to occupy. The study of mass-cultural forms produced by and for women has been included under the project of extending the boundaries of literary analysis beyond the traditional canon. Furthermore, some of the more convincing arguments for mass culture's utopian dimensions have come from feminists who have read forms such as soap operas, Harlequin romances, Hollywood films, and mass-circulation magazines as fantasies for women, for whom social conditions may prevent forms of protest other than cultural ones.

Thus, studies of mass culture for women are committed to exploring its progressive possibilities on feminist grounds. The point of departure for Jameson's utopian readings—the assumption that audiences are not the unwitting dupes of the culture industry—acquires additional urgency when the audience is female. In an exemplary instance of such work, Janice Radway argues that the women who read Harlequin romances appropriate the admittedly conservative ideologies these books promote for their own ends; she grants the female reader the power to control her own reading and suggests that to assume otherwise is to deny women any agency and to recapitulate sexist ideology. Unlike Jameson, Radway focuses not just on the texts of mass culture, but on the process of consumption, arguing that even if the texts are conservative, the *act* of reading can have subversive effects. For example, the woman for whom reading a romance is a way to claim her own private time or activity resists the demand that she devote her time to her children, her husband, or household tasks. Aware that such forms of resistance may do little to transform the social structures that lead women to seek the pleasure provided by romance novels in the first place, Radway nonetheless insists on the importance of recognizing the positive dimensions of consuming mass culture:

> It could be the case that these readers develop assertive techniques in a few restricted areas of their lives and thus do not use their newfound confidence and perceived power to challenge the fundamental hierarchy of control in their marriages. However, it is only fair *not* to assume this from the beginning in order to guard against the danger of automatically assigning greater weight to the *way* a real desire for change is channeled by a culture into nonthreatening form than to the desire itself. To do so would be to ignore the limited but nonetheless unmistakable and creative ways in which people resist the deleterious effects of their social situations.[10]

Radway's optimism depends on her shift of focus away from the texts of Harlequin romances to their function in the lives of readers, and she offers the hope that "the desire" for change will ultimately produce change. Her argument resembles Jameson's theory that the impulses awakened by mass culture can be put to other uses. Like Jameson, she distinguishes between desire and how desire is "channeled by a culture into nonthreatening form." In so doing, she relies on a version of the repressive hypothesis, implicitly claiming that the desires managed by mass culture precede, and are hence detachable from, the forms that give them expression. Using a psychoanalytic model, Radway describes the affective dynamics of romance reading in the following way: "Romances can be termed compensatory fiction because the act of reading them fulfills certain basic psychological needs for women that have been induced by the culture and its social structures but that often remain unmet in day-to-day existence as the result of concomitant restrictions on female activity.[11] Romances serve as a therapeutic outlet, fulfilling affective needs that are not met elsewhere. What is problematic about this model is that it takes the term "basic psychological needs" for granted without considering how those needs or affects might be constructed culturally and thus fulfilled by romances. Yet the task of analyzing "the way a real desire for change is channeled by a culture into nonthreatening form" remains crucial to understanding why the desires aroused by texts do not necessarily usher in resistance or rebellion.

For Radway, the progressive potential of mass culture also resides in the critic's rather than the reader's activity. Despite her charges of elitism against critics who speak patronizingly of Harlequin readers, Radway closes her analysis with a call for a coalition among women that presumes a distinction between the feminist readers of her book and the readers of romance: "I think it absolutely essential that we who are committed to social change learn not to overlook this minimal but nonetheless legitimate form of protest. We should seek it out not only to understand its origins and its utopian longing but also to learn how best to encourage it and bring it to fruition."[12] Radway adopts the voice of the "we who are committed to social change" and implies that this group is different from those who indulge in the "minimal" (but of course "legitimate") form of protest that reading romances represents. It sounds as though the critics are the intellectual vanguard charged with the task of "encouraging" and "bringing to fruition" the as-yet feeble impulses of working-class housewives. Radway's call to activism suggests that the progressive potential of mass culture depends on the work of critics who can capitalize on the pleasures of mass culture. It is important to remember this address, for it is a reminder that mass-culture consumption alone is not transformative unless the desires it awakens are mobilized in other ways.

Radway's analysis reveals how the terms in which feminist critics argue for the subversive power of mass culture often conflate the text or audience's activity with the critic's activity. Radway's most significant intervention, evident in the impact of her book among critics who are not primarily interested in the Harlequin romance itself, is her suggestion to critics that they need to analyze mass culture, not her claims for the subversive force of the romances. Critics who argue for the political and aesthetic reevaluation of mass culture or women's culture can confuse the critically interesting with the subversive, forgetting that a work does not have to be resistant to be worth interpreting, and that an intervention within the institution of literary criticism is not always a synecdoche for other forms of resistance. Within the context of feminist criticism of nineteenth-century popular culture, the subversive force of a work like Jane Tompkins's *Sensational Designs* lies not so much in her claims for the aesthetic or political power of the works she describes as in the fact that analyzing them drastically shifts the focus of literary criticism.[13] In other words, Tompkins's subversive power need not depend on the subversive power of the texts she analyzes. There has, however, been a tendency to equate the two, to assume that noncanonical texts must be proven subversive to be studied.

Nineteenth-century feminist critics have also been too willing to celebrate popular culture as a voice for female subjectivity. Less interested in the novel's status as mass culture than in how it provided a vehicle for women writers, a first generation of feminist critics focused on the nineteenth century in order to create an alternative tradition of women's writing. Often such criticism has assumed that a text authored by a woman is inherently subversive. Elaine Showalter, for example, restores the sensation novel to a position in literary history by arguing that it expresses women's discontent with marriage and with their social position, and furthermore that its conventions are specifically suited to expressing a female voice, since the genre's melodramatic incidents provide a language for female fantasies that cannot be depicted in realistic terms: "The sensationalists provided some of these excitements by inverting the stereotypes of the domestic novel and parodying the conventions of their male contemporaries. Sensation novels expressed female anger, frustration, and sexual energy more directly than had been done previously. Readers were introduced to a new kind of heroine, one who could put her hostility toward men into violent action."[14] Showalter focuses on the sensation novel as a forum for the expression of affects such as "anger, frustration, and sexual energy." The specific nature of the fantasies provided by the novels is less important than their function as a vehicle for their readers' emotional release. Yet, given that novels such as *East Lynne* and *Lady Audley's Secret* depict the punishment of their transgressive heroines, it is necessary to examine not just how the sensation novel expresses rebellious impulses but how it manages them.

Showalter's argument for the subversiveness of the woman-authored sensation novel is linked to her assumption that affective expression is subversive as well. The link between femininity and affect makes it possible to claim that the repression of affect is the mechanism for the repression or oppression of women and thus that the expression of affect is a means of liberation for women. The problem with these feminist readings of women's popular genres and the responses they produce is that they do not interrogate the significance of the fact that mass culture works within the category of affect, which is not natural, but a historical construction. Thus, if popular genres enable women to express feelings, or to gratify emotional needs, we need to ask why questions of happiness or dissatisfaction, both within the texts *and* in the criticism, are formulated in terms of affective needs and individual affective relations, such as romance and parenting. It is important to account for how modern culture produces affect as the measure of individual fulfillment, and particularly women's happiness, constructing individual affective bonds as central to pleasure. Attention to this historical construction must underlie any discussion of the politics of affect.

In order to pursue this project, feminist analysis can benefit from both Foucauldian and Marxist accounts of the history of private life. Such a conjunction of theories is not without its tensions, however, and like the tensions between Foucauldian and Marxist criticism, they tend to turn on questions of resistance. To the extent that Foucault seems to foreclose the possibility of resistance, feminists are likely to find his work problematic, whereas Foucauldian work often seems critical of feminist celebrations of subversion or resistance. I would argue that feminists who want to locate the subversive potential of mass culture must reckon with Foucault's model, which does not preclude the possibility of resistance, although it might make it more difficult. If affect can be a source of resistance, it is also, as the subsequent chapters will show, a mechanism for power. Affect operates as a form of power not on the model of punishment or overt violence, but on the model of discipline.[15] Foucault's model of disciplinary power is in fact quite useful for describing the position of middle-class women as prescribed by Victorian domestic ideology; the household as the domain of affective relations becomes the arena for a seemingly invisible enslavement or subjection. Moreover, the middle-class woman's suffering often takes the form of psychic or emotional rather than physical pain. It gives rise to a politics of affect according to which the expression of emotion can be liberatory. The political consequences of representing this pain as invisible and psychic, of representing it, for example, as hysteria, will be one of the primary concerns of this book.

One of the reasons for the tensions between Foucauldian and feminist analyses has been the assumption on the part of many literary critics that the only texts worth studying are those that produce or enact resistance. Hence, to the extent that Foucault's theories are taken to imply that resistance is always recuperated, feminist critics are hostile to his work. Judith Newton, for example, argues that Foucault's conception of power as operating through multiple sites, prevents the theorization of broad-based relations of domination and submission (along lines of gender and class, for example) necessary to produce resistance to power.[16] Her argument turns on a reading of Dickens's *Bleak House,* in which she challenges D. A. Miller's Foucauldian critique of the novel on the grounds that such a reading precludes the possibility of resistance. It is important, however, to distinguish between a critique of the Victorian novel and a critique of resistance.

The Victorian novel need not be defended in order to guarantee the possibility of social transformation. The strategic aims of this book differ from those of an earlier generation of feminists whose study of Victorian fiction by women challenged conceptions of the canon and ideologies of aesthetic value. In the wake of challenges to bourgeois feminism from feminists interested in race, class, and sexuality, Victorian fiction, including fiction by women, must be examined critically, particularly as other kinds of texts from colonial and post-colonial contexts, or from non-middle-class writers, provide new contexts within which to explore the hegemonic functions of texts more likely to legitimate than to challenge dominant ideologies. To this end, Foucault's work can be enormously useful to feminists especially because it helps to explain the role of ideologies of gender and affect and the role of the middle-class woman in the establishment of middle-class power.

On the other hand, the relations between Foucauldian and feminist criticism can sometimes grow too cozy when Foucault's work is used to endorse as progressive any form of activity that shows signs of resistance. The project of exploring the politics of mass culture or of affect is quite compatible with the concept of "micropolitics" frequently ascribed to Foucault. Like Foucault, critics of mass culture seek to authorize culture, sexuality, and desire as domains of resistance, thus countering Marxism's sometimes too-narrow emphasis on spheres of production, such as the marketplace or the workplace, as the only real sites of political transformation. Foucauldian and feminist critiques of Marxism converge in this respect. But the claim that domestic, personal, and sexual practices, or more generally, those domains traditionally designated as feminine and private, are political is not equivalent to the claim that they are *subversive*.[17] Foucault's suggestion that resistance is not exterior to power means that these domains can be both vehicles for resistance *and* vehicles for the imposition of power, and that their effects cannot be known in advance.[18]

The distinction that Foucault makes between punishment and discipline is crucial, and one that feminists often overlook. Disciplinary power is different from punishment because its effectiveness depends on its ability to mask itself and to appear in the guise of love or self-expression. This model is particularly applicable to institutions gendered as feminine, such as the household, and to the culture industry, which exert their power through the mobilization of pleasure and desire and not through an overt force that makes pain or oppression directly evident. Often these domains *appear* to be outside of power: the household seems to be nonpolitical, as does romance, as do women's activities more generally. In fact, it is the linking of these spheres with the feminine that often accomplishes the work of making them appear to be outside politics. Feminist work must contend with the quite powerful, and often conservative, effects of this strategy.[19] The project of examining the intersections of gender and power problematizes an earlier generation of feminist analysis that has tended to equate the feminine with the resistant.

If Foucault and feminism need not be at odds, then, it is only on condition that certain easy assumptions about resistance be themselves resisted. We cannot assume that female expression of feelings constitutes resistance, or that affect itself, because gendered as feminine or because apparently natural, is intrinsically subversive. We must attend to the ways that, for example, masculine affect, even when and often because gendered as feminine, operates as a particularly effective strategy of power, often effective because invisible. If sensationalism or the expression of affect challenges or transforms structures of power, it is only because it can also maintain or enforce those structures. By the same token, mass culture can be subversive, but it can also be conservative. Or it can be both simultaneously, producing, in other words, multiple and unpredictable effects.

Where Foucauldian analysis might exist in most uneasy tension with feminist analyses of mass culture, however, is in its critical stance towards the expression of desire. Janice Radway's and Tania Modleski's accounts of the utopian dimensions of women's popular forms don't include a thoroughgoing analysis of the regime of affect. To say that the utopian moment in women's texts consists, for example, in an idealized version of romance and domesticity or in their capacity to provide emotional fulfillment never gets to the problem of challenging the very structures of romance, domesticity, and affect that Foucault's work calls into question. Analyses of mass culture that locate its subversive potential in its capacity to produce or express subversive desires or affects must take into account Foucault's critique of the repressive hypothesis and question the assumption that affective expression is liberatory.

My own attempt to negotiate the tensions between feminist and Foucauldian analysis involves recourse to feminist and poststructuralist versions of psychoanalytic theory. Like Foucault's project, this work seeks to historicize the structures of fantasy and affect explored in psychoanalytic theory. Rather than rejecting Freud as hopelessly contaminated by sexist or essentialist assumptions, some poststructuralists and feminists have used psychoanalysis to analyze the relation between what are taken to be universal structures of affect and subjectivity and their particular forms within patriarchy, or more narrowly, within the modern nuclear family structure.

There are marked differences, though, between the assumptions of feminists, such as Nancy Chodorow and Jessica Benjamin, who are interested in object-relations, and those feminists whose work is informed by poststructuralism, such as many of the French feminists, Jacqueline Rose, or Jane Gallop. The former speculate about the differences that might exist between families where mothers are the primary caretakers and families where primary caretaking is not gendered. Chodorow and Benjamin both assume that certain processes of individuation and bonding are necessary features for the development of the psyche, but that, for example, the need for men to develop greater autonomy or the existence of "fluid boundaries" between mothers and daughters might be transformed under co-parenting. Such theories often fail to historicize the nuclear family structure and tend to assume that reforming the family can alleviate the harmful social effects of male aggression. Poststructuralist feminists, on the other hand, tend to argue that structures of violence are more intransigent, that historical or social transformation cannot entirely eliminate loss, anxiety, or aggression. Such theories invoke what appears to be a universal or ahistorical model of psychic processes in order to criticize both Marxist and feminist theories that posit the utopian prospect of a world without violence or a society composed of unrepressed, coherent, and healthy egos, a world in which the unconscious would cease to exist.

It might seem rather easy to reject the latter kind of psychoanalytic theory on the grounds that it is ahistorical. Here "history" and "theory" seem to be in conflict—with Marxism and feminism on the side of "history," challenging the ahistorical nature of psychoanalytic theory, and psychoanalysis on the side of theory, providing a critique of Marxist and feminist accounts of the historical production of pain or affect. Foucauldian analysis seems to be allied with Marxism and feminism in this debate, but it is important to remember that Foucault, like poststructuralist psychoanalytic theorists, is also critical of the utopianism formulated in terms of liberation from repression. The psychoanalytic institutions that operate by implanting the repressive hypothesis are not the same as psychoanalytic theory, which can be as critical as Foucault of the assumption that an essence of the self is "repressed" by culture and waiting to be released by therapeutic or political action. The apparent conflict between "history" and "theory" should be reconciled not by appeal to truth but by appeal to its political usefulness. The value of a theory, like the value of historical analysis, resides in its ability to challenge assumptions about "nature." Just as Foucault's theoretical apparatus provides a means of critically analyzing facile claims for resistance, so too does psychoanalysis question the assumptions that both Marxists and feminists make about the possibility of historical and political change.[20]

Psychoanalytic discourse also provides a useful tool for political and historical analysis because it challenges the empirical verifiability upon which historical analysis depends. To the extent that psychoanalysis questions the process by which the reality of events is appealed to in order to ground analysis, it opens up the necessity of allowing for the role of the unconscious and of fantasy within political processes. The process of reading the social text that produces the affectively charged figures of the mysterious woman or the suffering woman is not one in which fantasy is demystified in favor of "reality." Rather, sensationalized figures or fantasies actively construct "reality," and we can only substitute one figure for another, or one version of truth for another. Exploring the politics of affect involves a historical investigation of how a discourse about affect privatizes and personalizes political action. But it also transforms what we mean by "politics," opening up questions about how political life engages affective and psychic processes.

My work has required a theoretical framework in which the conflicting claims of Marxism, feminism, Foucauldianism, and psychoanalysis can be negotiated without assimilating any of them to a master-narrative provided by a single theoretical framework. My interest in different theoretical paradigms is governed not by whether or not they are "true" but by the political work that they do. The debate between "history" and "theory" is a mechanism by which political differences are negotiated. But the debate emerges precisely because it is not immediately clear whether historicization or theorization is the more radical strategy. Because the politics of theory, like the politics of affect, cannot be determined in advance, it is necessary to read individual texts to see how they enact and construct particular political agendas. I choose to negotiate contemporary debates about the politics of affect through a reading of nineteenth-century discourses of sensation, not so much to produce truths about the nineteenth century as to clarify the contemporary stakes of the politics of affect.

Three

Detective in the House: Subversion and Containment in *Lady Audley's Secret*

Although it has received little attention from literary critics until recently, *Lady Audley's Secret* by Mary Elizabeth Braddon was one of the best-selling novels, not only of the 1860s but of the entire latter half of the nineteenth century. It is one of the most important novels of the sensation genre, which emerged as a successor to and composite of forms such as the gothic novel, the Newgate novel, and the stage melodrama.[1] The sensation novel is distinct as a genre from its precursors because its crimes and mysteries occur, not in foreign countries or wild landscapes, not among the lower classes or the inhabitants of monasteries and convents, but in the stately homes of the aristocracy, whose lives are depicted in realistic detail. Rather than relegating terror to the exotic fringes of society, the sensation novel exploits the disparity between apparently stable families and marriages and the horrifying secrets and extremes of passion that disrupt them, in recognition (in the words of Henry James) that the "most mysterious of mysteries" are "at our own doors."[2] This constitutive principle of the genre is elaborated in *Lady Audley's Secret* itself:

> What do we know of the mysteries that may hang about the houses we enter? Foul deeds have been done under the most hospitable roofs; terrible crimes have been committed amid the fairest scenes, and have left no trace upon the spot where they were done. I do

not believe in mandrake, or in bloodstains that no time can efface. I believe rather that we may walk unconsciously in an atmosphere of crime, and breathe none the less freely. I believe that we may look into the smiling face of a murderer, and admire its tranquil beauty.[3]

As the last sentence suggests, the genre's concern with the deceptiveness of domestic tranquillity is linked to its representation of women. Lady Audley, whose defining characteristics are her golden-haired beauty and her capacity to commit murder, represents the genre in microcosm; the impossibility of recognizing her wickedness from her appearance adds to her power both to fascinate and to threaten others. Only the special skill of the detective can reveal her character. Whereas gothic novels depict the trials of courtship and threats to the purity of virgin heroines, sensation novels are more likely to represent marriage and to show women who produce evil rather than suffer from it. Plots revolve around the legal status of marriage, and the conflicts created by property and inheritance laws. The crime most peculiar to the sensation novel is bigamy, an offense in which a sexual relation or romance is directly under the jurisdiction of the law, and in which illicit passion infects marriage from within, rather than, as with adultery, from without.[4] The genre creates sensationalism by locating crime where one would least expect it—not only in the home but in the actions of a woman—and in the process violates the separation of the private and public spheres crucial to Victorian culture. According to both Victorian and contemporary critics, the affective power of the sensation novel's transgressive heroines has subversive tendencies.

The Sensational Portrait of a Lady

The Victorian critics, for example, were especially vehement about the sensation novel's dangerous portrayal of women whose sexuality and affects are uncontrolled. The figure of the criminal and sexualized woman, by violating the standards of feminine propriety, also threatened the social order. One critic remarked:

There is nothing more violently opposed to our moral sense, in all the contradictions to custom which they present to us, than the utter unrestraint in which the heroines of this order are allowed to expatiate and develop their impulsive, stormy, passionate characters. We believe it is one chief among their many dangers to youthful readers that they open out a picture of life free from all the perhaps irksome checks that confine their own existence.... The heroine of this class of novel is charming because she is undisciplined, and the victim of impulse; because she has never known restraint or has cast it aside, because in all these respects she is below the thoroughly trained and tried woman.[5]

The emphasis here on the danger of "impulse" that is "undisciplined" or without "restraint" reveals the link made between the unleashing of affect, especially in women, and threats to the social order. Psychic discipline becomes the prerequisite to moral and social stability, and women in particular bear the burden of representing virtue as the control of desire. In addition to gender difference, class difference is also implicitly represented in terms of the control of affect; although lower- or working-class women might not be sufficiently refined to manage their impulses, the sign of the middle-class woman's status is her ability to do so. As another critic's remarks about Lady Audley suggest, the woman who does not behave appropriately is unthinkable because femininity is so closely attached to sexual propriety:

> Lady Audley is at once the heroine and the monstrosity of the novel. In drawing her, the authoress may have intended to portray a female Mephistopheles; but, if so, she should have known that a woman cannot fill such a part. The nerves with which Lady Audley could meet unmoved the friend of the man she had murdered, are the nerves of a Lady Macbeth who is half unsexed, and not those of the timid, gentle, innocent creature Lady Audley is represented as being.... All this is very exciting; but is also very unnatural. The artistic faults of this novel are as grave as the ethical ones. Combined, they render it one of the most noxious books of modern times.[6]

According to this critic, the novel violates the natural relation between femininity and affect; Lady Audley's crime is that she lacks the affect appropriate to her sex, facing her enemies cold-bloodedly with "the nerves of a Lady Macbeth who is half unsexed." Uncomfortable with the discrepancy between Lady Audley's innocent appearance and her behavior, the critic declares her to be an aesthetic and ethical abomination. The claim that the sensation novel produces an "unnatural" excitement is thus grounded in assumptions about the naturalness of gender roles.

It is precisely this threat to gender difference that contemporary feminist critics have seized upon as the source of the sensation novel's appeal and subversiveness. Responding to criticism that sees the sensation novel as a minor and inferior genre, either blandly conventional or irrelevant to cultural and literary analysis, Elaine Showalter argues that the sensation novel gives expression to the violent passions and frustrations of women whose lives are occupied exclusively by romance and the home. She writes: "The sensationalists made crime and violence domestic, modern, and suburban; but their secrets were not simply solutions to mysteries and crimes; they were the secrets of women's dislike of their roles as daughters, wives, and mothers. These women novelists made a powerful appeal to the female audience by subverting the traditions of feminine fiction to suit their own imaginative impulses, by expressing a wide range of suppressed female emotions, and by tapping and satisfying fantasies of protest and escape."[7] Whereas the Victorian critics deplored women's expression of feeling, the contemporary feminist critic celebrates it; both, however, have assumed the repressive hypothesis, equating the unleashing of suppressed feelings with rebellion against social convention. Showalter's discussion of *Lady Audley's Secret* focuses on Lady Audley as the figure who defies conventional expectations by appearing to be demure and innocent when in fact she is capable of the "unfeminine assertiveness" required to commit bigamy, murder, and arson. She argues that the female reader identifies with "a new kind of heroine, one who could put her hostility toward men into violent action."[8] The secret that lies behind the novel's sensational mystery is that Lady Audley is neither insane nor criminal, but instead acts out of rational self-interest to protect her livelihood. Abandoned by her first husband, George Talboys, she commits bigamy because marriage is her only means to economic security. When he returns, she manages to take control of events and get rid of him; murder stands in for divorce, which was only beginning to be an imaginable solution to unhappy marriages and was still very difficult to obtain. Thus, Showalter argues that "as every woman reader must have sensed, Lady Audley's real secret is that she is *sane* and, moreover, representative."[9]

At the same time as Lady Audley's crimes satisfy female readers' fantasies of rebellion and affective expression, her sensational appeal within the narrative is also the product of a masculine fantasy about women's hidden powers. The story is largely told from the perspective of Robert Audley, the nephew who becomes a detective to investigate his aunt's mysterious past. The narrative rarely provides access to Lady Audley's inner life or point of view; instead its sensationalism emerges from descriptions of the haunting beauty that belies the heroine's criminal behavior. The power of Lady Audley's image is evident in one of the novel's more sensational scenes, in which Robert Audley and his friend George sneak into Lady Audley's private chambers, which have been locked in her absence. As if entering the womb that will reveal the mysteries of femininity, they creep along a "secret passage" to find a series of rooms cluttered with "womanly luxuries" (46). They discover not the woman herself, but an excess of the accessories that signify her femininity. "The atmosphere of the room was almost oppressive for the rich odors of perfumes . . . handsome dresses lay in a heap upon the ground . . . jewelry, ivory-backed hair-brushes, and exquisite china were scattered here and there" (46). Their quest culminates in the opportunity to examine the pre-Raphaelite portrait of Lady Audley, which hangs in the antechamber. Rather than confront Lady Audley herself, they seek the safety of a representation to satisfy their curiosity about the mysterious lady of the house; Robert explains, "I would give anything to see it, for I have only an imperfect notion of her face" (45).

The portrait shows Lady Audley as a "beautiful fiend" not because she in unfeminine but because the marks of her femininity are exaggerated:

> No one but a pre-Raphaelite would have so exaggerated every attribute of that delicate face as to give a lurid brightness to the blonde complexion, and a strange, sinister light to the deep blue eyes. . . . It was so like, and yet so unlike. It was as if you had burned strange-colored fires before my lady's face, and by their influence brought out new lines and new expressions never seen before. The perfection of feature, the brilliancy of coloring, were there; but I suppose the painter had copied quaint mediaeval monstrosities until his brain had grown bewildered, for my lady, in his portrait of her, had something of the aspect of a beautiful fiend. Her crimson dress, exaggerated like all the rest in this strange picture, hung about her in folds that looked like flames, her fair head peeping out of the lurid mass of color as if out of a raging furnace. (47)

Sensational representation is as much the domain of the male artist as of the female novelist. The lurid exaggeration of Lady Audley's beauty makes her frightening but also fascinating as she becomes the object of the male viewer's voyeurism. Once accentuated, the signs of her femininity—her blue eyes, her crimson dress, her fair hair—reveal her capacity to be a demon, confirming male suspicions of her dangerous powers. The fantasy of the beautiful woman as evil has its dividends for men as well as women.

By the end of the novel Lady Audley's rebellion is diagnosed as madness and she is exiled to an institution in Belgium to die of "maladie de langueur," while Robert Audley reestablishes the ideal of family life in "a dream of a fairy cottage" (285). By casting Lady Audley as a beautiful fiend, just as the pre-Raphaelite painter does, Robert Audley exorcises the threat she is taken to represent and consolidates the patriarchal family.

The portrait's fascinating allure, both for the men in the novel and for the readers of Braddon's description, lies in the ambiguities of its portrayal of Lady Audley's beauty. It at once reveals and obscures her "true" nature and identity. The portrait is an emblem of how sensational representations work more generally; Braddon's insistent focus on her heroine's appearance seduces the reader with both the possibility *and* the impossibility of making visible the contradictions that mark Lady Audley's identity. I have suggested that sensationalism derives its power from rendering concrete or visible what would otherwise be hidden; the image of the beautiful and transgressive woman becomes sensational when we know that she is evil and we both see and don't see her criminality in her appearance. If Lady Audley looked as evil as she supposedly is, she would be less sensational. (Her mother's insanity, for example, is more rather than less unsettling when it turns out that she has the appearance of a golden-haired child rather than a madwoman.) The sensation of repulsion produced by Lady Audley's criminality is indistinguishable from the fascination produced by her beauty; sensationalism consists in the indistinguishability of the two feelings. The *meaning* of the sensation or affect is thus constructed rather than natural, and the representation that produces it can signify both female transgression and its containment. The fact that neither sensational representations nor the feelings they produce have natural meanings is frequently obscured, however. Representations of beautiful and mysterious women seem naturally sensational, for example, because they engage the apparently natural erotic appeal of female beauty.

Subversion and the Critics

If the sensational paradox of the beautiful but evil woman can be used both to reinforce and to challenge ideologies of gender and affect, the critic's task is a difficult one. In particular, politically engaged critics, such as Marxists or feminists, who have an investment in literature's potential to subvert or resist dominant ideologies have to contend with the fact that the figure of the mysterious or criminal woman has just as often been mobilized in order to control femininity as to undermine it.[10] More skeptical of literature's oppositional functions, Foucauldian critics have provided useful challenges to claims that transgressive or outlaw figures are subversive. D. A. Miller's work has been one of the more prominent instances of a Foucauldian approach to the nineteenth-century novel, and his discussion of *Bleak House,* for example, offers a theory of the detective novel, one of the genres *Lady Audley's Secret* draws on, that implicitly challenges Showalter's feminist assessment of the sensation novel. Working from the view that literature contributes to rather than critiques dominant ideology and existing structures of power, Miller suggests that the detective plot functions to simplify complex social issues, an argument that implies that popular genres displace and efface real problems:

> The detective story gives obscurity a name and a local habitation: in that highly specific "mystery" whose ultimate uncovering motivates an equally specific program of detection. . . . In relation to an organization so complex that it often tempts its subjects to misunderstand it as chaos, the detective story realizes the possibility of an easily comprehensible version of order. And in the face—or facelessness—of a system where it is generally impossible to assign responsibility for its workings to any single person or group of persons, where even the process of victimization seems capricious, the detective story performs a drastic simplification of power as well. For unlike Chancery, the detective story is fully prepared to affirm the efficacy and priority of personal agency, be it that of the criminal figures who do the work of concealment or that of the detective figures who undo it.[11]

Miller suggests that the detective plot "solves" complex social problems by rewriting them in simpler terms; once good and evil become readily identifiable entities, evil can be exorcized.

In *Lady Audley's Secret,* for example, Lady Audley is the interloper whose insane behavior threatens the family; by uncovering the secret of her past and consigning her to the madhouse, the novel renders the family safe. Negotiating the tensions between marriage as an economic contract and marriage as an affective bond, the novel scapegoats her for the threat posed to the stability of marriage and the family when either impulse (economic gain or sexual desire) operates to exclude the other. A woman like Lady Audley can take advantage of a man and marry for money rather than love. And blindly infatuated men like Sir Michael and George can choose inappropriate objects of desire. Their desires (implicitly sexual) are figured as madness, "this fever, this longing, this restless, uncertain miserable hesitation, . . . this frenzied wish to be young again" (5). Such desire threatens social divisions when it leads men to choose women, such as Helen Talboys or Lucy Graham, who are outside their class. Yet, ultimately the blame for this error falls upon Lady Audley, whose beauty bewitches and tempts the helpless men. The novel is obsessed with the dangers of excessive passion and sexual madness, but it rewrites this dilemma as the problem of an individual woman's murderous instincts and inherited madness.

The construction of Lady Audley as the repository of dangerous secrets and impulses mobilizes Robert Audley's detective work, which controls the intrusions of this deceptive woman; he has the power to discover truth and administer the law. In an age before psychoanalysis, the detective, the new professional required by the law's intrusion into the family, sought out the family's tensions, its sexual undercurrents, its madwoman (the hysteric's precursor).[12] As the doctor with whom Audley consults in order to diagnose Lady Audley as insane remarks, "Physicians and lawyers are the confessors of this prosaic nineteenth century" (246). Just as the confessional function of the doctor culminates in the production of the psychoanalyst, so the conversion of lawyers into detectives disguises a new form of social control, allowing for a deinstitutionalized, private, and resolvable inquiry into the family. Read according to Miller's model, the detective plot in *Lady Audley's Secret* operates to explore and defuse domestic anxieties.

At the same time, however, detection and the family intersect differently in *Lady Audley's Secret* than they do in *Bleak House*. Miller argues that *Bleak House* uses the detective plot to create an alternative to the interminable processes of Chancery. The detective police represent an institution of power that, unlike Chancery, is containable and that guarantees the possibility of a sphere outside of the jurisdiction of the law, such as the family. Ultimately, *Bleak House* attempts to dissociate itself from this model too, using the dichotomy it establishes between Chancery and the police, which is aligned with the distinction between an unclosed narrative and the detective plot, to claim that its own narrative system is different from either alternative. In contrast, *Lady Audley's Secret,* for all its simplifications, doesn't separate detection from the family, producing no thematic or formal difference between public and private realms, or between realist and detective narratives. Because detection occurs in its midst, the family can no longer serve as a refuge and instead becomes the scene of conflict and anxiety. And rather than being a figure with untroubled authority, like Inspector Bucket,

Robert Audley, the detective, doubts his knowledge, efficacy, and motives. Even as it attempts to rewrite the tensions of domestic life in manageable terms, *Lady Audley's Secret* has a far from utopian view of the family, revealing it as a site of relations of power that involve both gender and class.[13] The novel's happy ending, in which the mystery is solved and the family is reconstructed, is less convincing than *Bleak House's* domestic finale. In *Lady Audley's Secret,* the family is not a refuge from problems that occur elsewhere, but a suddenly healed instance of an institution that has been riddled by conflict throughout the narrative.

Lady Audley's Secret might also seem more subversive than *Bleak House* because Braddon dares to represent her heroine as an unrepentant criminal. Lady Dedlock's story in Dickens's novel could easily provide the material for a sensation novel, but rather than killing the man who threatens to expose her shady past, she becomes the suffering heroine of a maternal melodrama and dies in a lurid episode that resembles the climax of Mrs. Henry Wood's *East Lynne.* Unwillingly separated from her illegitimate daughter Esther, Lady Dedlock must pay for her moral redemption as a mother by being killed off in the narrative. And as the suffering mother, not only does she hide her pain under a carefully wrought demeanor of coldness, but she is kept silent even by the narrator. Her cries of anguish, when they finally do break through, remain trapped and unheard deep within the chambers of Chesney Wold:

> As Sir Leicester basks in his library, and dozes over his newspaper, is there no influence in the house to startle him; not to say, to make the very trees at Chesney Wold fling up their knotted arms, the very portraits frown, the very armour stir?
>
> No. Words, sobs, and cries, are but air; and air is so shut in and shut out throughout the house in town, that sounds need be uttered trumpet-tongued indeed by my Lady in her chamber, to carry any faint vibration to Sir Leicester's ears; and yet this cry is in the house, going upward from a wild figure on its knees.
>
> "O my child, my child! Not dead in the first hours of her life, as my cruel sister told me; but sternly nurtured by her, after she had renounced me and told my name! O my child, O my child!"[14]

The chapter ends there, with the narrator providing the secret spectacle of Lady Dedlock's unheard cries for the reader but refraining from moving in more closely to represent her psychic state. Lady Dedlock remains for Dickens a figure; her secret past and deadened exterior represent the dead soul of the aristocracy. He is unwilling to disrupt that exterior to speak from her point of view, as he does, for example, in the case of Jo. Instead, Lady Dedlock's closely guarded secret becomes a vehicle for the reader's sensational thrills. Most evident in the sadomasochistic relation of surveillance between her and Tulkinghorn, Lady Dedlock's ability to mask her feelings makes her a fascinating mystery. This power is, however, a minimal form of resistance, ultimately one that she cannot maintain and one whose psychic cost is so high it destroys her:

> In truth she is not a hard lady naturally. . . . But so long accustomed to suppress emotion, and keep down reality; so long schooled for her own purposes, in that destructive school which shuts up the natural feelings of the heart, like flies in amber, and spreads one uniform and dreary gloss over the good and bad, the feeling and the unfeeling, the sensible and the senseless; she had subdued even her wonder until now.[15]

Dickens uses Lady Dedlock to promote a politics of affect, suggesting that the aristocracy's suppression of "the natural feelings of the heart" can only lead to destruction. This equation of the repression of feeling with moral and social decay is central to the nineteenth-century novel, and to the sensation novel in particular, and it frequently finds its particular expression in the figure of the silenced woman. Installed within a framework in which a male observer, whether narrator or detective, watches a woman, the spectacle of the suffering woman also makes possible the sensational thrill of uncovering a secret. Suppressed affect provides a vehicle for surveillance, and this apparatus remains hidden behind the lure of that which incites it.

Despite his interest in the sensational power of the woman with a secret, Dickens does not go as far as Braddon and make his heroine a murderer. Within Dickens's narrative, it is unthinkable that Lady Dedlock should be Tulkinghorn's murderer—that job is left to her double, Hortense, who despite her uncanny resemblance to Lady Dedlock, is differentiated from her employer by being a foreigner and a member of the working class. A similar strategy is evident in that other canonical precursor to the sensation novel, Charlotte Brontë's *Jane Eyre,* in which the middle-class heroine's more aggressive tendencies are projected onto the insane and racially other Bertha. Braddon's representation of the blond, feminine, and upper-class Lady Audley as capable of attempting murder does constitute a departure from the narrative conventions of mainstream Victorian fiction. Of the three sensation novels to be discussed in this book, *Lady Audley's Secret* seems the most subversive *if* the sensation novel's subversiveness is a function of its heroine's transgressiveness.

The figure of the mysterious and criminal woman is not, however, intrinsically subversive; it can be deployed both to challenge and to reinforce ideologies of gender and affect. Claims about *Lady Audley's Secret's* subversiveness might best be understood as strategic responses to other critics and readers. The feminist and Foucauldian approaches exemplified by Showalter and by Miller are not necessarily mutually exclusive, especially since both critics challenge traditional conceptions of literary and aesthetic value. Showalter argues for the subversiveness of the sensation novel in order to foreground the potential value of popular works by women, whereas Miller attacks the assumption that canonical novels criticize their social milieu or processes of representation. Miller's Foucauldian analysis shows how a canonical novel with an ostensibly critical perspective on Victorian society is in many ways implicated in the processes from which it tries to distance itself and less subversive than it might like to be. However, in the analysis of a popular and noncanonical novel such as *Lady Audley's Secret,* exactly the kind of narrative whose limits and blindnesses *Bleak House* might be assumed to transcend, it might be more urgent to see how the text, despite expectations to the contrary, contains subversive elements.[16] The availability of both readings is testimony to the impossibility of separating the mechanisms of subversion and recuperation or designating a particular literary text intrinsically liberatory or reactionary.

Emphasis on subversion or containment in the novel coincides with emphasis on the female criminal or the male detective in *Lady Audley's Secret*. One can read the novel from the detective or masculine point of view as a fantasy of control, surveillance, and power, in which threats to the family can be identified and contained. One can also read it from Lady Audley's or the woman's point of view as a fantasy of rebellion, in which women can take their revenge on a patriarchy that restrains them, and in which madness is a sign of resistance. The latter reading seems to be subsumed to the former by the end of the novel, however, when Lady Audley's rebellion ultimately fails. Less obvious is how Robert Audley's position of power as detective is undercut. Given that his perspective controls the narrative, it seems important not only to show how Braddon's female protagonist subverts traditional roles, but to question the female author's investment in her male protagonist. In doing so, I hope to resolve the apparent conflict between the feminist and Foucauldian paradigms.

Affect and Masculine Power

Criticism of the novel tends to focus almost exclusively on the "beautiful fiend," Lady Audley, thus repeating the text's fascination with the paradoxical character and lurid history of its mysterious heroine. Lady Audley becomes the fetishistic object even in feminist readings, her peculiar combination of beauty, madness, sanity, evil, and calculation serving as the figurative locus to explore the operations of Victorian ideologies of gender. The problem with such interpretations is that they imply that the detective's work is neutral, that he investigates the secrets of the female criminal while himself remaining an object of no particular interest. Yet the novel is sensational not just because crime occurs in the family, but because it occurs in the detective's own family; Robert Audley's best friend seems to have been murdered on his family estate and his aunt appears to be the murderer. This incestuous intermingling of familial relations and detection makes Robert Audley's role peculiar. Like the analyst, he is subject to countertransference; his investigations into a family drama reveal his own desires and blindnesses. He is caught up in an Oedipal drama with his uncle, sexually tied to both George and Clara Talboys, and afraid of his own madness, so that his investment in Lady Audley's secret is far from simple. The novel is not just about how the crime and its detection affect his family, but about how they affect him, as he finds his power both constituted and threatened by his simultaneous roles as detective and family member.

Read as Robert Audley's story, *Lady Audley's Secret* narrates his development from aimless son of the aristocracy, "an idle flaneur upon the smooth pathways that have no particular goal" (281), to a full-fledged member of the patriarchy—husband, father, homeowner, and active professional. The detective case is the means to both professional and sexual maturity. Prior to it, his professional status is ambiguous:

> Robert Audley was supposed to be a barrister. As a barrister was his name inscribed in the law-list; as a barrister he had chambers in Figtree Court, Temple; as a barrister he had eaten the allotted number of dinners, which form the sublime ordeal through which the forensic aspirant wades on to fame and fortune. If these things can make a man a barrister, Robert Audley decidedly was one. But he had never either had a brief, or tried to get a brief, or even wished to have a brief in all those five years, during which his name had been painted upon one of the doors in Figtree Court. (21)

Supported by an inheritance, Robert Audley can remain a member of the ruling class without having to do any work. Despite its mockery of his laziness, the passage suggests that even if the name on the door doesn't accurately describe the nature of his labor, it does designate his position of power as a member of an important social institution. Ostensibly he is unconventional, but his idleness comes from a class privilege that places him squarely within existing social structures. The novel emphasizes his marginality, suggesting that his reclusive habits and ample leisure time make him the ideal solitary investigator. Ultimately, however, he enforces the dominant social values and upholds the work ethic by finding purpose in his investigation. Once he becomes a detective, he administers the law by actively working, traveling from one end of the country to the other in search of evidence, and by doing so privately, without institutional support. The law turns into detection without declaring itself as such; Robert Audley looks like a family member or a curious gentleman asking after his friend. Detection exists in an odd no man's land between the legal, professional world and the family. Its ambiguous status keeps the boundary between family and professional life fluid, leaving open the question of whether Robert's new maturity is a result of professional discipline or changed familial relations.

As detection, professionalism, and the law infiltrate the family, the family in turn transforms detective work into romance. The incitement to detection for Robert Audley is not a crime but the arousal of affect. Prior to his engagement in George Talboy's life, his "listless, dawdling, indifferent, irresolute manner" and "lymphatic nature" indicate a lack, not only of professional ambition, but of romantic or sexual desire. He is a somewhat eccentric bachelor, even slightly effeminate in his tastes, preferring French novels to hunting. He is indifferent to women as sexual objects and to marriage as an economic benefit (as evidenced by his lack of attachment to his cousin Alicia, who is not only the obvious choice economically, but the most engaging woman in the novel). The moment that marks his change is not the need to find his friend George (itself replaced by the investigation of Lady Audley/Helen Talboys), but his meeting with George and their homoerotic attraction to one another. He first greets him "with an emphasis by no means usual to him." As he plays nurse to his newly widowed friend and then tries to solve the mystery of his disappearance, he finds new passion and direction in life. "The big dragoon was as helpless as a baby; and Robert Audley, the most vacillating and unenergetic of men, found himself called upon to act for another. He rose superior to himself, and equal to the occasion" (26). Suddenly, the passive and boyish Audley is in a position of power and responsibility and he acts accordingly. The language of the passage is distinctly sexualized; "vacillating" and "unenergetic" behavior implies impotence, "rising superior" its opposite. Robert's new professional demeanor is indistinguishable from the signs of attraction to George: "If any one had ventured to tell Mr. Robert Audley that he could possibly feel a strong attachment to any creature breathing, that cynical gentleman would have elevated his eyebrows in supreme contempt at the preposterous notion. Yet here he was, flurried and anxious, bewildering his brain by all manner of conjectures about his missing friend; and false to every attribute of his nature, walking fast" (55). The novel continually conflates the language of affect and the language of work. Their connection suggests that desire is not a natural drive, but is instead constructed in relation to social processes and institutions. Furthermore, the play of desire is integral to the workplace, rather than exorcised to the realm of leisure in the interests of efficiency. Romance and work are not causally related, such that one is more fundamental than the other, nor are they separate domains; this novel continually collapses distinctions between private and public realms, between the domestic and the professional spheres.

The sexualization of nonsexual domains is further underscored by the fact that the object of Robert Audley's desire is a man. Eve Sedgwick, arguing for the connections between the homosexual, the homoerotic, and the homosocial, has suggested that the link, as well as the distinction, between homosexuality and patriarchal power functions to define other relations of power besides those immediately connected to sex and gender:

> Psychoanalysis, the recent work of Foucault, and feminist historical scholarship all suggest that the place of drawing the boundary between the sexual and the not-sexual, like the place of drawing the boundary between the realms of the two genders, *is* variable, but is *not* arbitrary. That is . . . the placement of the boundaries in a particular society affects not merely the definitions of those terms themselves—sexual/nonsexual, masculine/feminine—but also the apportionment of forms of power that are not obviously sexual. . . . In any male-dominated society, there is a special relationship between male homosocial (*including* homosexual) desire and the structures for maintaining and transmitting patriarchal power: a relationship founded on an inherent and potentially active structural congruence.[17]

At the beginning of the novel, Robert's behavior, both sexual and professional, is gendered as nonmasculine; he is more like a boy, a woman, or a homosexual. Sexual manhood would seem to require his insertion into a set of relations with a woman, as husband or suitor, yet professional maturity demands that he relate to other men as colleagues. The two processes converge in his attraction to George Talboys, so that a man is the means by which he comes to work and to love. Furthermore, the distinction between home and work would seem to correspond to the boundary between the sexual and the nonsexual. Yet, detection starts to blur the boundaries by turning the home into a place of work, professionalizing the activity of identifying sexual deviance. At the same time, work becomes sexualized, motivated by desire. This mutual imbrication of the sexual and the nonsexual realms means that the structure of relations in the professional sphere— relations between men—carries over into the sexual domain, as evidenced by the homoerotic bond between George and Robert. Women in the novel merely serve as stand-ins for this homoerotic bond; Lady Audley becomes the ostensible object of detection, and Clara Talboys becomes the ostensible object of affection. The novel ends with the traditional closure of marriage supplemented by the reunion of the two male friends, George having returned from Australia because he "yearned for the strong grasp of [Bob's] hand" (285). Clara seems only to be the medium of exchange that allows for the culmination of the relation between the men. Lady Audley also serves as a means to this end, as the duplicitous woman whose seduction of Michael Audley and George Talboys must be exposed in order to rid the family of female evil and safeguard it for male bonding. The detective story whose focus is the crimes of Lady Audley masks the narrative of Robert Audley's accession to the world of male power by means of his affective ties to a male friend. Patriarchal culture privileges relations between men in every arena; rather than making him deviant, Robert's homoeroticism seems to fit him all the better to be the bearer of social values. The novel's homoerotic subtext not only reveals his investments, but intensifies the links between sexuality and work that the novel brings into play.

Affect and Masculine Weakness

Rather than acting as the police for desire, Robert Audley polices by virtue of his own desire, which is never completely dissociated from the domain he investigates. Thus, affect and power are linked rather than intrinsically opposed. It remains unclear, however, whether Audley's affective investment in the case strengthens or weakens his skills as a detective. Although the tie between Helen Talboys and Lady Audley is obvious at a very early stage, Robert continues to collect evidence because he is terrified by the effects of his knowledge. If his investigation of Lady Audley is bound up with his attraction to George, then his reluctance to divulge the secret of her identity reveals the other locus of his investments—his relation to his uncle. The closer he gets to the secret of George's disappearance, the more he resists conclusions that implicate and threaten his own family. His detective work produces an Oedipal family drama: as he shows signs of maturity, forming attachments outside his immediate family and acquiring professional responsibilities, he becomes enmeshed in an Oedipal rivalry with his uncle (explicitly described as his second father), whom he will eventually "kill" and replace as head of the family by revealing Lady Audley's secrets. His search constantly reflects back on himself: "Is the radius to grow narrower day by day until it draws a dark circle around the home of those I love?" (100). Because his work forces him back to his home and his relatives, his professional development depends on resolving family tensions, which increasingly seem to retard his investigations.

Thus the novel foregrounds the detective's role, making him less innocent or neutral than he first appears to be. Audley's sense of his own involvement produces guilt and self-loathing. He is implicated in the events that he uncovers in ways that he hesitates to acknowledge, desperately afraid of his new role: "His generous nature revolted at the office into which he had found himself drawn—the office of spy, the collector of damning facts that led on to horrible deductions" (128). Suddenly the guilt attaches to him rather than to the criminal. Ostensibly the innocent observer of events, he becomes an active participant in the drama he unfolds. He seems to produce the crime in the process of investigating it, making trouble where previously there was none. Surveillance is the problem, not Lady Audley: "He was forever haunted by the vision of his uncle's anguish, forever tortured by the thought of that ruin and desolation which, being brought about by his instrumentality, would seem in a manner his handiwork" (166). Afraid to disturb the patriarch's happiness with his young wife, he sees his work in terms of its effect on his uncle, not Lady Audley. The focus of the investigation shifts away from Lady Audley's history to the underlying relations of power between the son and his father-figure. Because of this relation, Robert and Lady Audley become rivals for Sir Michael's affection; the family romance subsumes the detective/criminal relation so that Robert shares the guilt with Lady Audley.

For Robert Audley, detection alternates between private nightmare, exposing horrifying and personal secrets, and neutral science, rationally revealing the truth, with the latter often a defense against the former. This distinction is explicitly elaborated in the chapter in which, pondering the information he has gathered, Robert first has the following dream about the case and then tries to codify his knowledge of the facts:

> In another dream he saw the grave of Helen Talboys open, and while he waited, with the cold horror lifting up his hair, to see the dead woman rise and stand before him with her stiff, charnel-house drapery clinging about her rigid limbs, his uncle's wife tripped gaily out of the open grave, dressed in the crimson velvet robes in which the artist had painted her, and with her ringlets flashing like red gold in the unearthly light that shone about her. (64)

George has only just disappeared, and Robert has uncovered only one of the many documents that will provide evidence for his discoveries, but his unconscious already knows the solution to the mystery. Not only does his dream reveal the connection between Helen Talboys and Lady Audley, but Lady Audley appears here in her "true" form, that is, endowed with all the power and ambiguity that her portrait reveals.

Unable to trust his dream's revelations, however, Robert gropes his way toward a more scientific method of detection:

> He drew up this record in short, detached sentences, which he numbered as he wrote. It ran thus: "Journal of Facts connected with the Disappearance of George Talboys, inclusive of Facts which have no apparent Relation to that Circumstance." . . . When Robert Audley had completed this brief record, which he drew up with great deliberation, and with frequent pauses for reflection, alterations and erasures, he sat for a long time contemplating the written page. (67–68)

In producing a record that is complete, neutral, quantitative, and epistemologically reliable, Robert Audley hopes to absolve himself of any personal responsibility for his discoveries. He can infinitely elaborate his work, painstakingly filling in the blanks in a list of facts that have nothing to do with him. His epistemological power, his capacity to note every detail, becomes a juridical power, the capacity to uncover criminals and bring them to justice. He intimidates Lady Audley with the claim that he can collect "a thousand circumstances so slight as to be forgotten by the criminal, but links of iron in the wonderful chain forged by the science of the detective officer" (81). The metaphor of the "chain" translates the wholeness of the evidence directly into the power of the law to capture criminals. He becomes the custodian of social justice, bolstered by the unassailable power of scientific evidence.

Yet, like Freud's appeals to the scientificity of his method, Robert Audley's claims for detection look like a defense against doubts and investments that his dream reveals. The dream work is immediate, subjective, and emotionally powerful, leaving him less in control of his knowledge. In addition to revealing Lady Audley's secret identity, it makes him a central figure in the unfolding drama, as his own unconscious comes into play:

> But into all these dreams the places he had last been in, and the people with whom he had last been concerned, were dimly interwoven—sometimes his uncle, sometimes Alicia; oftenest of all my lady; the trout stream in Essex; the lime-walk at the Court. Once he was walking in the black shadows of this long avenue, with Lady Audley hanging on his arm, when suddenly they heard a great knocking in the distance, and his uncle's wife wound her slender arms around him, crying out that it was the day of judgment, and that all wicked secrets must now be told. Looking at her as she shrieked this in his ear, he saw that her face had grown ghastly white, and that her beautiful golden ringlets were changing into serpents, and slowly creeping down her fair neck. (64–65)

At first he dreams about the people and places of his investigations, but as in life, he is inexorably led back to Audley Court and to his own family relations. At the moment of revelation he is caught with Lady Audley, whose position as "his uncle's wife" is explicitly emphasized and whose intimate embrace seems to indicate an illicit union. The unveiling of the truth is figured as the last judgment, a horrifying and apocalyptic moment. In this context, the "wicked secrets" seem likely to be Robert's desires rather than Lady Audley's past. Lady Audley is transformed into Medusa, revealing the threatening power that her appearance normally hides. Her "golden ringlets" are constantly used as a synecdoche for her beauty, which in turn constitutes her identity; their mutation dramatically signifies her complete duplicity. Yet, this vision of Lady Audley's evil may reveal more about the beholder than the beheld. Freud's remarks on the Medusa's head are helpful in this context, explaining, as they do, how a representation of the threat posed by a woman can also be reassuring: "The hair upon the Medusa's head is frequently represented in works of art in the form of snakes, and these once again are derived from the castration complex. It is a remarkable fact that, however frightening they may be in themselves, they nevertheless serve actually as a mitigation of the horror, for they replace the penis, the absence of which is the cause of the horror."[18] This logic applies to how the novel functions in general. By fixing a particular danger or anxiety in the person of Lady Audley, it can then control and ultimately exorcise it. Robert's sexualized dream reveals how he will be able to restore the family to peace by first convincing himself that his aunt is evil. The dream thus reveals as much about the process of detection as it does about the secret to be detected.

The dream also transforms Robert's detection into an Oedipal scene. Both Alicia and Sir Michael misrecognize Robert's suspicion of Lady Audley as desire for her, taking the obsession of the detective for the obsession of the lover. The attention he pays to her, the emotions his discoveries produce, the threat those discoveries pose to his uncle—all of these phenomena are seen as the behavior of an infatuated son. Detection begins to resemble incest and brings with it all the guilt and anxiety that might attach to a forbidden desire. Once again work and romance are indistinguishable, the one masking as the other. Robert's dream reveals the complexity of his position, whereas the rational labor of making lists represses it.

Uncomfortable with the disruption his power creates, Robert must find a way to absolve himself of responsibility for his discoveries. He can only bring himself to pursue his case by setting the two families, the Talboys and the Audleys, against one another. He must choose between his love for his uncle and his love for George Talboys, between his position as dutiful son and his position as lover: "I've a comfortable little fortune in the three per cents; I'm heir presumptive to my uncle's title; and I know of a certain dear little girl who, as I think, would do her best to make me happy; but I declare that I would freely give up all, and stand penniless in the world to-morrow, if this mystery could be satisfactorily cleared away, and George Talboys could stand by my side" (105). His affection for George Talboys is directly opposed to the future he would have by remaining within his own family. His uncle represents the law of the father; loyalty and obedience to him installs Robert in a social position that includes income, position, and a wife. Detection and homoerotic affection are transgressive. Rather than simply being anarchic, Robert searches for an outside authority to guide his actions. He goes to George's father, hoping to pit one patriarch against another. When Mr. Talboys refuses this role, he inserts Clara, George's sister, in his place: "I accept the dominion of that pale girl, with the statuesque features and the calm brown eyes. I recognize the power of a mind superior to my own, and I yield to it, and bow down to it. I've been acting for myself, and thinking for myself, for the last few months, and I'm tired of the unnatural business" (136). Robert must have his work authorized by an outside source who functions as a substitute for his uncle. He resists the development his detection demands of him, seeking to remain the submissive boy.

The transfer of authority to a woman is crucial. Clara also functions as a repository for Robert's desire, standing in for George Talboys as well as for his father.[19] This conveniently resolves the problem of homoerotic love; he can have the woman who looks like George and who herself transfers onto him her love for her brother, the only man she has loved. The change in gender of the love object and the authority figure also enables Robert, under the guise of misogyny, to play out his ambivalent relation to sexual involvement and patriarchal power:

> I hate women. They're bold, brazen, abominable creatures, invented for the annoyance and destruction of their superiors. Look at this business of poor George's! It's all woman's work from one end to the other. He marries a woman, and his father casts him off penniless and professionless. He hears of the woman's death and he breaks his heart—his good, honest manly heart, worth a million of the treacherous lumps of self-interest and mercenary calculation which beats in women's breasts. He goes to a woman's house and he is never seen alive again. And now I find myself driven into a corner by another woman, of whose existence I had never thought until this day. (137)

Robert compares Clara's effect on him to Lady Audley's effect on George, and thus raises the possibility that his infatuation with her is no less misguided or illusory. Like Lady Audley, Clara functions for Robert by means of his image of her physical appearance; "her brown eyes" guide him in his search. At the same time, this female object of desire is constantly denigrated in part because Robert's affection for her is seen as a power she holds over him. The hostility for a father and the affection for a man that could never be expressed directly can be manifested toward a woman.

The novel's use of women as means of exchange for relations between men and then as scapegoats for their anxieties points to the difficulty of locating the text's subversiveness in its representation of a female criminal or madwoman. One can't specify the novel's effect as either subversion or recuperation because both processes occur simultaneously. The passages that are most misogynist can also be read as covert expressions of female power and aggression. Robert's speech about "petticoat government," for example, prompted by his simultaneous resentment of and relief about Clara's effect on him, both elevates and denigrates women:

> What a wonderful solution to life's enigma there is in petticoat government! . . . Who ever heard of a woman taking life as it ought to be taken? . . . It is because women are never lazy. They don't know what it is to be quiet. They are Semiramides, and Cleopatras, and Joans of Arc, Queen Elizabeths, and Catharines the Second, and they riot in battle, and murder, and clamor and desperation. . . . To call them the weaker sex is to utter a hideous mockery. They are the stronger sex, the noisier, the more persevering, the most self-assertive sex. They want freedom of opinion, variety of occupation, do they? Let them have it. (136–137)

Having articulated the nature of female power, Robert Audley goes on to say, "I hate women." Although the passage can be read as a sign of the novel's subversive tendencies, its context must also be accounted for. Robert Audley views women as powerful and rebellious in order to contain them. The production of Lady Audley's secret, of her madness, crime, and deviance, is how the novel can then convert marginality into something that can be brought under control, ridding the family of that which threatens it. The representation of Lady Audley as a villain is as much the product of a reactionary conservatism as of a covert feminism, and the appeal to her as a figure of resistance is accordingly problematic.

Male Madness

Yet the novel has also worked to question the detective's authority, by revealing how women are used to stabilize the complex forces of desire and investment that inform Robert Audley's work. If the novel has policed illicit female behavior (by first producing it as deviant), it has also subverted its own processes of containment by showing the weaknesses of its detective. The novel's oppositions—between madness and sanity, desire and work, detective and criminal—converge in the figure of Robert Audley, who becomes simultaneously the representative of dominant ideology and the isolated madman, the new patriarch and the homosexual who dodges traditional masculine roles. The interpenetration of family and law, and of desire and discipline, in his work corresponds to a confusion between processes of containment and subversion. The following passage, for example, depicts him as a social outcast, whose detective work undermines his sanity and thus links him to Lady Audley:

> He had dropped away from his old friends. He had shrunk from those men as if he had, indeed, been a detective police officer, stained with vile associations and unfit company for honest gentlemen. He had drawn himself away from all familiar haunts, and shut himself in his lonely rooms with the perpetual trouble of his mind for his sole companion, until he had grown as nervous as habitual solitude will eventually make the strongest and the wisest man, however he may vaunt himself of his strength and wisdom. (264)

Madness becomes a term to apply not merely to a scapegoat but to anyone. The novel is extremely sensitive to the normalcy of madness, to how excesses of emotion can be produced by constraints that impinge on all individuals. In one of *Lady Audley's Secret*'s more remarkable passages, for example, the narrator meditates on a rather more mundane, but no less severe, form of madness than Lady Audley's, a madness produced by the effects of mid-Victorian capitalism on everyday life:

> Who has not felt, in the first madness of sorrow, an unreasoning rage against the mute propriety of chairs and tables, the stiff squareness of Turkey carpets, the unbending obstinacy of the outward apparatus of existence? We want to root up gigantic trees in a primeval forest, and to tear their huge branches asunder in our convulsive grasp; and the utmost that we can do for the relief of our passion is to knock over an easy-chair, or smash a few shillings' worth of Mr. Copeland's manufacture.
>
> Madhouses are large and only too numerous; yet surely it is strange they are not larger, when we think of how many helpless wretches must beat their brains against this hopeless persistency of the orderly outward world, as compared with the storm and tempest, the riot and confusion within—when we remember how many minds must tremble upon the narrow boundary between reason and unreason, mad to-day and sane tomorrow, mad yesterday and sane to-day. (135)

The protest here seems to be against the commodification and regulation of experience, against how "carpets," "easy chairs," and "Mr. Copeland's manufacture" suppress not only forbidden desires but all desires. The cathartic possibility of unleashing emotion by "root[ing] up gigantic trees in a primeval forest" has been rendered impossible in the face of the "mute propriety" of the commodities now manufactured from the raw materials provided by the forest. Despite the implicit utopianism of the fantasy that in some prior age affect could be more readily expressed, the narrator's complaint does suggest an important discrepancy between psychic life and commodification. What Marx, for example, calls "alienation" is here expressed as the inadequate relation between the "hopeless persistency of the orderly outward world" and the "storm and tempest, the riot and confusion within." If madness is not just a female problem, the sensation novel can be considered a means for expressing the feelings and experiences for which capitalist culture provides no other outlet. The passage reveals what may be a less manageable problem than Lady Audley's madness, which can be attributed to her femininity. Ventriloquizing Robert Audley's position in this passage, Braddon inhabits the position of her male protagonist in a way that challenges the gendering of the distinction between sanity and insanity. She feminizes Robert Audley and empowers Lady Audley by granting them both emotional lives. Robert Audley becomes more sympathetic and less authoritative when his power as detective and patriarch appears unstable.

At the same time, however, Robert Audley's marginality, like Lady Audley's subversiveness, is converted into an operation of the law; his desire, his homoeroticism, and his asociality are all mobilized for the policing of the family. The aristocratic son who refuses to join the mainstream has posed a threat to conservative values. The eccentricity that makes him a good detective ultimately brings him back to the fold, and he emerges as a guardian of the status quo. The class whose very prosperity seems to be producing deviants holds its own. By the end of the novel Robert can return to being a lawyer, and his profession is now revealed to be as thoroughly enmeshed in the world of the family and romance as detection was: "Mr. Audley is a rising man upon the home circuit by this time, and has distinguished himself in the great breach of promise case of Hobbs v. Nobbs, and has convulsed the court by his deliciously comic rendering of the faithless Nobb's [sic] amatory correspondence" (285). Labor and romance interpenetrate again; master of a legal system that presides over courtship and the family, Robert Audley not only uses his knowledge of love professionally, but is ironically superior about it.

Yet, although the sensation novel refuses the family as a refuge, anxiously subjecting it to scrutiny and the law, it also makes it the only place where resistance could occur, since it must come, not from some readily identifiable space outside of power, but from places that, because saturated by both the law and desire, serve as regions within which to change the economy of their relations. Jameson's articulation of the utopian possibilities of mass culture, his claim that "even the most degraded works . . . have as their underlying impulse—albeit in what is often distorted and repressed, unconscious form—our deepest fantasies about the nature of social life, both as we live it now, and as we feel in our bones it ought rather to be lived" resembles Foucault's caution against seeing sites of resistance as distinct from the systems of power that produce them.[20] Both would agree that one cannot find a text somehow outside ideology or unequivocally critical in its relation to society. *Lady Audley's Secret* prevents one from looking to the family, desire, madness, or affect as guarantees of resistance or intrinsically disruptive forces. The novel relentlessly erases the boundaries between sexuality and work, the family and the law, and the private and the public spheres to reveal that one confronts rather than escapes each domain through the other. The fact that subversive forces can be recuperated or that anxieties can be contained doesn't mean that utopian prospects are impossible. Instead, they must be glimpsed from within conservative ideologies as the possibility of another way in which Lady Audley's madness or Robert Audley's disaffectedness might find their expression.

The Sensational Portrait of a Commodity

If Lady Audley is finally neither criminal nor insane, then the sensational and compelling portrait of her might be said to posit a secret where in fact there is none. The apparent discrepancy between her feminine appearance and her unfeminine behavior can be resolved by rejecting the ideology of femininity upon which it is based or by redefining femininity to include Lady Audley's bid for power. The pre-Raphaelite portrait might then be said not to hide but to reveal the power of femininity. Like her "insane" mother, who is not an ugly demon, but a childlike blond beauty, Lady Audley invites the viewer to "see" madness and femininity differently. Yet the portrait's sensational power does not disappear with the demystification of its secret; the secret that it has no secret becomes the source of its continued affective power. It consolidates a more pervasive, albeit socially constructed, form of madness, produced by consumer culture and contemporary urban life, rather than a madness that can be attributed to crime, heredity, or femininity.

The pre-Raphaelite portrait that captures Lady Audley's ambiguous power so well might be juxtaposed against another portrait of a woman whose appearance is deceiving. In *Bleak House,* Lady Dedlock's image appears among a group of pin-up portraits, known as the Galaxy Gallery of British Beauty, with which Mr. Weevle lovingly decorates his humble lodgings:

> But what Mr. Weevle prizes most, of all his few possessions . . . is a choice collection of copper-plate impressions from that truly national work, The Divinities of Albion, or Galaxy Gallery of British Beauty, representing ladies of title and fashion in every variety of smirk that art, combined with capital, is capable of producing. With these magnificent portraits . . . he decorates his apartment; and as the Galaxy Gallery of British Beauty wears every variety of fancy dress, plays every variety of musical instrument, fondles every variety of dog, ogles every variety of prospect, and is backed up by every variety of flower-pot and balustrade, the result is very imposing.[21]

The portrait of Lady Dedlock, deemed by Guppy to be a "speaking likeness," seems to be particularly compelling, but its appeal derives as much from the commodities it displays as from the woman whom they adorn: "She is represented on a terrace, with a pedestal upon the terrace, and a vase upon the pedestal, and her shawl upon the vase, and a prodigious piece of fur upon the shawl, and her arm on the prodigious piece of fur, and a bracelet on her arm."[22] Lady Dedlock almost disappears beneath the catalogue of the objects that surround her, but in fact they are both figuratively, as metonyms, and literally, as the commodities purchased with her wealth, signs of her power. The portrait reveals mass culture's power to sensationalize capitalism by using female display as a vehicle for representing consumer culture. Erotic fetishism is set in motion to produce commodity fetishism. A prototype of advertisements, and such cultural traditions as the gossip magazine and the star system, the Galaxy Gallery of British Beauty demonstrates mass culture's power to combine "art and capital," selling products by selling the life-styles with which they are associated.[23] Mr. Weevle's "weakness" for "fashion" finds its satisfaction in the gossip columns of the newspapers: "To . . . read about the brilliant and distinguished meteors that are shooting across the fashionable sky in every direction, is unspeakable consolation to him. . . . Mr. Weevle reverts from this intelligence, to the Galaxy portraits implicated; and seems to know the originals, and to be known of them."[24] Like mass culture in general, the portraits offer up the life-styles of the rich and famous in order to provide the "unspeakable consolation" of making the powerful classes accessible and knowable. Rendered visible in the sensational and iconic portraits of beautiful women, capitalism's power literally acquires a body and a face. The sensation novel's quest to uncover the secrets of beautiful women satisfies the craving to know and to see consumer culture. The fascination that women like Lady Dedlock and Lady Audley hold for audiences is thus not simply an erotic one, nor can it be demystified or dispelled by analyzing or revising the ideologies of gender upon which it is based. Providing a body for capitalism, a picture of the luxuries it can provide, these women exhibit the power not just of sex but of money. Thus, the sensation novel is not simply a vehicle for repressed female desire, and the liberation of the impulses it represents as criminal or insane would not alone suffice to render it unnecessary. In *Lady Audley's Secret*'s politics of affect, it is not just sexual desire, whether repressed or liberated, that is at stake; the novel sets into motion the relation between affect and capitalism by displaying the beautiful and rebellious woman as the figure for the desiring consumer and the desired commodity. Whether the sensationalized woman provides a deceptive face for capitalism remains to be seen in the chapters that follow.

Four

Ghostlier Determinations:
The Economy of Sensation and
The Woman in White

> Do you believe in dreams? I hope, for your own sake, that you do.
> See what Scripture says about dreams and their fulfillment, and take
> the warning I send you before it is too late.
> —the woman in white in *The Woman in White*

> And they said unto him, We have dreamed a dream, and there is no
> interpreter of it. And Joseph said unto them, Do not interpretations
> belong to God? Tell me them, I pray you.
> —Genesis 40:8

> When the work of interpretation has been completed, we perceive
> that a dream is the fulfilment of a wish.
> —Freud, *The Interpretation of Dreams*

The "Preamble" to Wilkie Collins's *The Woman in White* claims for the narrative the status of a legal document necessitated by the inadequacy of the judicial system in uncovering and prosecuting all crimes. Because the "Law is still . . . the pre-engaged servant of the long purse," operating in the service of those with power and wealth, it remains the task of a poor man and amateur detective, Walter Hartright, to investigate and defend the interests of Laura Fairlie, the victim of legal loopholes that disenfranchise her of both her inheritance and her identity. As the primary narrator of the story of crime and its investigation, Hartright aspires to "present the truth always in its most direct and most intelligible aspect." To carry out this project, he enlists the supporting testimony of eyewitness accounts other than his own and arranges these texts in logical order so as to "trace the course of one complete series of events."[1]

This description of the novel as an objective and rational document seems oddly inaccurate, given that *The Woman in White* was one of the most famous sensation novels, noted for its suspense and excitement. Following *The Woman in White*'s publication in 1860, the sensation genre became the publishing phenomenon of the decade. In the preface to the 1860 edition of *The Woman in White,* Collins refers to the "two main elements in the attraction of all stories—the interest of curiosity, and the excitement of surprise."[2] It does not seem to be his intention that the reader listening to a story told "as the Judge might once have heard it" should respond with impartial objectivity (33). Instead, his mystery narrative invites the reader not just to participate in a process of rational inquiry but to enjoy the thrill of being shocked by the unexpected.

The absence in the "Preamble" of any reference to the narrative's sensationalism perhaps signals a disavowal of the way the sensation novel promotes an extension of the operation of the law by locating the private confines of the family as the domain of crime.[3] Sensational responses are central to the quasi-legal procedure of uncovering the secrets that crop up everywhere in the novel. Characters are alerted to the presence of a mystery by their own bodily sensations of fear, excitement, and suspense. Similarly, the reader who is startled by the "excitement of surprise" is prompted to satisfy the "interest of curiosity" that might also motivate legal inquiry. The extension of the law beyond its usual boundaries installs a hermeneutics of suspicion in which every fact that excites a sensation merits investigation.

We might suspect that Walter Hartright, the writer of the "Preamble," is hiding more than just his narrative's sensational qualities. He is, after all, more central to the novel both as narrator and as character than his claims to pluralism and disinterestedness admit. The story he introduces is not only about Laura Fairlie's persecution ("what a Woman's patience can endure") but also about how his discovery of it ("what a Man's resolution can achieve") serves as a vehicle for his accession to patriarchal power and property, making it possible for him to marry her despite their class difference. His pursuit of justice allows him to further his own interests, and by unmasking the crimes of aristocratic men like Sir Percival Glyde and Laura's sexually immoral father, he finally assumes their social position. In lamenting the fact that the legal system is not extensive enough to protect Laura Fairlie from exploitation by her husband, he fails to acknowledge that its lapses afford him the opportunity to step in where the patriarchal fathers and lawyers leave off.

Like Robert Audley in *Lady Audley's Secret,* Walter Hartright takes on the role of detective because he is personally involved in the lives of those affected by a domestic crime, not because he represents a public institution. In both cases, the detective's invasion of the family's privacy is obscured by his familiarity, and his inquiry owes its success to the privileged access to information provided by his intimacy with the family. However, in *The Woman in White,* women are the victims rather than the instigators of disruptions within the family; whereas Robert Audley assumes his authority by exposing Lady Audley's crimes and secrets, Walter Hartright champions the cause of Marian and Laura, who are unable to defend themselves against the male villains without his help. In the previous chapter, I suggested that Robert Audley's role as detective made it difficult to consider Lady Audley's rebellion to be unequivocally subversive, since her criminal behavior provides the rationale for investigating the family and purging it of its disruptive elements. *The Woman in White* seems even less promising for feminists interested in the subversive possibilities of sensationalism because the female characters have to be protected from the crimes made possible by the husband's legal prerogatives. The sensational power of Lady Audley's deceptive appearance is matched in *The Woman in White* by the sensational power of women placed in vulnerable positions. The thrill generated when Anne Catherick appears alone on the road at night, when Laura is sequestered by her husband first in her own house and then in a madhouse, or when Marian pursues her dangerous investigation of Sir Percival and Count Fosco provides the occasion for men to rescue helpless women. The sensational episodes thus seem to underwrite the consolidation of male power rather than signaling the disruption of the family by female transgression. Indeed, *Lady Audley's Secret* has been described as a feminist revision of Collins's novel, the founding text of the sensation genre. By making her villain female rather than male, Braddon appears to turn the genre on its head.

Despite their differences, however, the two novels share the use of the fascinating and sensational allure of the woman with a secret. Like Lady Audley, Laura Fairlie and Anne Catherick have an almost iconic status; their abrupt appearances are like visual images, capable of setting in motion the same sensational responses that Lady Audley's portrait provokes. The model for Lady Audley, if derived from *The Woman in White,* is as much the sensational female characters as it is the villains Sir Percival Glyde and Count Fosco, who do not have the same visual power of the women. Thus, it is worth investigating the relation between affect and gender at stake in *The Woman in White*'s spectacle of the mystery woman. Just as the portrait of Lady Audley exemplifies the sensational power of Braddon's novel, so is Anne Catherick's appearance on the road the paradigmatic scene in Collins's. What sort of sensational power is invested in the figure of woman in these texts? And why, in both cases, does that sensational image strike such fear and terror in the hearts of men? For just as *Lady Audley's Secret* chronicles Robert Audley's sensational responses to women, *The Woman in White* focuses on Walter Hartright's nervous reactions to the sensationalized representations of women. Whether the women are guilty or innocent, their sensational appearances spark anxiety, which often feminizes the men who respond so viscerally, and set in motion a masculine quest for knowledge.

The figure of the mystery woman is at the center of the most sensational moments in *The Woman in White*—Walter's encounter with Anne Catherick on the road to London, his realization that Laura Fairlie is identical in appearance to Anne, and Laura's return from the dead in the cemetery. I want to argue that these sensationalized appearances enable the more materially determined narrative of Walter's accession to power to be represented as though it were the product of chance occurrences, uncanny repetitions, and fated events. His rise up the social hierarchy is catalyzed by another kind of sensational moment—falling in love with Laura Fairlie—but this event is obscured by its links with those other sensational events (sensational both because extraordinary and because they produce bodily responses) described in the rhetoric of fate and chance. The disruptive energy of Walter's secret love for Laura is diffused by his ability to uncover other secrets, such as Sir Percival's false identity, Anne Catherick's mysterious origins, Laura's resemblance to Anne, Count Fosco's Italian past, or Sir Percival's plot against Laura, that are more criminal or repressed than his own. As his romance with Laura becomes entangled with the mystery of Anne Catherick, Walter constructs a sensational narrative about fate and chance that provides an alternative to a more materialist explanation, and thus suggests that the unlikely event of his marriage to Laura Fairlie can become a reality.

Long before he has any evidence to do so, for example, he is obsessed with the idea of Sir Percival's secret and overcome with a foreboding sense that misfortune will come to Laura Fairlie:

> Judging by the ordinary rules of evidence, I had not the shadow of a reason, thus far, for connecting Sir Percival Glyde with the suspicious words of inquiry that had been spoken to me by the woman in white. And yet, I did connect him with them. Was it because he had now become associated in my mind with Miss Fairlie, Miss Fairlie being, in her turn, associated with Anne Catherick, since the night when I had discovered the ominous likeness between them? Had the events of the morning so unnerved me already that I was at the mercy of any delusion which common chances and common coincidences might suggest to my imagination? . . . The foreboding of some undiscoverable danger lying hid from us all in the darkness of the future was strong on me. The doubt whether I was not linked already to a chain of events which even my approaching departure from Cumberland would be powerless to snap asunder—the doubt whether we any of us saw the end as the end would really be— gathered more and more darkly over my mind. (101)

The passage maps the mental process by which Walter comes to "associate" Sir Percival with Laura Fairlie, and Laura in turn with Anne Catherick, a process that, rather than following "the ordinary rules of evidence," seems to be inspired by the associative powers of the unconscious. The affective charge of his relation to the two women plays itself out through the transfer of that affect to the person of Sir Percival, who becomes his rival for possession of Laura. Walter's belief that events are controlled by some invisible force, even as it renders him helpless, gives him the hope of rescue from the social position to which he is confined.

Walter's melodramatic conviction that "the end" to the foreseen cannot be predicted arises from his disturbing, but nonetheless indubitable, physical sensations. He describes himself as being "at the mercy of any delusion" because of the "unnerving" nature of his encounter with the woman in white and his uncanny recognition of her resemblance to Laura Fairlie. Bodily sensation, because it is involuntary, becomes a symptom of the self's subjection to the shock of chance or surprise events, and underwrites the construction of a sensational or melodramatic narrative. Walter's incapacity to control his own body, even as it renders him anxious, permits him to rise to power without appearing to aspire to it. The dramatic revelation of Sir Percival's illegitimacy and Count Fosco's membership in the Brotherhood makes it possible for the bourgeois hero to ascend to the status of the aristocracy as if by magic. However, before his confrontations with these two men, which are almost like chivalric duels, take place, Walter has a series of shocking encounters with "the woman in white" and her double, Laura, the affective power of which needs to be explained.

In arguing that the sensational narrative, which intertwines romance, male secrets, and the rhetoric of chance and fate, mystifies the story of Walter's class mobility, I do not want simply to replace one story with the other. This would be to lapse into the logic of false consciousness, to explain away without explaining the force of sensation. Rather, it is necessary to consider what dividends might accrue by routing Walter's desire and rise to power through the sensational. As D. A. Miller has suggested, *The Woman in White* provides a locus for examining "the value, meaning, and use that modern culture . . . finds in the nervous state."[4] I want to look carefully at the early scenes in the novel that are centrally concerned with the creation of both sensation and Walter Hartright's desire in order to examine how, in addition to providing a cover for his class aspirations, they carry an affective power that seems to exceed this explanation. It does not seem accidental that this excess seems to center on the bodies of two women, whose extraordinary effect on Walter is increased rather than dispelled by his discovery that they resemble one another. The thrill exerted by Anne and Laura's resemblance is not demystified by the revelation that they have the same father. We don't really care what the reason is, we want an excuse to be shocked and prefer an interesting story to a legal document.[5] The rather predictable story of the young art instructor falling in love with his beautiful student is complicated by its occurrence in the midst of the mystery about Anne Catherick. Walter stresses the immediacy of his love for Laura, relying on her natural beauty as an alibi for how his desire transcends the economic exigencies that govern her marriage to Sir Percival Glyde and that promote her persecution. We could say that his story of "love at first sight" is a mystification, that he reads the signs of her position as if they emanated naturally from her body rather than being a function of her social position. What's odd about his claim to love Laura at first sight is that the novel itself seems to demystify it by having Laura's appearance preceded by Anne's. Why, after all, does Walter not fall in love with Anne Catherick, given that she looks the same as Laura? The fact that he doesn't suggests that his love for Laura must be determined by her social class, but because the text itself reveals this so readily, we must consider how sensational plotting complicates any simple material or social interpretation of romance.

Rather than demystifying Walter's love for Laura, the woman in white's relation to her double seems only to add further sensational intrigue to the romance, which itself sensationalizes and masks Walter's class transition. A reading of the sequence of events that leads to the awakening of Walter's desire suggests that his attraction to Laura is inhabited from the start by his experience of Anne Catherick and, furthermore, that the shock of his encounter with Anne Catherick is connected to his expectations about Laura. There is no primal event in which love arises naturally or instantaneously as an uncontrollable physical sensation, but rather a structure of determinations that patterns events. Although Anne's resemblance to Laura can be explained by social determination, the women's startling similarity plays out another kind of determination, one that follows the logic of Freud's notion of *Nachträglichkeit* or deferred action.

The Shock of the Women in White

Although future events will ultimately confirm the significance of his experience, Walter Hartright's first perceptions of Laura Fairlie and Anne Catherick acquire much of their sensational force from his own investments. Walking home on the last evening before he departs for his new position at Limmeridge House, Walter indulges in a fantasy prompted by Pesca's fairytale story about his prospects for marrying one of the ladies of the house, the first of a series of prophecies that will ultimately be fulfilled. He loses the customary constraint required by his position as art instructor, a profession in which the sign of his class difference is his desexualization. A male version of the female governess, whose class position and relation to the family are ambiguous, Walter appears to harbor some resentment about being "admitted among beautiful and captivating women much as a harmless domestic animal is admitted among them" (89). His professional training demands that he separate himself from his body and his feelings as though they were detachable possessions: "I had trained myself to leave all the sympathies natural to my age in my employer's outer hall, as coolly as I left my umbrella there" (89). Rather than being natural, the bodily sensations of desire are constructed by the exigencies of social position, since Walter's "situation in life [is] considered a guarantee against any of [his] female pupils feeling more than the most ordinary interest in [him]" (89). These passages reveal how class differences are secured by the management of sexual desire, which far from being a natural force, is so tied to class politics that Walter's pupils are assumed not to be susceptible to any but the "most ordinary interest." Rather than being forbidden or repressed by social restrictions, desire or sensation does not even appear when the social configuration is inappropriate. It cannot be said, then, that Walter's attraction to Laura, and her feelings for him, are the product of natural impulses that transcend social determination. The link between sexuality and class identity suggests that what is forbidden is not sexuality in and of itself but the class transgression that love between an instructor and his pupil might represent. Thus, Walter's love for Laura is not independent of his class identity but a product of his desire to change it.

This narrative is not one that Walter can openly admit, however, and his encounter with the woman in white sets in place the notion that sexuality is repressed by class hierarchies rather than being a mechanism for their preservation. As he walks home, the return of this repressed sexuality is catalyzed by his heightened sensitivity to the landscape, as if to suggest that, freed from the confines of the social world, he can recover a more natural sensibility:

> The prospect of going to bed in my airless chambers, and the prospect of gradual suffocation, seemed, in my present restless frame of mind and body, to be one and the same thing. I determined to stroll home in the purer air by the most roundabout way I could take; to follow the white winding paths across the lonely heath. . . . So long as I was proceeding by this first and prettiest part of my night walk my mind remained passively open to the impressions produced by the view; and I thought but little on any subject—indeed, so far as my own sensations were concerned, I can hardly say that I thought at all.
>
> But when I had left the heath and had turned into the by-road, where there was less to see, the ideas naturally engendered by the approaching change in my habits and occupations gradually drew more and more of my attention exclusively to themselves. By the time I had arrived at the end of the road I had become completely absorbed in my own fanciful visions of Limmeridge House, of Mr. Fairlie, and of the two ladies whose practice in the art of water-color painting I was so soon to superintend. (46–47)

Walter allows himself to be carried along by the landscape, forsaking his usual rationality and direction for the "most roundabout way" (just as the mystery story takes a detour through sensation to arrive at rational explanations). He gives himself over to the outside world, letting his mind "remain pa sively open to impressions" that remain unmediated "sensations" rather than formulated thoughts. Even when his consciousness turns inward to speculations on the future, and his dispersed attention narrows to a single focus so that he is "completely absorbed" by visions that "[draw] more and more of [his] attention exclusively to themselves," Walter's mind is still the passive receiving medium of ideas that are "naturally engendered" rather than produced of his own volition. The taboo on "fanciful visions" is loosened by his ability to disavow any responsibility for them.

Given the already charged relation between Walter's state of mind and the landscape, it is hard not to read Anne Catherick's startling appearance as though it were a response to his questions about the future:

> I had now arrived at that particular point of my walk where four roads met. . . . I had mechanically turned in this latter direction [back to London], and was strolling along the lonely high-road— idly wondering, I remember, what the Cumberland young ladies would look like—when, in one moment, every drop of blood in my body was brought to a stop by the touch of a hand laid lightly and suddenly on my shoulder from behind me. (47)

Walter's emphasis on his passivity as he "idly" speculates about the future and "mechanically" proceeds towards his destination suggests that he is subject to a determination outside his control, that the event has not been willed or desired in any way. The woman in white's touch abruptly returns him to his body, interrupting the flow of mental and bodily activity by bringing "every drop of blood . . . to a stop." Walter becomes the sentient flesh-and-blood creature that he cannot be in the workplace. The shock of this physical event resonates across the text, underwriting the mystery of Anne Catherick's behavior. The explanation for Walter's physically traumatic experience is presumed to lie with the woman who is its ostensible cause. Yet, one possible meaning for the event might be derived from the speculation that precedes it. The woman in white might be seen as the harbinger of the ladies at Limmeridge House, but one that allows Walter to disavow any responsibility for his desire to form a romantic liaison with one of them. Rather than being removed from the social world, the encounter with Anne Catherick magically suggests that Walter's fantasy might become a reality.

Walter avoids admitting his physical shock might be related to his transgressive desire by constructing the woman in white as a figure of mystery. His sensational response thus becomes the product of an identity or a story that remains hidden from him. The single instant of his terror must be installed within a larger narrative that will locate and rationalize that fear as residing outside of himself. "Far too seriously startled by the suddenness with which this extraordinary apparition [stands] before [him]," Walter finds himself "quite unable to account for" the woman's presence (47–48). He describes his attempt to determine her identity or motives from her physical appearance, the illegibility of which allows him to construct her body as the sign of and potential solution to her mysteriousness: "All I could discern distinctly by the moonlight"; "The voice, little as I had heard of it"; "her dress . . . so far as I could guess" (48). Anne Catherick's body provides a series of clues that, if correctly read, might provide the explanation for her cataclysmic effect.

In describing his response to Anne Catherick, Walter is particularly concerned to ward off any suggestion of a sexual subtext to the encounter, but he confirms by negation the link between heightened affect and sexual desire. His guilt about the sympathy he feels when "the loneliness and helplessness of the woman touched [him]" suggests that he fears that his response will be construed as sexual attraction. Disturbed by his own sense of helplessness, when his "natural impulse to assist her and to spare her" overcomes "the judgment, the caution, the worldly tact, which an older, wiser, and colder man might have summoned to help him in this strange emergency," Walter must reassure himself that he has not fallen into the clutches of a woman of ill repute (49). "The one thing of which I felt certain was, that the grossest of mankind could not have misconstrued her motive in speaking, even at that suspiciously late hour and in that suspiciously lonely place" (48). The narrative is marked by retroactive justification, indicating that Walter is still haunted by uncertainty about his behavior and its significance. His feelings of sympathy seem uncomfortably ambiguous, perhaps in part because they take the form of an uncontrollable bodily response that resembles sexual desire:

What could I do? Here was a stranger utterly and helplessly at my mercy—and that stranger a forlorn woman. No house was near; no one was passing whom I could consult; and no earthly right existed on my part to give me a power of control over her, even if I had known how to exercise it. I trace these lines, self-distrustfully, with the shadows of after-events darkening the very paper I write on; and still I say, what could I do? (50)

Walter casts his aid to Anne Catherick as the equivalent of a sexual fall, emphasizing his own helplessness and lack of control as much as hers. Writing about his acquiescence to her request to be left alone, he describes his utterance of the word "yes" as though it were as cataclysmic in its consequences as a woman's sexual consent: "One word! . . . Oh me! and I tremble, now, when I write it" (50). The writing of the past causes him to reexperience his earlier sensations, and the future contaminates his account so much that "the shadows of after-events [darken] the very paper" he writes on. Past and present grow confused, and the affect the episode produces seems to be caused as much by subsequent events as by the encounter itself. Is Anne Catherick's significance apparent to Walter when he meets her, or is it only constructed retroactively, in light of "after-events"? He "traces the lines" of his writing as if the script, rather than the event itself, might be the source of meaning. The physical nature of the encounter becomes both alibi and dilemma because Walter can only describe himself as the victim of a bodily sensation that overtakes all rational considerations: "Remember that I was young; remember that the hand which touched me was a woman's" (50). This moment attains the status of an event that shapes the course of his future life, marking his break from the "quiet, decent, conventionally domestic atmosphere of [his] mother's cottage" (50).

Walter's lurid rendering of the encounter with the woman in white leaves ambiguous the question of whether its significance lies within the event itself or in its relation to future events. We are caught between body and text; is the moment charged because of the force of his physical experience of having "every drop of blood . . . brought to a stop" or because Anne Catherick will turn out to resemble Laura Fairlie and will become embroiled in Sir Percival's plot and secret past? It is not clear whether the physical shock of the event must be diffused or parried by the sense that future events are determined by it, or whether Walter is locating the affect attached to subsequent events in the single telling instance of his encounter with Anne Catherick. Walter tells the story as though his response to Anne Catherick itself determines what follows: "What had I done? Assisted the victim of the most horrible of all false imprisonments to escape; or cast loose on the wide world of London an unfortunate creature, whose actions it was my duty, and every man's duty, mercifully to control? I turned sick at heart when the question occurred to me, and when I felt self-reproachfully that it was asked too late" (55). Walter's rather hysterical pronouncements about the consequences of his action suggest that it is being loaded with a significance that cannot be found within the event itself. Thus, the establishment of the encounter with Anne Catherick as a primal event might be seen as a screen narrative for the more questionable act of falling in love with Laura Fairlie, which then simply becomes one more of the events somehow set in motion by his inability to respond adequately to the first episode. His sense of having acted "too late" in questioning his behavior might also apply to his belated guilt about falling in love with Laura. In this instance, and in the affectively charged scenes that follow, Walter seeks to locate the significance of events not just in their relation to a larger temporal sequence but in their dramatic sensational force. Physical sensations that threaten to overwhelm the perceiver must be transformed into mysteries to be explained. But if this shock is a primal event, it is one produced through the mechanism Freud describes as deferred action;[6] sensation is not in itself meaningful except when it has been endowed with meaning after the fact of its occurrence. Thus, one of the meanings of Walter's response to Anne Catherick has to do not with the woman herself, but with how she is tied to his subsequent response to Laura.

The Shock of Repetition

Among the more immediate aftereffects of Walter's encounter with the woman in white is how it heightens the striking force of his visual first impressions of Marian and Laura Fairlie. The memory of Anne Catherick is mingled with his anticipation of the other women. "What shall I see in my dreams tonight? . . . the woman in white? or the unknown inhabitants of this Cumberland mansion?" (57). Marian Halcombe, the sight of whose ugly and masculine face provides the shocking conclusion to Walter's scrutiny of her figure, confirms the idea that the female body and the male perception of it are legible indicators of sexual attraction. Fresh from his ambivalence about Anne Catherick and his response to her, Walter finds in Marian a woman whose body provokes immediate physical repulsion. In Laura he finds the exact opposite.

Suspense builds for Walter's first encounter with Laura, which is delayed by his meetings with other members of the household, and his enlistment of Marian's help to investigate the woman in white's references to Limmeridge House and the Fairlies. Primed by previous events, Walter begins to "wonder . . . whether [his] introduction to Miss Fairlie would disappoint the expectations that [he] had been forming of her" (74). Although he accounts for his attraction as a case of love at first sight, it is difficult not to see it as a function of a series of expectations and prior events. When the moment finally arrives, he interrupts his narrative to alert us to his difficulties in describing the immediate effects of his experience because the event must be mediated by his language about it and by the history in which it is installed: "How can I describe her? How can I separate her from my own sensations, and from all that has happened in the later time? How can I see her again as she looked to me when my eyes first rested on her—as she should look, now, to the eyes that are about to see her in these pages?" (74). The burden of Walter's narrative is to explain his love for Laura as the unavoidable effect of her appearance. His alibi for social transgression is his helpless susceptibility to the physical sensation produced by her body. "I let the charm of her presence lure me from the recollection of myself and my position" (78). Describing Laura as the "first woman who quickened [his] pulses," he attempts to chronicle the "sensations that crowded on [him], when [his] eyes first looked upon her" (76). In order to recreate this experience for the reader, he must convert his text into an image in order that the eyes that read it become "eyes that are about to see her."

Yet there is very little that is immediate about Walter's account of the event. He uses a drawing he has made in order to recall her freshly to mind, as though she is a representation not a person or as though what he is really recalling is his perception of her rather than the woman herself. Furthermore, he ascribes the power of Laura's appearance to her body's status as the material instantiation of linguistic figures and mental ideas. She is the lyric love poem come to life; her eyes, for example, are "of that soft, limpid, turquoise blue, so often sung by the poets, so seldom seen in real life" and convey "the light of a purer and better world" (75). Invoking a Platonic metaphysics, Walter describes Laura as the embodiment of ideal form.

> Does my poor portrait of her, my fond, patient labour of long and happy days, show me these things? Ah, how few of them are in the dim mechanical drawing, and how many in the mind with which I regard it! A fair, delicate girl, . . . that is all the drawing can say; all, perhaps that even the deeper reach of thought and pen can say in their language, either. The woman who first gives life, light, and form to our shadowy conceptions of beauty, fills a void in our spiritual nature that has remained unknown to us till she appeared. Sympathies that lie too deep for words, too deep almost for thoughts, are touched, at such times, by other charms than those which the senses feel and which the resources of expression can realise. The mystery which underlies the beauty of women is never

raised above the reach of all expression until it has claimed kindred
with the deeper mystery in our own souls. Then, and then only, has
it passed beyond the narrow region on which light falls, in this
world, from the pencil and the pen. (75–76)

Rather than being a body, Laura is a physical representation of Walter's spir-
itual life, the entity that "fills a void" and "gives form" to "shadowy conceptions." Although this idealist rhetoric seems oddly out of context in a
sensation novel, it aptly describes many of its sensational moments, which
derive their force from the "mystery" of a prediction or an expectation becoming a reality. Thus, we could read Laura's embodiment of his "shadowy
conceptions" as the fulfillment of a dream already firmly in place. Like his
response to Anne Catherick, the immediacy of Walter's sensations is not in
itself significant, for those sensations are always mediated and in part produced by a textual understanding of the event. Furthermore, by describing
his pen and his language as incapable of rendering "the mystery which underlies the beauty of women," Walter poses as the insoluble mystery of the
novel Laura's physical attractiveness.

   Walter's declaration that his response to Laura is immediate and instan-
taneous also seems suspicious because his first impressions of her are inhabited by his memory of Anne Catherick, even though he is at this point
unaware of how substantial the link between the two women is. Some mystery in addition to the "mystery" of the soul is created by her appearance:

> Mingling with the vivid impression produced by the charm of her
> fair face and head . . . was another impression, which, in a shadowy
> way, suggested to me the idea of something wanting. At one time it
> seemed like something wanting in *her*: at another, like something
> wanting in myself, which hindered me from understanding her as I
> ought. . . . Something wanting, something wanting—and where it
> was, and what it was, I could not say. (76–77)

Although he does not yet recognize the "something wanting" as her resemblance to Anne, Walter's perception of Laura as the complete embodiment
of his desire seems to depend on her disturbing lack. His first encounter
with her, freighted with significance as the moment at which his love originates, will turn out to have the "shadow" of a prior event and of another
woman cast over it. It is possible to read the locution "something wanting"
as a description of Walter's own desire, and his "sense of an incomplete-
ness" as an attempt to find the lack in "the harmony and charm of her face"

that suggests she requires his love to be truly whole. Laura's body would thus again become a symbol for his affective state. However, the solution to the mystery of "something wanting," that Walter has forgotten that Laura resembles Anne, complicates this relation between her body and his sensations, since it suggests that Laura's body exerts its sensational attraction only because it serves as the sign of something other than itself. She becomes attractive when her body ceases to be merely a body and becomes a sign or text.

Walter's identification of the "something missing" occurs when Marian reads her mother's letter, in which she explains her acquaintance with Anne Catherick. Walter's narrative alternates suspensefully between the text of the letter and the image of Laura; as in the earlier encounters with both Anne Catherick and Laura Fairlie, a woman's body arrives to fill the void created by narrative expectation. Walter is like a voyeur aroused simultaneously by an image and a text, and carried to a greater pitch of excitement by his ability to project Marian's text onto Laura's body. As Marian asks him about the woman in white, Laura flits at a distance across his field of vision: "My eyes fixed upon the white gleam of her muslin gown and head-dress in the moonlight, and a sensation, for which I can find no name—a sensation that quickened my pulse, and raised a fluttering at my heart—began to steal over me" (85). Walter reexperiences the sensation, a quickening of the pulses, he felt when falling in love with Laura. Her figure provides a locus to which he can assign the name of his unrepresentable sensation, the locus that allows him to "fix" his eyes while his mind wanders in a combination of aimlessness and excitement, much like the pleasure of sexuality. He is both voyeur and fetishist here, taking pleasure in the view of Laura at a distance, and seeking to locate in her clothing the source of his pleasure.[7] As when he encountered Anne Catherick, his state of suspended tension begins to narrow to a single focus: "All my attention was concentrated on the white gleam of Miss Fairlie's muslin dress" (85). Even as Marian announces the "extraordinary caprice of accidental resemblance," Walter comes to the same realization through the repetition of an earlier sensation. It is not clear whether his memory is triggered by Laura's resemblance to Anne or by the recurrence of his own feeling.

> A thrill of the same feeling which ran through me when the touch was laid upon my shoulder on the lonely high-road chilled me again.
> There stood Miss Fairlie, a white figure, alone in the moonlight;

in her attitude, in the turn of her head, in her complexion, in the shape of her face, the living image, at that distance and under those circumstances, of the woman in white! The doubt which had troubled my mind for hours and hours past flashed into conviction in an instant. That "something wanting" was my own recognition of the ominous likeness between the fugitive from the asylum and my pupil at Limmeridge House. (86)

The "something wanting" is not a thing but a relation. As Neil Hertz suggests, what is uncanny is not the content of what is repeated but the fact of repetition.[8] Although this moment would seem to be startling because it repeats Walter's encounter with Anne Catherick, as he experiences "a thrill of the same feeling," it would have to be more precisely described as a moment of deferred action. He constructs his encounter with Anne Catherick as meaningful because she resembles Laura, a significance only made possible by his acquaintance with Laura after the fact of his encounter with Anne. That original event acquires significance because of its relation to subsequent events, even though Walter has attempted to describe it as shocking in and of itself. Two primal moments with these women merge in this one, as Walter relives his encounter with Anne and recovers the solution to his sense of "something wanting" in Laura.

If the fact of repetition is more important than the content of repetition, we have reason to be wary of how Walter gives that content a dark significance, reading the relation between the women as an "ominous likeness" rather than merely an "accidental resemblance." His response to the shock of repetition is to turn it into a meaningful harbinger of the future: "To associate that forlorn, friendless, lost woman, even by an accidental likeness only, with Miss Fairlie, seems like casting a shadow on the future of the bright creature who stands looking at us now" (86). This reaction bears out Freud's suggestion that the uncanny sensations produced by "involuntary repetition . . . [force] upon us the idea of something fateful and inescapable when otherwise we should have spoken only of 'chance.'"[9] The hidden forces that Walter senses at work will ultimately manifest when the image Laura presents becomes a reality. This confirmation of "the idea of something fateful and inescapable" finally seems to supersede the shock produced by the events themselves. Having discovered the connection between Laura and the woman in white, Walter is reassured against the confusion he has experienced: his "doubt . . . flashes into conviction in an instant." He regains control by being able to attribute his feelings to the supernatural coincidence of uncanny resemblance, and any possibility of his "thrill" having a sexual content is dispelled. He has produced a mystery or secret that displaces or replaces the secret of his own love for Laura. The easing of anxiety produced by his "conviction" suggests that the production of mystery, rather than simply producing further affect, also manages it.

For at the same time as Walter discovers the mystery of the relation between Anne and Laura, he also confesses his love for Laura: "The poor weak words, which have failed to describe Miss Fairlie, have succeeded in betraying the sensations she awakened in me" (88). He depicts himself as the victim of sensations that affect him in spite of himself ("my hardly-earned self-control was as completely lost to me as if I had never possessed it" [90]), implying that love is beyond considerations of social class. He confesses that which must remain a secret, although he doesn't manage to escape Marian's scrutiny, and her announcement that she has "discovered [his] secret" leads to his departure from his position.

We might read Walter's subsequent detective work as a form of paranoid projection; he discovers the secrets that the other men who threaten his position possess in order to ward off discovery of his own secret. He disposes of Sir Percival and Count Fosco not simply by uncovering their plot to substitute Laura Fairlie for Anne Catherick but by threatening to expose their personal ghosts in the closet, secrets so threatening to their reputations that Walter can use his knowledge to blackmail these rivals into silence. He becomes a trader in secrets, using his discovery of Sir Percival's illegitimate birth and Count Fosco's membership in the Brotherhood in exchange for making public Laura Fairlie's hidden identity and his love for her. For both men, a single fact about their past dominates their entire identity and fate, and these secrets are represented by a single all-telling mark or text. Of Fosco's membership in the Italian secret society, Pesca tells Walter, "We are identified with the Brotherhood by a secret mark, which we all bear, which lasts while our lives last" (596).

Similarly, the secret of Sir Percival's illegitimacy is revealed by the absence of any notation of his birth in the second copy of the church registry. According to Walter, "That space told the whole story!" (529). With melodramatic excess, he ascribes to this fact explanatory power over all of Sir Percival's actions: "Who could wonder now at the brute-restlessness of the wretch's life—at his desperate alternations between abject duplicity and reckless violence—at the madness of guilty distrust that had made him imprison Anne Catherick in the Asylum, and had given him over to the vile conspiracy against his wife, on the bare suspicion that the one and the other knew his terrible secret?" (530). The novel derives its sensational force from casting events as the result of a single hidden cause. Furthermore, to know or to reveal a secret is to wield an enormous power, since Walter's discovery of the registry gives him access to property that is the equivalent of all that Sir Percival owns: "This was the Secret, and it was mine! A word from me, and house, lands, baronetcy, were gone from him for ever" (530). Because secrets render discourse powerful enough to strip a man of his possessions and his identity, Walter can rise in social position by acquiring knowledge. The sensational force of uncovering secrets obscures their function as a means to social mobility.

Walter's success depends not only on unmasking secrets but also on producing them. Faced with the painful impossibility of his love for Laura, he invents a mystery that allows him to believe that his feelings are more than just the result of a broken heart: "Poignant as it was, the sense of suffering caused by the miserable end of my brief, presumptuous love seemed blunted and deadened by the still stronger sense of something impending, something invisibly threatening that Time was holding over our heads" (101). The production of anxiety acts as a way of diffusing and managing another anxiety. Given Walter's own secret and the desire for social mobility that it represents, it is not surprising that he should be so eager to believe Anne Catherick's claim that Sir Percival has a "Secret," a word that he writes with a capital letter in order to reflect its ominous power. His one hope for the success of his romance is that some dramatic turn of events will alter the outcome that social convention would normally dictate. He cannot rely on his own desires or actions, but must instead count on chance events or the working of a larger fate to rescue him. Thus, long before he has any reasonable evidence for Sir Percival's or Count Fosco's criminal behavior, Walter is susceptible to the possibility that secrets exist and that some hidden fact will alter his fortunes. The "delusions" he feels compelled to construct from "common chances" and "common coincidences," such as Anne and Laura's resemblance, are perhaps not quite so irrational as he might like to think (101). Forced to leave Limmeridge House because of his own secret and because of Laura's commitment to Sir Percival, he can only hope that the future will hold dreadful consequences. The overshadowing of his "sense of suffering" by the "still stronger sense of something obscurely impending" suggests that "Time" will rescue him from his misery (101). It is to Walter's psychic, and, ultimately, economic and social benefit to believe in forces of determination that will bring about apocalyptic events and to believe that he cannot predict their outcome. Belief in chance allows him to hope that it will accrue to his good fortune. As Derrida says, "To believe in chance can just as well indicate that one believes in the existence of chance as that one does *not,* above all, believe in chance, since one looks for and finds a hidden meaning at all costs."[10]

The Body's Secret and the Secret's Body

The language of fate and chance events, which leads Walter to pursue Sir Percival and Count Fosco, is first generated by the bodily resemblance of Anne Catherick and Laura Fairlie. This mysterious coincidence is connected to yet another male secret, their father's sexual indiscretion, which produced the illegitimate Anne. Their blood relation further strengthens the social reading of their difference; they share a common parentage, but because Anne is illegitimate she is destined for the life that makes her body bear the marks of suffering. Furthermore, Walter's assumption of the family property is rendered morally secure by the fact that the father's crime ensures the instability of his transmission of property. Had there been no Anne Catherick, Laura's fortune might have been safe from the plots of Count Fosco and Sir Percival, and because she embodies the secret of her father's sexual promiscuity, Walter can finally reconsolidate the family line by replacing him: "But for the fatal resemblance between the two daughters of one father, the conspiracy of which Anne had been the innocent instrument and Laura the innocent victim could never have been planned. With what unerring and terrible directness the long chain of circumstances led down from the thoughtless wrong committed by the father to the heartless injury inflicted on the child!" (575). Walter seeks to locate a direct link between the father's "thoughtless wrong" and subsequent events, again invoking the metaphor of the "chain" that Robert Audley uses to describe his discoveries. Causality is given an emotional valence as he speaks of the "unerring and terrible directness" of this teleology. But where exactly did the crime occur, given that the effects of the "fatal resemblance" exceed its origin? The father's indiscretion provides no guarantee that a conspiracy will take place. The lineage of heredity somehow becomes responsible for determining all further events, but the causality here is not as necessary as the language suggests. The resemblance between Anne and Laura becomes a literalization of the law that the "sins of the father are visited upon the children," but that literal reality must be acted upon before "heartless injury" makes "accidental resemblance" a "fatal resemblance." The crime of the father gets written on the bodies of the two women, which bear the traces of his secret in an immediately visible form. Their "resemblance" is striking in part because it renders concrete, literally embodies, the hidden causality that connects them.

The compelling affect produced by both Anne's and Laura's appearance also seems related to Walter's sexual attraction. But sexual desire is not an explanation in itself, since it is socially constructed. Walter's glorification of Laura's physical appearance can be seen as a version of commodity fetishism, which is described by Marx as a process of sensationalizing objects, or creating a mystery that substitutes for a recognition of the true source of their power: "The mysterious character of the commodity-form consists therefore simply in the fact that the commodity reflects the social characteristics of men's own labour as objective characteristics of the products of labor themselves, as the socio-natural properties of these things."[11] Walter makes the mistake of reading social relations as inhering in an object when he attributes Laura's attractiveness to her physical beauty. This is made evident by the fact that the only difference between her and Anne Catherick is their social class, and this can be the only explanation for why Walter loves Laura rather than Anne. If Laura's body does not naturally possess the characteristics that make her desirable, then the fascination she exerts must be explained by appeal to a theory of how objects become cathected, which is one way of describing Marx's notion of commodity fetishism. He explains commodity fetishism in specifically visual terms, a suggestive analogy since Walter's relation to Anne and Laura is so insistently visual:

> Through this substitution, the products of labour become commodities, sensuous things which are at the same time suprasensible or social. In the same way, the impression made by a thing on the optic nerve is perceived not as a subjective excitation of that nerve but as the objective form of a thing outside the eye. In the act of seeing, of course, light is really transmitted from one thing, the external object, to another thing, the eye. It is a physical relation between physical things. As against this, the commodity-form, and the value-relation of the products of labour within which it appears, have absolutely no connection with the physical nature of the commodity and the material . . . relations arising out of this. It is nothing but the definite social relation between men themselves which assumes here, for them, the fantastic form of a relation between things.[12]

Just as the commodity fetishist takes the evidence of sight as confirmation of the commodity's objective and intrinsic value, so Walter Hartright uses the immediacy of sight in order to locate the source of his desire in Laura's body rather than in social relations. And indeed Laura is a kind of commodity, the acquisition of which guarantees to its possessor social property; however, because her status as a site of property or position is mediated by the sexual attractiveness of her body, her power can be simultaneously mystified and naturalized. The sexualizing or sensationalizing of her body is the mechanism for romance, which is then the means to social mobility, and the steps in this process are collapsed when her body itself is seen as the source of her appeal. Furthermore, the "definite social relation" that might explain the difference and similarity between Laura and Anne assumes in this sensational text "the fantastic form of a relation between things." The substitution of Laura for Anne seems to work two ways, both establishing and denying the importance of the body as a marker of identity and social position. On the one hand, if Laura can be sequestered away as Anne Catherick, and actually come to look like her, it would suggest that identity is contingent, that the body is not a guarantee of individuality, but can be molded or propped upon to create another identity. On the other hand, Walter and Marian's discovery of Laura in the asylum works to suggest that she really is Laura and not Anne. Their instant recognition of her, even when she is disguised, implies that they see, beyond the trappings of society and the machinations of Fosco, an essential Laura. Of course, this real Laura is finally no more than body, since she is reduced to a state of childlike dependency once her memory and identity are stripped away by trauma. However, this is the only Laura who is necessary and desirable for Walter's purposes because he can then act as her parent and bring her back to life, while still being sure of her utter dependency on him and her conformity to his ideal of femininity.

The mystery that is created by Laura's and Anne's bodies can be connected to Marx's description of commodity fetishism as the production of a secret: "Value, therefore, does not have its description branded on its forehead; it rather transforms every product of labour into a social hieroglyphic. Later on, men try to decipher the hieroglyphic, to get behind the secret of their own social product."[13] We might understand from this passage how to read the sensation novel's interest in secrets, its fascination with uncovering the mystery of the object. The reference to value branded on the forehead conjures up the fantasy enabled by Fosco's brand, the possibility that a secret could be as easy to discover as a mark on the body. Similarly, Laura and Anne's sensational power seems to derive from the immediate legibility of their bodies, but also from their bodies' status as a "hieroglyphic," or a mystery to be decoded. The connection between the two women is broached but then mystified as the product of fate or chance. Thus, the sensation novel provides a narrative for social determination but obscures it by rendering it in the form of fatal determination. Furthermore, because the fetishization of the woman's body takes on an erotic quality, the explanation for its power tends to take the form of a sexual, rather than economic, narrative.

It is difficult to say whether Anne and Laura are fascinating because they are bodies or because they are signs. Walter melodramatically concludes from the likeness between the two: "If ever sorrow or suffering set their profaning marks on the youth and beauty of Miss Fairlie's face, then, and then only, Anne Catherick and she would be the twin-sisters of chance resemblance, the living reflections of one another" (120). When this prediction is fulfilled, this sentence is repeated almost verbatim; the moment of bodily repetition is echoed by a textual repetition. "The sorrow and suffering . . . *had* set their profaning marks on the youth and beauty of her face; and the fatal resemblance which I had once seen and shuddered at seeing, in idea only, was now a real and living resemblance" (454). The textual repetition suggests that Laura's body is only the vehicle for the sensational shock produced by the concept of "fatal resemblance." At the same time, though, the shock also seems to derive from the fact that what was at first only an abstract concept is now, not just figuratively but literally, in Laura's flesh. The sensational, the possibility of "fatal resemblance," has been made "sensation-al," that is visibly evident and tangibly experienced. In other words, Laura is both a body and a sign, and the physicality of the body as sign, which makes possible the sensational experience of the sign as a body, naturalizes its meaning. Effaced by the emphasis on repetition are the social circumstances that make this repetition of bodies possible. The difference between Laura and Anne could be read as the difference between a rich woman, safely ensconced in domestic comfort, and a poor woman confined to an asylum. Identity is a product not of intrinsic qualities but of social determinations, which mark the body sufficiently that identical women can have different appearances. When placed in similar circumstances, the two women become indistinguishable; however, the text is structured to make this event seem to be the mysterious product of "chance" or "fate." What might have seemed a fantastic possibility, the "idea" of "fatal resemblance," has become as "real and living" as Laura's flesh-and-blood body and the physical sensation of shock that it produces.

But it is important to remember that Laura is not a natural body; her body has been constructed as the sign or embodiment of the idea of chance or fate. When she becomes Anne revivified, and her body enacts the drama narrated in the letter, she appears as a "white figure" and a "living image" rather than a real body. The language suggests that, even as a body, Laura is a figure for something else. This, in fact, is the implication of Marx's account of the fetishized commodity's affective power; although it is a mistake to locate the object's power in its natural properties, its function as a sign or material embodiment of social relations makes it fascinating.

The question to ask, then, is not just what the female body signifies, but why it so powerfully sensationalizes or embodies other meanings. Laura's and Anne's bodies make it possible to connect physical sensations or bodily responses to lurid tales. *The Woman in White*'s sensationalism fulfills the desire to make what the body fears meaningful, translating ordinary events into the extraordinary. Constructed as the repository of secrets, the woman's body both reveals and conceals, making visible, because it embodies them, otherwise invisible social determinations, and at the same time embodying invisibility, characterized as the beautiful woman's unfathomable charm.

I suggested that *Lady Audley's Secret* scapegoats women for what might be a more general modern affective predicament, the madness produced by middle-class consumer society. Similarly, *The Woman in White* opens up the possibility that the anxiety produced by women might be a reassuring cover for a different affective dilemma, one prompted by the effects of urban development and industrialization. During one of his journeys to inquire about Sir Percival, Walter describes in gothic tones a very different landscape than the one in which he encountered Anne Catherick:

> Is there any wilderness of sand in the deserts of Arabia, is there any prospect of desolation among the ruins of Palestine, which can rival the repelling effect on the eye, and the depressing influence on the mind, of an English country town in the first stage of its existence, and in the transition state of its prosperity? I asked myself that question as I passed through the clean desolation, the neat ugliness, the prim torpor of the streets of Wellingham. And the tradesmen who stared after me from their lonely shops—the trees that dropped helpless in their arid exile of unfinished crescents and squares—the dead house-carcasses that waited in vain for the vivifying human element to animate them with the breath of life—every creature

that I saw, every object that I passed, seemed to answer with one accord: The deserts of Arabia are innocent of our civilised desolation—the ruins of Palestine are incapable of our modern gloom! (503)

Walter transfers onto the landscape the hidden narrative of his own accession to power, observing with horror the waste and desolation that may be its by-products.[14] The colonialist discourse that measures progress and civilization in England against the desolation of the "deserts of Arabia" and the "ruins of Palestine" seems to turn against its beneficiaries; rather than creating new forms of happiness, the expansion made possible by new technologies ushers in a new form of anxiety. Home threatens to become as alien and alienating as the foreign and barren landscapes of the East are presumed to be.

Juxtaposed with Marx's account of commodity fetishism, this passage reveals a similar tendency to characterize capitalism in terms of the inversion of natural relations between people and objects; objects become personified and people, objectified. In Collins's text, the commodity at first seems to be defetishized; no longer animated with the life of the labor that makes it, the "dead house-carcasses" stand in "arid exile." Yet the objects that lack "the vivifying human element" still seem able to express the feelings that the human subject cannot articulate. Walter anthropomorphizes the products of capitalism even as he pronounces them dead, and they declare "with one accord" that one of the products of urban advancement is a new affect, "modern gloom."

One of the forms of and defenses against the new affects created by "the repelling effect" and "depressing influence" of capitalism might be the heightened affective experiences provided by the sensation novel. It offers escape from depression, but oddly enough does so by producing anxiety. Yet this might not seem so paradoxical if we keep in mind the other affect generated by capitalism—the fear that it will deaden affect. Capitalism's perceived ability to dehumanize necessitates the reassuring production of affect that guarantees individual subjectivity. Marx's account of commodity fetishism suggests that capitalism threatens to render the self's experience or sensations unreliable because the perception of the commodity is so cut off from the social relations that produce it. Sensationalism of the kind produced by *The Woman in White* confirms affective experience, making, for example, Walter's sensational encounters with women meaningful. The fear of not knowing what the woman represents or who she even is turns out to be far less frightening than the possibility of not having *any* affect at all.

The relation between capitalism and affective life suggests why Laura Fairlie's sensational power cannot simply be demystified by a narrative about Walter's material ambitions. *The Woman in White* demonstrates how affect can be made melodramatic in order to enable male accession to power, and in order to repress or mystify (both in the sense of obscuring and in the sense of making mysterious or sensational) the mechanisms by which this is made possible. Walter's sensational attraction to Laura Fairlie depends on both the mystification of how, as a marriageable woman, she represents his means to social success, and the mystification of her body as significant in itself rather than as the marker of social relations. Her resemblance to Anne Catherick both reveals the nature of those social relations, and reconceals them by enabling a story about determination in the form of fate. This form of determination allows Walter to believe that his accession to power is not the result of his own transgressive ambition or desire, but is somehow "in the cards." Furthermore, in so far as the resemblance is a function of chance, a realization made possible by his accidental encounter, he can also believe that social determination does not prevent his rise in power, that accidents can happen and can be significant enough to change the course of events. This continues to be one of the social functions of sensation; it encourages the belief that events are extraordinary or arbitrary and thus that change occurs miraculously rather than through more mundane or painstaking processes. Both fate and chance, although seemingly opposed, are invoked to obscure the nature of social determination.

But in addition to disguising a narrative about material determination, *The Woman in White's* sensational moments make social relations as visible or tangible as they could ever be if they must always be embodied in objects that are "only" their signs. Walter's psychic fascination with the two women is the product of the fantasy that it might be possible to make social relations visible in single cataclysmic events. This is a fantasy that Marx shares with him to the extent that he hopes to make capitalism visible by telling a story about the worker in the factory. Yet the assumption that sensational and beautiful women hide the "real" story of capitalism-evident in the factory or in the gloomy landscape of Wellingham is one that my discussion of *Capital* will question. The de-fetishization of the commodity and of women can be as misogynist as their fetishization, stemming from the assumption that their seductions are false and trivial, and that they distract attention from the real truth or more morally and politically productive impulses. The mystery of the woman in white reveals why sensation might continue to exert its thrill, even when demystified by Marxist analysis, for Marx's own notion of the commodity implies that, if correctly seen, objects have the capacity to render social relations visible or concrete. If the woman in white and her double are affectively powerful because they are signs, and not just bodies, this is no less true for the reader of culture than it is for the fortune-hunter.

Five

Crying for Power:
East Lynne and Maternal Melodrama

> She rose to her feet and looked at me steadily. Her voice was cold saying: "Then in that case I think you had better leave now."
>
> I said: "I thought I might take a look around first, if you don't mind. There might be something you missed."
>
> "I don't think that is necessary," she said. "This is my house. I'll thank you to leave now, Mr. Vance."
>
> I said: "And if I don't leave, you'll get somebody who will. Take a chair again, Mrs. Fallbrook. I'll just glance through. This gun, you know, is kind of queer."
>
> "But I told you I found it lying on the stairs," she said angrily. "I don't know anything else about it. I don't know anything about guns at all. I—I never shot one in my life." She opened a large blue bag and pulled a handkerchief out of it and sniffled.
>
> "That's your story," I said. "I don't have to get stuck with it."
>
> She put her left hand out to me with a pathetic gesture, like the erring wife in *East Lynne.*
>
> —Raymond Chandler, *The Lady in the Lake*

In addition to indicating that mass culture has its own forms of intertextuality, Raymond Chandler's allusion to *East Lynne* highlights the contradictory dimensions of Mrs. Henry Wood's "erring wife," who is at once transgressive adulteress and suffering victim. Philip Marlowe's suspicion of sentimentality, evident in his disdain for Mrs. Fallbrook's teary-eyed display, proves to be the streetwise common sense of an experienced detective.[1] Mrs. Fallbrook eventually of course turns out not to be Mrs. Fallbrook at all, but rather the evil femme fatale who is the villainess in so many of Chandler's novels, a woman who feigns feminine helplessness to disguise the fact that she is a murderer. The temptresses of hard-boiled detective fiction and film noir would seem to have more in common with a sensation novel heroine like Mary Elizabeth Braddon's Lady Audley than with the weepy Isabel Vane. Despite Chandler's misogynist implication that women use tears as a form of manipulation, his reference to *East Lynne* indicates that the woman who emulates Isabel Vane by crying in distress may not be as helpless as her tears would suggest. In the many stage and film productions of *East Lynne,* for example, actresses who dramatized to excess the emotions of the powerless and sentimental heroine used the role to affirm their artistic skills.[2] For the reader of *East Lynne* as well, playing the pathetic woman is not the same as being the pathetic woman. The reader who identifies sympathetically with the suffering Isabel Vane by crying, like the actress who works herself into an emotional passion, can derive both pleasure and power from tears.

This drama of affects, which Mrs. Henry Wood stages so effectively in her lavish descriptions of her women characters' public and private displays of emotion and their hidden inner states, raises questions about the political consequences of the construction of the figure of the suffering woman. As a sensation novel, *East Lynne,* like the melodramas and sentimental fiction to which it is also linked, derives its affective power by setting in motion two assumptions: that patriarchal culture does violence to women by forcing them to hide their feelings, and that the expression of those feelings will alleviate their suffering. The figure of the woman with a secret, whose sensational power is evident in novels such as *Lady Audley's Secret* and *The Woman in White,* becomes in *East Lynne* the woman whose secret is her feelings. It could be said that the nineteenth-century novel in general, faced with the mystery of female identity, looked inside women and discovered there a world of psychic pain and repressed feelings. But it is more accurate to say that nineteenth-century culture *invented* the suffering woman, and that she serves political purposes beyond the need to tell her story.

The gendering of genres such as melodrama and sentimental fiction as feminine is evident in Raymond Chandler's hard-boiled detective fiction, a masculine genre in which, as the above quotation suggests, feminine mass-cultural forms are belittled. In recent years, however, the denigration of feminine genres has been questioned, and melodrama has attracted the attention of feminists eager to explain its appeal to women and willing to argue that it has the capacity to empower them.[3] By focusing on *East*

Lynne's peculiar mix of sensation novel and melodrama, female transgression and female victimization, I seek to explore the political consequences of literary affects in which pain is mixed with pleasure and of texts that aim to produce tears. The sisterly resemblance between the heroines of the sensation novel, detective fiction, and film noir, despite the differing audiences and periods of those forms, attests to the enduring affective power of the female figure who combines rebelliousness and silent suffering.

Whereas *The Woman in White* seems to be addressed to a male audience and to dramatize masculine control over the threat of feminizing sensation, and *Lady Audley's Secret* plays out a fantasy of female rebellion, *East Lynne* transforms a narrative of female transgression into a lavish story about female suffering, a suffering that seems to exceed any moral or didactic requirement that the heroine be punished for her sins.[4] Unlike *Lady Audley's Secret* and *The Woman in White*, *East Lynne*'s sensational appeal has as much to do with its capacity to make its audience cry as it does with its capacity to generate mystery or suspense, but its sensational thrills resemble those of the other novels since they are also produced by the investigation and revelation of secrets. Although the secret in this instance turns on the melodramatic repression of affect, *East Lynne* also contains the bigamy, adultery, mistaken identity, murder, and catastrophe characteristic of the sensation genre. First serialized in the *New Monthly Magazine* in 1860, *East Lynne* sold almost half a million copies in England, making it one of the most popular novels of the nineteenth century, and its popularity as a stage play and a film continued well into this century.

Its aristocratic heroine, Isabel Vane, is left destitute when her profligate father dies, but is rescued by an upwardly mobile lawyer, Archibald Carlyle, who buys her father's estate and whom she agrees to marry even though she is not in love with him. Childlike and overly sensitive, Isabel is made miserable by Carlyle's overbearing sister, and she struggles to resist her attraction to the charming Francis Levison and her jealous fears about her husband's friendship with Barbara Hare. Urged on by Levison's insinuations that her suspicions are legitimate, she runs off with him, abandoning her husband and children. Although she instantly repents her action, Isabel must now live with the consequences of her fatal mistake. Levison, who is an irresponsible cad, refuses to marry her; tormented by guilt and regret, she is left alone with the child she has borne by him. After a railroad accident kills her illegitimate child and leaves her severely disfigured, she returns to East Lynne in disguise to serve as governess to the children she has abandoned. There she is forced to endure the spectacle of her husband's marriage to her former rival, Barbara Hare, and to watch helplessly as her son dies, unable to reveal to him that she is his mother. Succumbing finally to grief and overwrought nerves, Isabel weakens and dies, although not before her husband forgives her at her deathbed.

The sensation novel's capacity to make its readers enjoy suffering, or to transform pain into pleasure, suggests that mass culture's affective powers and political effects are complex. As Diderot, one of the first critics of melodrama, which, like the novel in general, emerged in the eighteenth century, asks: "Does not life give us enough trouble without our inventing additional imaginary ones? Why allow sadness to creep into the world, even of our amusements? The remark of one who knows not the pleasure of being touched and giving way to tears."[5] Like sensationalism, melodrama has a double function, at once registering and displacing other sentiments. It is possible to read Isabel's dilemmas as the result of her position as a woman; she is left destitute when her father dies, forced to marry a man she does not love in order to survive, tyrannized in her new household by her husband's sister, and separated from her children, the worst of all fates for a woman if her natural destiny is to be a mother. Female readers could easily respond to her plight as a dramatization of the difficulties that attend womanhood. Yet, in addition to providing an outlet for the expression of suffering, *East Lynne* accomplishes the more complex task of converting pain into pleasure. Tears bring pleasure because they allow the origins of suffering to be misrecognized. The novel's sensationalism effaces the material causes of Isabel's suffering by representing it as the product of the repression of her feelings.

The Repression of Feelings and the Production of Pleasure

Each of the three parts of *East Lynne* creates melodrama from a different form of unexpressed and specifically female suffering: in the first part, Isabel is silent in the face of her impoverishment at her father's death, her unfulfillable desire for Levison, her forced marriage to Carlyle, and her subjection in her new household; in the second part, she suffers the consequences of the remorse and isolation that her adultery produces; in the third part, she agonizes over her proximity to her children and her remarried husband while being forced to hide her identity. In each case, however, the focus is on forms of suffering that are represented as circumstantial or locally, rather than socially, remediable; furthermore, the suffering is invisible except to the reader, who has privileged access to Isabel's feelings. That the formula is a general one suggests why Isabel's predicament might be moving for audiences other than middle-class women.

Even before she leaves her husband, Isabel is depicted as a woman who can only respond emotionally to the conditions of her life because she is prevented from overt action. As Franco Moretti suggests, "Tears are always the product of *powerlessness*. They presuppose two mutually opposed facts: that it is clear how the present state of things should be changed—and that this change is *impossible*."[6] Isabel's powerlessness stems from her economic dependence first on her father and then on her husband. The novel, however, represents this economic problem as an emotional one, focusing on her inability to express herself, rather than on her inability to support herself. Constantly misunderstood and incapable of correcting those misperceptions, she suffers in silence. For example, her relation to her husband's domineering sister, Miss Corny, who usurps her position as head of the household, is described as follows:

> [Miss Corny] deferred outwardly to Lady Isabel as the mistress but the real mistress was herself, Isabel little more than an automaton. Her impulses were checked, her wishes frustrated, her actions tacitly condemned by the imperiously willed Miss Carlyle: poor Isabel, with the refined manner and the timid and sensitive temperament, had no chance against the strong-minded woman, and she was in a state of galling subjection in her own house. Mr. Carlyle suspected it not.[7]

Isabel's misery takes the form of being "checked," "frustrated," "condemned," and left an "automaton" whose desires are divorced from her actions. The reader is presented with the spectacle of her interior life, gaining access to the private and invisible drama that goes unnoticed by those around her. Isabel simply decides to *"put up"* with Miss Corny, adopting the strategy of submission that will later be played out in more exaggerated terms when she returns to East Lynne.[8] Her position dramatizes for the reader the emotional costs of women's economic dependence, which forces them to accept hardships without complaint. By depicting Isabel's suffering as the result of her silence, however, the novel can suggest that relief would be provided if she could only articulate her feelings.

> More timid and sensitive by nature than many would believe or can imagine, reared in seclusion more simply and quietly than falls to the general lot of peers' daughters, and completely inexperienced,

> Isabel was unfit to battle with the world, totally unfit to battle with Miss Carlyle. The penniless state in which she was left at her father's death ... had imbued her with a deep consciousness of humilia- tion; and, far from rebelling at or despising the small establishment ... provided for her by Mr. Carlyle, she felt thankful to him for it. .... Oh, that she had had the courage to speak out openly to her hus- band! that he might, by a single word of earnest love and assurance, have taken the weight from her heart, and rejoiced it with the truth. But Isabel never did: when Miss Corny lapsed into her grumbling mood, she would hear in silence, or gently bend her aching fore- head in her hands, never retorting. (142)

This passage formulates the more general problem of women's economic vulnerability in terms of the specific problem of Isabel's confinement to silence. Because Isabel's dilemma is her muteness rather than the economic conditions that underlie her marriage, a solution that would not entail ma- terial social transformation can be offered. Isabel need only have the "cour- age to speak out" in order for her problems to be corrected. The depiction of her position in terms of hidden affects makes it possible for the reader to imagine that women could alleviate their oppression by articulating their feelings.

Once Isabel makes the fatal error of leaving her husband, however, she reaches a point of no return, a point at which "change is impossible." Moretti argues that melodrama derives its emotional impact from its depic- tion of a protagonist who arrives at recognition "too late." Isabel, for ex- ample, can never recover the life she has abandoned even when she realizes that she has been led astray by Levison and that her husband does in fact love her. Moretti points out that the simplest way for recognition to be "too late" is for it to occur at the point of death, when "time is irrever- sible."[9] For the Victorian middle-class woman, sexual transgression is equiv- alent to death, since she dies socially when she falls into disgrace. Having taken "a blind leap in a moment of wild passion," Isabel finds herself "plunged into an abyss of horror, from which there was never more any escape; never more, never more" (237). Rather than dying, she lives in an emotional purgatory, plagued by remorse and guilt that can never be ex- pressed. "She would take [her cross] up from henceforth daily and hourly, and bear it as she best might: she had fully earned all its weight and its sharp pain, and must not shrink from her burden" (250). The silent suffering she endured during her marriage now becomes her earned punishment. Yet, even though Isabel's passive martyrdom is necessitated by her error, for the female reader it might bear poignant resemblance to the demands that marriage makes on women. It is significant that, in her address to her readers warning them of the consequences of abandoning marriage, the narrator recommends a form of submission very much like Isabel's penitential forbearance:

> Lady—wife—mother! Should you ever be tempted to abandon your home, so will you awake! Whatever trials may be the lot of your married life, though they may magnify themselves to your crushed spirit as beyond the endurance of woman to bear, *resolve* to bear them; fall down upon your knees and pray to be enabled to bear them: pray for patience; pray for strength to resist the demon that would urge you so to escape; bear unto death, rather than forfeit your fair name and your good conscience; for be assured that the alternative, if you rush on to it, will be found far worse than death! (237).

By identifying with Isabel, the reader can express the pain she might feel about the necessity of her own silent endurance. Just as Isabel is absolutely helpless to change her position, the reader can imagine that her own position allows for nothing other than passive submission to fate. Rather than being forced to question the social and material conditions that render her helpless, she can receive confirmation that heroic suffering is the only avenue of response.

The reader can also derive comfort even while crying about Isabel's misfortunes because they can be identified as the result of accidental or contingent circumstances that enable what Moretti calls the "if only" structure of melodrama. By enabling the wishful fantasy that Isabel might have been happy "if only" she had not left her husband, the novel effaces the more pervasive problem of women's confinement to marriage, and the impossibility of escaping it. We are told that "but for that most fatal misapprehension regarding her husband, the jealous belief, fanned by Captain Levison, that his love was given to Barbara Hare, and that the two were uniting to deceive her, she would never have forgotten herself." The narrator encourages the reader to believe that Isabel might have remained with her husband and escaped suffering "if only" she had not been the victim of circumstance.

> In talking over a bygone misfortune, we sometimes make the remark, or hear it made, "Circumstances worked against it." Such and

such a thing might have turned out differently, we say, had the sur-
rounding circumstances been more favorable, but they were in opposition: they were dead against it. Now, if ever attendant
circumstances can be said to have borne a baneful influence upon
any person in this world, they most assuredly did at the present
time upon Lady Isabel Carlyle. (204)

If Isabel's fate can be attributed to a series of unfortunate "circumstances,"
the reader can avoid confronting the extent to which her problems are
caused by her social position as a woman. Melodramas like *East Lynne* are
pleasurable because they provide readers with the satisfaction of locating
the source of a woman's pain. Furthermore, in making that source a matter
of circumstance, they also provide them with the satisfaction of being able
to locate a remedy for suffering. Readers can thus displace feelings that
might be the product of a more systemic and nameless oppression onto a
situation in which pain can be expressed because the conditions that produce it are so clear.

Neil Hertz would call this kind of sensational representation an "end
of the line" moment. The affective power of such representations stems
from their capacity to make tangible or expressible anxieties that would
otherwise be more diffuse. In speaking of how the political threat posed by
revolutionary politics in nineteenth-century France is represented by the
figure of the sexually threatening woman, Hertz invokes Freud's logic in
"Medusa's Head," in which Freud explains how the representation of a
threat can be reassuring. Hertz argues that when a political threat is represented as a sexual threat, "the field is narrowed to the point where a complex of historical factors can be ignored in favor of a thrilling encounter in
which intimations of sheer weakness and sheer power are exchanged."[10]
Isabel's sensationalized suffering can be traced to a single cataclysmic event,
her departure from East Lynne, rather than being symptomatic of all marriages or of the general position of women in the social structure. An analysis of her difficulties in terms of the latter would have to be much more
complex, and a political agenda that would solve the problems might be
difficult to formulate. Although *East Lynne* can certainly be read as an implicit critique of the condition of women, its appeal also lies in the fact that
it makes the dilemma clear enough to produce tears. The tears themselves
are reassuring because there is a tangible reason to cry. Whether the figure
of the suffering woman sentimentalizes or sensationalizes the more general
problem of the oppression of woman for good or ill depends on the availability of other strategies for the explanation or transformation of the pain of

the middle-class woman. For women without a feminist critique of marriage or a political or collective outlet for struggle, sentimental or melodramatic fiction might serve as a vehicle for the affective expression of pain that would otherwise go unnoticed. In order to assess the use of the politics of affect for specifically feminist purposes, it is necessary to examine the relation between gender and affect.

Femininity and the Discourse of Affect

East Lynne makes Isabel's suffering tangible or "sensation-al" by representing it as a state of repressed but tormenting affects. Each of the female roles that she occupies, the silenced and submissive wife and daughter, the passionate but transgressive lover, and the abandoning and abandoned mother, places her in a position where she cannot express her feelings. The linking of femininity with the possession of a rich and hidden affective life suggests why feminism might adopt as its political agenda the project of giving a voice to women who have hitherto been silenced. By representing female identity in terms of being emotional, the novel makes the oppression of women equivalent to the repression of affect. Isabel, for example, must constantly suppress both her suffering and her desire, both painful and pleasurable feelings. Repression rather than oppression is the focus of the novel's drama; women whose feelings are generated by their structural position bear the additional burden of being forced to hide those feelings, stay silent, and put up with their lot in life. Because Isabel's pain seems to derive from the need to deny her suffering, it is possible to imagine that expression would relieve her of her burdens.

This feminist politics of affect would have to account, however, for Foucault's claim that the repressive hypothesis can be a way to produce discipline rather than a means to overcome it. If a discourse about repression *precedes* and produces affect, then it is not possible to celebrate the expression of feeling or the overcoming of repression as the mechanism by which women can liberate themselves. *East Lynne's* ideological work consists in the establishment of a link between femininity and affect, which then enables the melodrama of the seemingly irreducible conflicts between motherhood or domesticity and sexual desire. When the reader is encouraged to sympathize with Isabel's predicament as an affective one, she is already installed within a discourse that associates the problem of womanhood with the problem of expressing affect. Such a strategy is effective because the fact that affective experience is physical makes it seem natural. Isabel's emotions become the precursors of Freud's hysterical symptoms, bodily responses that seem uncontrollable and that speak of pains and suffering that cannot be overtly expressed.

Throughout *East Lynne,* femininity is consistently aligned with or defined in terms of susceptibility to feeling. Not just Isabel, but many of the other women in the novel experience affective states that are physical and difficult to restrain. Barbara Hare, for example, suffers the pain of being unable to express her love for Carlyle; upon learning that he has married Isabel she retreats to her bedroom to burst into tears, desperate to hide her response. The violence of her reaction could be attributed to the pressures of a social propriety that demands that a woman disguise unrequited desire. When Barbara is finally so overcome by Carlyle's marriage that she confesses her love for him, she is guilty of what is an understandable lapse, but a lapse nonetheless:

> There are moments in a woman's life when she is betrayed into forgetting the ordinary rules of conduct and propriety; when she is betrayed into making a scene. It may not often occur; perhaps never to a cold, secretive nature, where impulse, feeling, and above all, temper, are under strict control. Her love, her jealousy, the never-dying pain always preying on her heart-strings since the marriage took place, her keen sense of the humiliation which had come home to her, were all rising fiercely, bubbling up with fiery heat. The evening she had just passed in their company . . . [was] working her up to that state of nervous excitement when temper, tongue, and imagination fly off at a mad tangent. She felt like one isolated for ever, shut out from all that could make life dear; *they* were the world, she was out of it. (137)

Although it is not entirely clear whether Barbara's indulgence of her feelings is culpable, her suffering resembles the punishment that Isabel receives for her transgression; she is forced to watch others enjoy happiness while she remains excluded by her hidden anguish. The ambiguity stems from the double emotional burden of "a woman's life"; she must at once control her emotions and be controlled by them to the point of madness. In contrast to Barbara's state of emotional intensity, Mr. Carlyle is "utterly unconscious of the storm that was raging within her" (137), and thinks her declaration of undying love "sentimental rubbish" (140). Men don't simply control their emotions; they are less susceptible to the position of weakness that produces emotion in the first place.

Barbara's passion, like Isabel's desire for Levison, is so uncontrollable that it bursts involuntarily to the surface. Affect is thus naturalized as an involuntary physical response, and this representation enables the corollary belief that repression of affect is bad, expression of affect liberating. Women don't suffer from a system of oppression, one symptom of which is silenced affect; instead they suffer from capricious impulses that they are helpless to control. By representing affect as natural rather than socially constructed, *East Lynne* can displace the social sources of suffering onto a natural force.

This naturalization of affect needs to be understood in terms of how ideologies of marriage and romance construct female experience. By representing sexual desire as a natural and fatalistic force, for example, the novel can suggest that a woman's submission to adulterous passion is not her own fault. *East Lynne* broaches the relatively radical possibility that a woman forced to marry in order to ensure her livelihood might not be entirely happy with her lot in life and might selfishly seek happiness by pursuing her sexual desire for another man: "Love never yet came for the *trying:* it is a capricious passion, and generally comes without the knowledge and against the will" (166). The novel ultimately begs the question it raises about the possible absence of affect in marriage by depicting the emergence of Isabel's passion for Carlyle upon her return to East Lynne. The mistiming of her love suggests that she has simply been a victim of bad luck. Defending her heroine for what might seem like a presumptuous indulgence, the narrator attributes Isabel's newfound affection to the vagaries of chance: "That mysterious passion called by the name of love . . . had not been given to him. It was now. I told you some chapters back that the world goes round by the rules of contrary . . . and we go round with it" (496). The implication is that nothing can be done to eliminate the possible disparity between love and marriage, and that the best to be hoped for is their chance combination. Because Isabel does finally come to love Carlyle, the reader can mourn the fact that it did not happen earlier and be comforted that this fortuitous possibility would be the solution to the apparent lawlessness of feeling. What is avoided is the initial implication that the demands of affect and the demands of economic need might not coincide in marriage, and that the entire institution is thus suspect.

As apparently natural as biological characteristics, susceptibility to affect is similarly effective as a ground for gender difference. Although the narrator's pragmatic advice to women to control their emotions suggests that their affects might be produced by their relative social and economic powerlessness, she always preaches submission and acceptance, rather than challenging the underlying economic structures that force women to marry in the first place. In one of her moralizing addresses, she suggests that women must renounce their desire for passion because men will always lose their initial interest in romance. The law of desire is that it fades through habit, but this law impinges differently on men and women:

> It was not that his love had faded, but that time and custom had wrought their natural effects. Look at children with their toys; a boy with a new drum, a girl with a new doll. . . . Do not we all, men and women, become indifferent to our toys when we hold them securely in possession? Young lady, when he, who is soon to be your lord and master, protests to you that he shall always be as ardent a lover as he is now, believe him if you like, but don't reproach him when the disappointment comes. He does not wilfully deceive you; he only forgets that it is in the constitution of man to change, the very essence of his nature . . . you will do well to put up with it, for it will never now be otherwise. Never: the heyday of early love, of youth, and of novelty is past. (166)

The passage moves from an assertion of a law that applies to all "men and women" to an address aimed specifically at women who must adjust to the nature of men's affections. The metaphor of children with their toys implies that women are the commodified possessions and playthings of men, to be enjoyed for a time and then put aside in favor of more mature activities. Interested in love as a form of play, Isabel is constantly figured as the child who doesn't want to grow up; rather than adopting the duties of household manager that Miss Corny attends to, she spends her time waiting for Mr. Carlyle to come home, and coaxing him to walk in the garden and indulge in idle leisure. The narrator here offers up the lesson of endurance repeated so frequently in the novel—a woman's work is always to "bear the cross" of unrequited feeling. Isabel's position in the latter part of the novel would thus seem to be an instance of a general female predicament, not just a fate she has brought upon herself through her own actions. The narrator's lessons in repression are not necessarily inspired by moral principles, but by a pragmatism about the nature of men's affections.

The novel also wavers between depicting Isabel's susceptibility to feeling as the general condition of women and depicting it as a condition peculiar to her own situation by emphasizing the class differences between Isabel and Carlyle. The middle-class woman reader can simultaneously identify with Isabel as a woman and disavow that identification by constructing her as too aristocratic. Isabel's melodramatic affects can be read as the

aristocracy's form of decadence, which must be renounced by the bour-
geoisie in favor of the work and discipline that allows them to attain the
status of the class they aspire to displace. Miss Corny, with her parsimonious
stiffness, scorns her brother's laxness in neglecting work to be with his
child-bride. Isabel is the commodity or plaything whose value cannot be
readily identified. "They go strolling out together, or she sings to him, he
hanging over her as if she were gold; to judge by appearances, she is more
precious to him than any gold that ever was coined into money" (134). Yet,
Isabel is in fact as precious as gold to the extent that she been instrumental
in consolidating Carlyle's rise to power. Although, due to her father's profli-
gacy, he doesn't have to marry her to acquire East Lynne, the marriage does
cover over the aggressive displacement of the family heritage that his buy-
ing power makes possible. Isabel brings social cachet with her good looks
and delicate charm; in her white dress and diamonds she embodies the
power of the aristocracy. Carlyle operates with a form of economic utility
that extends beyond strictly material objects; he also buys the sensitivity that
can be more readily indulged in by those who are born to property and
position. Although the novel espouses the bourgeois values of hard work
and the suppression of feeling necessary to work, it also seems aware of the
value of cultural and emotional capital. Bourgeois patriarchal structures depend upon the emotional life of women and the aristocracy, but this need
must be disavowed and the threatening power of affects must be managed.
The exigencies of bourgeois mobility make different emotional demands
of men and women. The aristocratic Isabel still has something to say to the
bourgeois woman being told by the author of *East Lynne* to put up with the
coldness and indifference of men, but she is different enough to make it
possible for Barbara to serve as an alternative locus of identification. Barbara is the patient and suffering lover, who finally gets the man she loves
through her endurance, the middle-class version of passion.

Emotion is also gendered in the novel by being depicted as that
which, like women, distorts reality. This connection raises the question of
the novel's relation to its own narrative strategies, which include both sensationalism and realism. Mrs. Wood's chronicling of small-town life implies
that the prosaic realist narrative is the locus of truth, yet she also attends in
melodramatic excess to how this reality is lived by women, and she narrates
a story about emotions and interiority as well as including the details of
social context. Mrs. Hare's belief in dreams, the women who exaggerate
when they gossip, the poisonous paranoia of jealousy—all of those forms
of female behavior that attend to the life of romance and feeling are fictions,

but given that Mrs. Hare's dreams prove to be right, and that gossip is a means by which facts are transmitted, the distinction between fact and fiction, or realism and sensation blurs. The novel wavers between dismissing the fantasies generated by affect as distortions and valorizing them as an important dimension of a reality that includes the lives of women.

Of Isabel's jealousy, the error of perception that leads to an error of action, the narrator says:

> There never was a passion in this world, there never will be one, so fantastic, so delusive, so powerful as jealousy. Mr. Carlyle dismissed the episode from his thoughts; he believed his wife's emotion to have arisen simply from a feverish dream, and never supposed but that, with the dream, its recollection would pass away from her. . . . Shakespeare calls jealousy yellow and green: I think it may be called black and white, for it most assuredly views white as black, and black as white. The most fanciful surmises wear the aspect of truth, the greatest improbabilities appear as consistent realities. (153)

Although truth and reality are here invoked as though they were as different from "fanciful surmises" and "the greatest improbabilities" as white is from black, the distinction is not in fact clear. Instead, a different kind of reality must be reckoned with when one speaks of the emotions, a reality associated with women. Isabel's jealousy is quite palpable to her, even though her husband dismisses it as a "feverish dream," and despite its "fantastic" and "delusive" nature it will be "powerful" enough to induce her to leave him. Implicit in the passage is the suggestion that men are deficient in being unable to attend to this reality, remaining in prosaic ignorance of the intensities of passion. Throughout the novel, the fiercest battles occur between women; Isabel's enemies are Barbara and Miss Corny, her rivals for Mr. Carlyle's affections. Dependent on the protection and support of men, women are more susceptible to the fears of exclusion and isolation that foster jealousy. The language of the passage depicts emotions on the model of ideology, without being clear about whether they are a form of "false consciousness," or whether, in Althusserian terms, they are more like "lived experience," registering and producing a reality that cannot be rendered false by invoking scientific fact. The former hypothesis seems finally to be adopted in so far as Isabel is forced to recognize the "error" of her jealousy, but at the same time the error seems highly understandable and in part produced by Mr. Carlyle's incapacity to read her inner life more sensitively. If affective experience and sensational narrative construct rather than falsify reality, the distinction between realism and sensationalism that casts the former as true and masculine and the latter as false and feminine is challenged.

In the process of gendering affect, and defining femininity in terms of susceptibility to affect, *East Lynne* sets in place an important cultural formation. In addition to charging the middle-class woman with maintaining the domestic sphere as a haven from the workplace, producing the family, and ornamenting male power through consumption and self-display, nineteenth-century culture charges women with the job of maintaining affective relations as mothers, daughters, wives, and lovers.[11] The affective power of women, which underwrites the sexual division of labor that assigns women to the affective tasks of the home and men to the economic tasks of the public sphere, is at once crucial to the capitalist social structure and threatening to it. Affect must be simultaneously produced and regulated; hence, the valorization of the tender, sentimental, loving woman, and the denigration of the oversexualized, hysterical, irrational, or overly sentimental woman. This productive contradiction plays itself out in *East Lynne* in the class distinction between excessive, aristocratic affective display and correct, disciplined, bourgeois affective display, and in the simultaneously sympathetic and judgmental attitude of the narrator towards Isabel's heightened sensations. Melodrama's focus on the conflicts between seemingly opposed affects, especially sexual desire and domestic affection, works to authorize and naturalize the regime of affect.

Once affect and femininity are linked, a certain kind of cultural work has already been done, and the attempt to realign them in order to produce a more liberated, and less repressed, female subject does nothing to challenge the very connection that produces gender and power differences in the first place. The causes of female suffering are structural and only symptomatically take the form of affects such as hysteria, depression, anxiety, passion, or despair. I am not suggesting that at the phenomenological level women do not have real feelings, only that how such feelings are represented, as well as the fact that they are represented, whether for the purpose of marginalizing women or for the purpose of benevolently attending to their unmet needs, is marked by history and ideology. To recommend the expression of feeling as an antidote to pain is to forget that the very description of feelings as repressed is already a way of representing the presence of feelings and emphasizing their significance. Repression is not simply a neutral or biological state; the positing of repression carries with it the ideological weight of a theory about how feelings become repressed in the first place.

Individualist accounts of the causes of repression fail to explain how the family and private life are themselves structured as the domain of affect under capitalism. Melodrama's capacity to challenge ideologies of affect is limited by its founding assumption that middle-class happiness depends on the emotional well-being produced by intense one-on-one bonds, such as romantic ties. Constructing not only emotional solutions but emotional problems, melodrama fails to challenge the social structures that make affect important at all.

The Maternal Melodrama

Melodrama's capacity to represent social problems as emotional problems and to naturalize affective experience are particularly evident in maternal melodramas. Generating affect from the spectacle of the mother separated from her child, the maternal melodrama presumes that nothing is more natural and inevitable than a mother's love. Conflict occurs when maternal affect seems to preclude or be precluded by other "feminine" impulses or duties, such as romance or marital responsibilities. In the twentieth century, the maternal melodrama has also negotiated the tensions created by women's presence in the workplace, although often with the insidious implication that a woman's "natural" desire to mother is at odds with the "unnatural" or "unfeminine" desire for a professional career. Although less apparently transgressive or threatening than sexual desire, maternal affect is often portrayed in melodrama as dangerously excessive or dangerously absent. Good mothers can then be distinguished from bad mothers, who can be identified by their tendencies to mother too much or too little. Isabel, for example, is guilty of both sins, first abandoning her children and then being so attached to them that she is driven to return to East Lynne, defying the edict that, as a fallen woman, she renounce her bond to them. Thus, like sexual desire, maternal desire must be put into play but also regulated, and it is dangerous when it is not balanced correctly, or when it becomes too narcissistic. A woman's desire is thus placed in the service of the social order, in the name of feminine propriety, familial harmony, and domestic stability. The construction of female desire as natural to all women masks how this construction in fact works in the interest of patriarchal and capitalist social structures. This highly functional economy is covered over in melodramatic scenarios that pit maternal desire against sexual desire or professional ambition and that make women individually responsible for their affective dilemmas.

Maternal melodrama is an extremely useful guide to the social functions of melodramatic and sentimental representations because it is difficult to challenge the naturalness of maternal affect. The sensational power of a mother's separation from her children is testimony to the force with which ideologies of maternity are taken for granted. In *East Lynne*, for example, Isabel's return to her former home to serve as governess provides the occasion for episodes that painfully accentuate the consequences of her transgression. She endures the double burden of watching her husband lavish the attention that had once been hers on his new wife and of having to hide her anguish for fear of revealing her identity. More painful, though, then her exclusion from marriage is her relation to her children.

Christian Viviani describes the basic structure of maternal melodrama in the following way:

> A woman is separated from her child, falls from her social class and founders in disgrace. The child grows up in respectability and enters established society where he stands for progress. . . .The mother watches the social rise of her child from afar; she cannot risk jeopardizing his fortunes by contamination with her own bad repute. Chance draws them together again, and the partial or total rehabilitation of the mother is accomplished, often through a cathartic trial scene.[12]

Elaborating on the assumptions about motherhood that underlie the genre, Mary Ann Doane observes: "Maternal melodramas are scenarios of separation, of separation and return, or of threatened separation—dramas which play out all the permutations of the mother/child relation. . . .All of the texts bring into play the contradictory position of the mother within patriarchal society—a position formulated by the injunction that she focus desire on the child and the subsequent demand to give up the child to the social order."[13] Disguised as her children's governess, Isabel occupies this contradictory maternal position. She simultaneously takes care of her children with excessive passion and represses her maternal feelings in order to maintain her disguise. Maternal melodrama emerges out of the same ideological configuration that first links femininity and affect and then defines feminine virtue as the management of affect. Maternal affect, like sexual desire, is at once required and in danger of becoming excessive.

Still, there is a significant difference between the melodrama generated by Isabel's separation from her children and the melodrama generated by her adultery, a difference that depends on the construction of the mother's bond to her children as natural. In justifying Isabel's desire to return to East Lynne, the narrator makes the following remarks: "But now, about the state of her mind? I do not know how to describe the vain yearning, the inward fever, the restless longing for what might not be. Longing for what? For her children. Let a mother, be she a duchess or be she an apple-woman at a standing, be separated for a while from her little children: let *her* answer how she yearns for them" (327). The reader might be prompted to answer the narrator's questions by proposing that Isabel yearns for romance; the language is very similar to that used to describe her passion for Levison. Instead, however, adult heterosexual desire has now been replaced by what seems to be a more rudimentary and fierce impulse, that which ties the mother to her child. Maternal sentiment is depicted as universal, transcending class boundaries to affect "duchess" and "apple-woman" alike.[14] Placed outside of the contingencies of social hierarchies and circumstance, motherhood does not pose the same threat to Isabel that her position as a wife does. Whereas she fears the possibility of being displaced by another woman in her husband's affections, she can depend on the biological link to her children to guarantee the stability of her bond with them. Her anxieties about their welfare stem from the assumption that her role as mother cannot be assumed by anyone else. She has "abandoned [her children] to be trained by strangers," leaving them without the love that only a mother can provide. Abandonment becomes a violation of natural law: "A brute animal deaf and dumb clings to its offspring: but *she* abandoned hers" (332). Isabel's fears about her children's welfare seem vindicated by the fact that Barbara Hare displays far more affection for her natural children than for her stepchildren. As Isabel's daughter observes: "Lady Isabel was our very own mamma. This mamma is not" (359). Isabel need not fear replacement in her children's affections, even if she has been displaced by Barbara as Carlyle's wife. The suffering caused by her separation from her children again conforms to the melodramatic formula of making it possible for the reader to identify the source and solution for that pain. Because the union between mother and child is a natural affective relation, its disruption can only be the result of contingent circumstances that might have been otherwise.

The special nature of maternal love makes Isabel's position at East Lynne extremely precarious. She is in constant danger of exposing her identity because she displays a concern for her children that would be appropriate only for a mother. To those who think she is merely a governess, her behavior appears excessive and odd; she is reprimanded for spending her salary on toys for the children, and discouraged from allowing her ailing son, William, to sleep in her room. In scene after scene, she must hide the tears prompted by her anxiety about William's health and the children's questions about the mother who abandoned them. Whereas Isabel's passion for Levison and her renewed longing for her husband might seem morally questionable, the need to suppress her maternal sentiments appears cruel and unnatural. Motherhood allows women to express intense affect that is socially sanctioned, and Isabel's struggle to curb her maternal instincts only confirms that those instincts are natural.

The novel thus constructs motherhood as a form of intimacy, which, unlike the passion of heterosexual romance, is not in danger of being transgressive or temporary. One of the reasons why this construction is so difficult to challenge is that it appears to serve the interests not only of patriarchy but of women themselves. Janice Radway, for example, locates the source of the pleasures provided by a contemporary popular form, the Harlequin romance, in the connection it establishes between mothering and romance. She argues that Harlequin romances provide for women the fantasy of a romantic relationship that recreates the nurturing, intimacy, and dependency that exist between mother and child. Furthermore, just as romantic ideals can be modeled on maternal ideals, as women seek a sexual relationship that imitates the parent-child relationship, mothering can be substitute for romance, when women construct their children as their lovers. Nancy Chodorow, from whose work Radway draws her analysis, argues that women can derive pleasure from mothering by identifying with the child for whom they care, and that they adopt this strategy to compensate for the fact that men do not provide for their emotional needs.[15] Through her children, the mother can recreate the fantasy of family intimacy that she has not been able to realize in an adult relationship.

In *East Lynne,* Isabel's relation to her dying son William demonstrates how the bond between mother and child can be constructed as a romantic relationship; she both casts her son as her lover and narcissistically identifies with him as a version of herself. When she first encounters her two eldest children, they are described as replicas of herself: "A graceful girl of eight years old, a fragile boy a year younger, both bearing her own once lovely features, her once bright and delicate complexion, her large, soft, brown eyes. How utterly her heart yearned to them!" (348). Furthermore, her biological connection to William is stressed in the frequent references to the fact that he has inherited his illness from her. Because she is genetically responsible for her son's weakness and fragility, Isabel's desire to mother him becomes a natural necessity. William's illness makes him as helpless as an infant, and in devoting her total attention to him Isabel can recreate the earliest moments of the intimacy between mother and child. That it is her son and not her daughter that figures so prominently in the narrative suggests that he is as much a substitute for her husband as a figure for her own identification. At moments when William sleeps, Isabel can establish contact with him without fear of detection. Such interludes carry an erotic undercurrent: "She glided down upon her knees, her breath in contact with his. Her eyes were wet: but that she might wake him, she would have taken the sleeper on to her bosom, and caressed him there" (357). Carlyle's final reunion with Isabel is described in very similar terms: "He leaned over her, he pushed aside the hair from her brow with his gentle hand, his tears dropping on her face. . . . Lower and lower bent he his head, until his breath nearly mingled with hers" (518). Such scenes of intimacy require that one person be in a state of total passivity in order to receive the ministrations of the other. Isabel receives forgiveness and relief when her former husband tends to her as she has tended to her dying son. Only when she is as weak and dependent as a child can she receive the erotic fulfillment that she has been denied.

If these moments of intimacy are fantasies about regression to a state of infancy, they depend on a conception of that state as one in which the ties between mother and child are unimpaired by any outside intervention, and in which identities merge. There has been controversy among feminist critics, however, about how to describe these early stages of intersubjective relations. Disagreements turn on whether the woman-centered or matriarchal pre-Oedipal phase should be considered a patriarchal fantasy or a threat to patriarchy and hence the locus of feminist fantasy. Implicitly adopting the latter hypothesis, feminist theorists such as Nancy Chodorow describe the pre-Oedipal phase as a utopian moment, free of the conflicts between mother and child brought on by the Oedipal crisis and consolidated by patriarchal culture's emphasis on individuality and autonomy. Chodorow's theories have underwritten feminist work that revalorizes the pre-Oedipal phase and the fluid boundaries that exist between mother and child as a model for social relations that resist patriarchal structures.

Adopting the view that the pre-Oedipal phase is patriarchal society's nostalgic and melodramatic fantasy of a natural Edenic state that exists prior to the imposition of the Oedipal structures of culture, feminists such as Jane Gallop, Julia Kristeva, and Jacqueline Rose have criticized the work that has emerged from Chodorow's theories and from object-relations theory. Influenced by poststructuralist readings of Freud and psychoanalytic discourse, these feminists argue that the pre-Oedipal state is itself permeated by the specter of loss and separation.[16] Julia Kristeva, for example, suggests that the pre-Oedipal phase is a triadic rather than binary structure in which the third term is the desire of the mother for an Other, a position occupied in patriarchal culture by the father.[17] Crucial to the formation of identity for the child is the abjection of the mother, the need to renounce the enveloping unity of the mother-child dyad that prevents the emergence of an independent identity or subjectivity.

Such theories correct feminist utopian fantasies of a world in which aggression and loss would not exist and critique feminist theories that attribute all psychic difficulties to patriarchy. They reveal the sentimentalization of motherhood and the pre-Oedipal phase implicit in Chodorow's model of parenting and the studies it has influenced. By insisting on the violent nature of the early relations between mother (or primary caretaker) and child, poststructuralist psychoanalytic feminists implicitly challenge the very distinction between the Oedipal and pre-Oedipal stages, a fictional narrative of psychic development that has sometimes been insufficiently deconstructed by those feminists who merely revalue the pre-Oedipal phase without questioning Freud's characterization of it. Whether or not Freud himself already complicated the pre-Oedipal phase, as close readers like Kristeva suggest, the important point is that it is impossible to claim an originary moment of bliss, followed by a fall into the discontents of civilization. In a move that resembles Foucault's critique of the repressive hypothesis, poststructuralist psychoanalytic theorists challenge the temporal paradigm that posits, as prior to the repressive work of culture, a state of natural affective plenitude. They do so by suggesting that so-called primary processes, such as the pleasure principle, are inhabited at the outset by contradiction, which leads to the necessity of positing beyond the pleasure principle such concepts as primary masochism or the death drive.[18]

A Foucauldian approach to affect and psychoanalytic models might seem to require the rejection of poststructuralist psychoanalytic theories on the grounds that they remain bound to Freudian categories even when they acknowledge that these processes are theoretical constructions. I would, however, claim that psychoanalytic discourse remains useful to and compatible with Foucauldian analysis because it illuminates how socially constructed affective processes are naturalized and deconstructs theories (including Freud's) that posit a primary or natural affective bond. For example, the melodrama in which sexual and maternal desires are in conflict turns on assumptions about which affective bond is primary. Yet the conflict itself may be a historical product of social formations that construct the family as the locus of intense one-on-one affective relations, which then give rise to triangular family romances or melodramas in which these relations are in conflict with one another. As a theorist of the middle-class and patriarchal nuclear family, Freud identifies one such family romance, the Oedipal drama in which the son and the father compete for the mother's attention. Revisions of Freud, including those by feminists, have focused attention on the affective bonds Freud tends to neglect, such as those between mothers and daughters, and they have questioned the universality of his models given his assumption that only women function as primary caretakers or as mothers. But even once the assumptions about the gender of parent, or child, or lover have been challenged, it is important more generally to deconstruct theories that assume the existence of primary affective bonds at all. Within at the very least the modern nuclear family, parent-child bonds and heterosexual romance are mutually constitutive, the one propped upon the other. One cannot say definitively that heterosexual romance is a substitute for or modeled upon the infant's earliest relations to the primary caretaker (in patriarchal society, usually the mother), especially when, as Chodorow notes, maternal love begins to model itself after heterosexual romance. Thus, feminist psychoanalytic theories, such as Chodorow's and Jessica Benjamin's, which propose that reforming primary relations, by means such as co-parenting, would eliminate sexist social structures, are problematic because they still take primary affective bonds and the family for granted.[19]

The impossibility of specifying which bond within the family is primary suggests that intense one-on-one affective bonds are a historical product. The privileging of private possessive individual bonds and the establishment of romance and motherhood as utopian containment mechanisms must be analyzed in the context of affective economies outside the family. Without a history of the construction of affect, the cultural work of melodrama, which takes for granted and naturalizes sexual, romantic, and familial desire, or personal affective relations, cannot be adequately understood.

The deconstruction of primary bonding also illuminates how the structures of affective life within modern middle-class culture construct and are constructed by the distinction between heterosexuality and homosexuality. The distinction between romance and parenting is held in place by the ideological formations that establish heterosexuality as a norm. Freud's account of the Oedipal family romance assumes, for example, that the son identifies with the father and desires the mother. Even as he challenges the distinction between romance and parenting by acknowledging the possibility of mother-son incest and father-daughter incest, Freud rarely considers the possibility that same-sex affective bonds between parent and child could be erotically charged. Although Chodorow and feminists supplement

Freud by focusing on mother-daughter relations, they tend to idealize these affective relations by assuming that they are neither conflicted nor erotic. In explaining the apparent difficulty with which a girl moves from the homo-social or homoerotic bond with her mother to a heterosexual bond with a male lover, Chodorow privileges the undercurrent of homosocial bonding in adult women's lives (the result of a continued bond with the mother). A different picture of the nuclear family produced by capitalist social struc-tures begins to emerge if one assumes that both homosocial and hetero-social relations are charged with love and aggression, taking on different forms within different social structures, forms that are especially marked when these bonds are eroticized or sexualized or when their sexualization is socially prohibited. The problem with a great deal of feminist theorizing about both motherhood and sisterhood is that it is insufficiently attentive to the aggression or violence that can inhabit same-sex relations between women. Often such blindness is the understandable product of the need to correct patriarchal culture's total silence about relations between women, which then gives rise to the tendency to idealize relations between women as an antidote to patriarchy.[20] I have found poststructuralist psychoanalytic theory, which remains vigilantly skeptical of any natural or unproblematic primary bond, more useful for my investigation of the social functions of melodrama. It avoids the political and theoretical dead ends that emerge when conflict between women undermines utopian conceptions of woman-centered social structures.

A history of the construction of primary affective bonds and the con-struction of the modern family would include the project of analyzing alter-natives to the assumption that the mother-child bond is natural and sacred. The difficulty of challenging such an assumption is evidenced by its perva-siveness even within feminist theories that seek to disrupt patriarchal social structures. In fact, even though the maternal melodrama largely works to naturalize the ideology of maternal affect, it also contains moments that challenge this ideology. One of the subversive dimensions of the sensation novel is its challenge to the links between femininity and maternity. Not least of Lady Audley's transgressions, for example, is her absolute willing-ness to leave her child. Far from being natural, maternal love, according to her, is subject to material determination; deserted by her husband with a son to support, she says, "I did not love the child, for he had been left a burden upon my hands."[21] Like Lady Audley, Isabel Vane seems perfectly capable of leaving her children or overlooking her maternal affects in order to pursue other desires, in this case her sexual desire for Sir Francis Levison.

The sensation novel also challenges maternal ideology when it focuses on the potentially erotic and/or narcissistic nature of mother-child
bonds. I have already suggested that Isabel's attachment to her son William
might have less to do with self-sacrificing maternal love and more to do with
his position as a substitute for her husband or for herself. Less obvious is
the submerged maternal melodrama within *The Woman in White,* the story
of Marian Halcombe's relation to her half-sister Laura Fairlie. As protective
of her younger and frailer sister as a mother, Marian might also be described as in love with her sister and hence fiercely jealous of her attachment to Walter Hartright and her obligation to marry Sir Percival. Yet, one
measure of the novel's investment in heterosexuality, even to the extent of
disrupting gender roles, is its construction of Marian as masculine. As such
she becomes the rival to Laura's suitors, but is clearly incapable of assuming
the position of husband because she is not really (that is, biologically) a
man. The novel can't really posit a homoerotic relation between women
except on the model of sexual inversion, that is, by making Marian masculine. Nor can Marian be maternal because that would make her obsessive
attachment to Laura incestuous. It is difficult for homosocial relations between women ever to compete with the heterosexual and patriarchal demand that a woman's primary affective attachment be to her husband.

The maternal melodrama, however, functions as one patriarchal narrative structure that enables the possibility of a resistance to that law
through the mother's attachment to her child. When the child is a son, the
law seems less disrupted, for the son simply seems to be like the father, and
the mother's love simply reinforces patriarchal relations. Mother-daughter
maternal melodramas, though, contain some interesting variations on the
pattern even when they ultimately reinforce the ideology of maternal affection as natural and nonerotic. Hollywood films that focus on mother-
daughter relations, such as *Stella Dallas, Mildred Pierce,* and *Imitation of
Life,* break the pattern to the extent that they propose the possibility that
relations between mothers and daughters are far from ideal. The excessive
love of Mildred for Vida, of Annie for Sarah Jane, or of Stella for Laurel
becomes transgressive to the extent that it prevents their daughters from
assuming the social position they seek. The mother's obsessive love for the
daughter emerges from identification with her, but also carries traces of an
erotic bond because it precludes the mother's need for romance.

Another Hollywood film, *Now, Voyager,* uses the maternal melodrama
to subvert the cultural restrictions on a woman's sexual desire. When Charlotte Vale adopts the daughter of her married lover, mothering and romance
are equated. (Charlotte, for example, states that holding Tina is like having

Jerry in her arms.) Only by accepting a heterosexual norm that demands that women find husbands in order to find affective fulfillment is it possible to suggest that mothering is a substitute for heterosexual romance. *Now, Voyager* is ambivalent about its endorsement of this ideology, and for that reason emotionally powerful, as it both challenges and reproduces the nuclear family. What remains unquestioned, however, is the assumption that emotional gratification requires a single, exclusive bond between individuals, and it is this ideological axiom, so crucial to modern culture, that melodrama installs in place and rarely, if ever, challenges.

Questioning this ideology, feminist psychoanalytic theories that emphasize the conflictual aspects of the pre-Oedipal phase are strategically useful for illuminating *East Lynne*'s maternal melodrama. They suggest that Isabel's anxiety about separation from her children might carry such affective force because it stands in for women's fears about the inevitable or structural separation that inhabits even maternal relations. At the same time, however, as the novel expresses this anxiety, it reassures the reader by representing Isabel's loss of her maternal bond with her children as a contingent dilemma, rather than as a more intransigent condition. She is barred from unmediated intimacy with her children, first because she abandons them and then because she cannot reveal her identity to them. William's death also enables the belief that the separation of mother and child is the product of a cruel but accidental fate and not an inevitable psychological necessity. Thus, even as the reader cries over Isabel's losses, she can indulge in the fantasy that if Isabel had not left her children or that if she could identify herself as their mother, harmony would be restored. By dramatizing the disruption of the mother-child bond, the maternal melodrama reinforces the belief that that bond is natural and eternal.

The death of Isabel's son William is arguably the most affectively powerful scene in the entire novel. Echoing other famous sentimental moments in nineteenth-century fiction, such as the death of Little Nell in Dickens's *The Old Curiosity Shop* and the death of Eva in *Uncle Tom's Cabin,* the child's death is a vehicle for the spectacle of Isabel's maternal suffering. Her anguish about the death of her child is intensified by the fact that because she cannot identify herself as his mother, she must hide her grief. In this respect, the maternal melodrama plays out the same melodramatic structure that marked the earlier sections of the novel, generating affect by focusing on its repression. Isabel attempts to reassure William when he expresses doubts about whether or not his mother really loves him, but "No, not even at that last hour when the world was closing on him dared she say, I am your mother" (493). By denying the reader the satisfaction of a final reunion between mother and child, the narrative enables the fantasy that Isabel need only utter the words that she is William's mother for all to be resolved. The tears the reader might shed at this moment can provide pleasure, because they are prompted by the identification of the cause of pain and of its antidote. The reader can cry about the impossibility of seeing resolution enacted, while being saved from the anxiety of not being able to locate the problem or its cure. The suffering caused by Isabel's need to remain silent is graphically depicted when William is on the verge of death. As Mr. Carlyle tends to his son, Isabel presents the following mute spectacle: "Down on her knees, her face buried in the counterpane, a corner of it stuffed into her mouth that it might help to stifle her agony, knelt Lady Isabel" (491). Repression is literalized as Isabel must physically prevent herself from expressing her feelings. Such scenes work to suggest the power that the removal of repression might have to change one's life; once again, the novel provides pleasurable tears by representing a potentially unresolvable problem, the inevitable separation of mother and child, as an affective problem.

The melodrama of Isabel's adultery and the maternal melodrama represent two different ways in which a narrative about contingency effaces more intransigent problems. In the first case, the possibility that Isabel's suffering is the product of her position as a woman is both represented and domesticated by depicting her tragedy as the result of a series of contingent accidents. In crying about Isabel's fate, the reader expresses her discontent with the position of women and her sense that she is powerless to change it. At the same time, tears become a mechanism for containing this anxiety because they are produced by the fantasy that Isabel's fate could have been different if particular circumstances had been different. When the narrative shifts to maternal melodrama, a story about contingency again effaces a structural problem. Isabel's accidental separation from her children acts as a locus for anxieties about mother-child relations, while encouraging the belief that, because the maternal bond is inviolable, a familial utopia could have been achieved if Isabel had not left her home. In the first case, what is effaced are the historical conditions that determine women's lives, conditions that might be altered if it were not assumed that tears are the only available response. In the second case, what is effaced is the structural inevitability of loss and separation even in the context of the mother-child dyad.

The difference between these two readings can be formulated as the difference between a Marxist reading and a psychoanalytic reading, or between a historical and a structural account of the sources of suffering. In the

first case, the representation of suffering as contingent is read as an efface-
ment of social conflicts that require systemic rather than local remedy.
Melodrama encourages a fatalistic submission to social conditions that are
historically specific and thus transformable. In the second case, melodrama
masks the pain of inevitable psychic conflicts by representing it as the product of specific circumstances. The difference between the two readings
turns on whether or not the dilemmas that melodrama effaces are amenable
to social change. To answer this question with a definitive yes would be to
enact the melodramatic structure in my own reading, that is, to offer an
identifiable, and hence reassuring, reason for discontent. At the same time,
to give a definitive no, on the grounds that pain is a structural necessity,
would be to run this risk in a different way, vindicating melodrama's invita-
tion to cry because we can do nothing about the painful price of subjectivity. Perhaps the conflict between the two readings suggests that the politics
of melodrama is indeterminate. To argue that the affect generated by melodrama contributes to a conservative politics, that books like *East Lynne*
would be unnecessary if social relations were changed, is to suggest that all
affect and indeed all culture is false consciousness and that in a world where
affects could be translated into deeds such mediations would wither away.
Melodrama instead might be a reminder of the difficulties involved in locating the real causes of pain or the real cures for pain. Certainly, in relation to
East Lynne, it is possible to identify social changes that would alleviate Isabel's suffering, but when concrete solutions to social problems cannot be
easily specified, melodrama's shorthand formulas for representing pain and
its antidote may be necessary. At such moments, melodrama provides the
reassuring confirmation that there is good reason to cry.

Maternal Sentiment and Political Activism

Psychoanalytic theory provides a way to challenge and de-naturalize the
ideology of maternal affect that *East Lynne*'s melodrama draws upon and
reproduces. Another crucial strategy for historicizing this ideology is to examine its class-specific and race-specific origins. Some of the most compelling maternal melodramas and sentimental fictions of the nineteenth-
century concern the institution of slavery in nineteenth-century America.
Harriet Beecher Stowe's *Uncle Tom's Cabin,* for example, enjoyed the same
kind of popularity as the sensation novel both in the United States and in
Britain. Stowe's novel suggests the powerful potential of sentimental or affectively sensational fiction, since she encourages the abolition of slavery

by reaching not just the minds but the hearts of middle-class female readers. The maternal melodrama is one of Stowe's central tactics; she uses middle-class maternal sentiment in order to mobilize abolitionist sentiment, generating the affective power of her text out of the representation of slavery as a system that separates slave women from their children. The horrors of slavery are thus depicted in terms of its disruption of familial affective ties. As in *East Lynne,* the power of these scenes depends upon the reader's assumption that maternal affection is natural, which leads to the conviction that slavery, because it threatens maternal affect, is unnatural and inhuman.

Stowe's mobilization of the politics of affect depends on her text's ability to encourage white middle-class women to identify with black slave women. By equating the middle-class family with the slave family, she legitimates slaves as people, who, because they have feelings, cannot be treated as commodities. More generally, the novel uses affect to promote an abolitionist agenda by suggesting that humanness is defined as the possession of feelings. The reader who is forced to acknowledge that slaves have feelings and generate sympathetic responses must also agree that slaves must be treated as humans.

Effective as Stowe's equation of middle-class mothers and slave mothers might be, this gesture also constitutes a profoundly deceptive sleight of hand in so far as it is blind to the *differences* between white middle-class women and black slave women.[22] The maternal melodrama in *Uncle Tom's Cabin* threatens to erase the social circumstances that separate black women from their children, who are taken from them not through accident or misfortune but through an institution that does not literally kill individuals, although it may produce "social death." The melodrama that substitutes necessity or fate for social circumstances is evident in the following polemical address, which is similar in form to Mrs. Henry Wood's admonitions to her readers, if more ambitious in its aims:

> And you, mothers of America,—you who have learned, by the cradles of your own children, to love and feel for all mankind,—by the sacred love you bear your child; by your joy in his beautiful, spotless infancy; by the motherly pity and tenderness with which you guide his growing years; by the anxieties of his education; by the prayers you breathe for his soul's eternal good;—I beseech you, pity the mother who has all your affections, and not one legal right to protect, guide, or educate, the child of her bosom! By the sick hour of your child; by those dying eyes, which you can never forget; by those last cries, that wrung your heart when you could neither help nor save; by the desolation of that empty cradle, that silent

nursery,—I beseech you, pity those mothers that are constantly made childless by the American slave-trade! And say, mothers of America, is this a thing to be defended, sympathized with, passed over in silence?[23]

Stowe equates the death of a child with the selling of a child into slavery, thus erasing the distinction between a natural fact and a social one. Her address to the "mothers of America" is in fact not all-inclusive; it is addressed to middle-class women, who, precisely because they are not slaves, are powerful enough to exert some influence to change the social system. Their power comes to them by virtue of the feelings naturally engendered by the circumstances of mothering, the "sentimental power" that Jane Tompkins has described in order to explain the cultural work of *Uncle Tom's Cabin* as both popular fiction and as proto-feminist novel.[24] Tompkins's claims for Stowe's cultural subversiveness rest on the unquestioned division between the races implicit in Stowe's vision of a world run, not by the disenfranchised, but by white women who possess domestic managerial power. Tompkins argues that "Stowe reconceives the role of men in human history: while Negroes, children, mothers, and grandmothers do the world's primary work, men groom themselves contentedly in a corner."[25] In declaring the common ground between "Negroes, children, mothers, and grandmothers," Tompkins neglects to consider that the division of labor within the slave household involves "Negroes" doing the primary work, while white women manage the household economy, or use the leisure time made available by others' labor to do the good work of preaching and writing about abolition. The class and race differences that separate women are effaced by Stowe's maternal melodrama and by Tompkins's feminist celebration of her politics of affect. Although the establishment of common ground may have been necessary to sway the sympathies that Stowe hopes to mobilize, it runs the risk of producing a situation in which the benevolent gestures and affects of middle-class women, rather than the activities of the slaves themselves, lead to abolition.

A critique of Stowe's maternal melodrama raises questions about whether the politics of affect is specific to middle-class women. Although it is beyond the scope of this book to do so, I would suggest that the answer to that question would involve a careful examination of the uses of melodrama and sentimentality in the narratives of non-middle-class women. Recent feminist work on the African-American literary tradition suggests that melodrama has been put to important uses by African-American women writers from Harriet Jacobs and Frances Harper to Toni Morrison and Alice

Walker.[26] The genre of slave narrative, for example, represents a complex borrowing of the strategies of domestic and sentimental fiction in order to portray the violations slavery imposes upon women's maternal and sexual desires. The politics of sexuality and maternal affect is complicated by the sexual violation of slave women by their masters and the "family" relations produced by miscegenation. The maternal melodrama's assumption that motherhood is a universal category would be challenged by a discussion of the particular status of motherhood under slavery, which denied women their status as humans or mothers, and denied their mixed-race children any claim to an identity derived from their fathers.[27] Toni Morrison's *Beloved,* the story of an escaped slave mother who kills her own child in order to prevent its return to slavery, both uses and revises the maternal melodrama by suggesting that maternal affection could take the form of murder. Morrison's narrative historicizes and denaturalizes the assumption of an unproblematic bond between mother and child that the maternal melodrama works to construct. Morrison also describes *Beloved* as an attempt to revise the genre of slave narrative by chronicling the "monstrous features" that nineteenth-century slave narratives "kept veiled" in the interest of not alienating readers. One of the mechanisms for that veiling was sentimental discourse, but Morrison does not necessarily reject melodrama or sensationalism in favor of realism, since she prefers "truth" to "fact" and seeks to depict or recreate the "emotional memory—what the nerves and skin remember as well as how it appeared."[28] Attention to specificities of race and class need not preclude the use of maternal melodrama or maternal affect for politically progressive purposes.

One of the political implications of the maternal melodrama, whether deployed by African-American or by middle-class white women, is that it allows the effects of social violence to be measured in terms of psychic pain and not just physical or literal violence. The conflict I have staged between a Marxist and a psychoanalytic reading, or between a social and a psychic account of the source of pain, need not lead to an impasse of interpretation or of political action. The way out of this theoretical and political dilemma is provided by a feminism that attends to the historical construction of affect in order to account both for the contingency of the division between private affective experience and public life and the relative intransigence of this distinction as a discursive paradigm that continues to structure everyday life.

As Douglas Crimp has suggested about political activism in the face of the AIDS crisis, one need not choose between "mourning and militancy," or between affective experience and political action.[29] The most effective activism might require both mourning *and* militancy, the recognition both of what can be changed because AIDS is not simply a biological problem but a social one, and of what cannot be changed in the face of death. The repression of mourning because of the need to confront without sentimentality how sexism, racism, and homophobia structure the incidence and treatment of AIDS might constitute a dangerous avoidance of the reality of suffering, an avoidance that creates not just individual psychic distress but political difficulties. The expression of feeling and activism need not be at odds, although they often are when affect is represented or experienced as natural or inevitable.

Attention to gender difference can illuminate how melodrama has functioned both to install women in their place and to allow them to mourn that position. Maternal melodrama, in particular, because of the privileged place within bourgeois culture of motherhood as the central instance of natural bonding, also reveals the historical nature of such ideologies and the constructed nature of affective experience. The fact that both maternal melodramas and feminist theories of affect and mothering are so readily blind to this history, displaying a tendency to idealize a utopian mother-child intimacy, is a sign of the intransigent appeal of such fantasies within political discourse itself. Such fantasies continue to structure political and theoretical discourse. Although it may be crucial to examine the premises of utopian aspirations and the ideologies of affect that underlie them, it is not necessarily the case that fantasy always has detrimental effects. Whether the theoretical positing of aggression within intimacy has any political purchase depends on the extent to which at particular times and places this possibility is negated. Within bourgeois culture, motherhood has frequently been constructed around this blindness. The questioning of maternal affection is a crucial task for feminists engaged in a critique of the family. The continued resonance of maternal melodrama in contemporary discourses about issues such as abortion, child-care, surrogate parenting, and single-parent homes, many of which take for granted that the biology of mothering has necessary social consequences, is of utmost political consequence. Whenever a social problem is dramatized through the sensational figure of a mother separated from her child, melodrama is producing not just tears but social policy.

Six

The Inside Story: On Sympathy in *Daniel Deronda*

Although Gwendolen Harleth might be considered one more of the many egoists who populate George Eliot's fiction, her reign as "the princess in exile" whose only concern is to do as she likes is short-lived.[1] Again and again Gwendolen is forced to do what she doesn't like. When her family loses its money, she can no longer live in the style to which she is accustomed; since she can't be an actress and won't be a governess, she can only marry to maintain her livelihood and social status; once married she is subjected to Grandcourt's "empire of fear." Gwendolen's desires are contained more often than they are realized, by a series of circumstances that would seem to provide more than ample punishment for the blindness and presumption of her initial ambitions. However, the frustration of her will does more than reveal the price of egoism; it has the advantage of producing an interior psychological life that the novel carefully depicts. Under Grandcourt's power, her will and rebellious energy go underground, creating the domain that will be documented by Eliot's psychological realism and mobilized by Daniel's moral guidance. Grandcourt ensures that Gwendolen's feelings have no outlet, and he actively fosters her inward resistance in order to feel the power of being able to keep her silent. The enforced secrecy of her thoughts only increases their intensity and richness. Her psyche becomes a mysterious underworld: "Fantasies moved within her like ghosts, making no break in her more acknowledged consciousness and finding no obstruction in it; dark rays doing their work invisibly in the broad light."[2] The narrator insists on the absolute separation of the "broad light" of conscious life from the "dark rays" of the unconscious. However, both Eliot, the realist author, and Deronda, the sympathetic mentor, have access to these "dark rays," and the invisibility of Gwendolen's mental life guarantees the privileged sensitivity of those who have the power to discern it. Eliot's is a realism of depths, not surfaces, positing the self as interior and penetrable only by special techniques. In order to represent Gwendolen's psychology, however, the novel depends on Grandcourt's repressive power to confine her to a secret mental life. The result is a peculiar complicity between Daniel's and the narrator's politics of sympathy and Grandcourt's emotional terrorism.

Despite Eliot's famous scorn for "silly novels by lady novelists," her construction of the dramatic interiority that makes Gwendolen both capable of sympathy and deserving of it owes a large debt to the sensation novel.[3] Part rebel and part victim, Gwendolen resembles both the transgressive and the suffering heroines of the sensation genre. Eliot, however, retains her respectability as a high-culture novelist by converting sensational events into sensational psychological dilemmas. Grandcourt terrorizes Gwendolen by forcing her to submit mutely to his wishes rather than by threatening her life or her property. Gwendolen responds by merely fantasizing about murdering him or fleeing from the marriage, although she suffers so much guilt about her transgressive wishes that she must melodramatically confess them to Daniel as if they were actual deeds. And although Grandcourt doesn't actually commit bigamy, Gwendolen considers her marriage to him to be its moral equivalent, as she anxiously guards her secret knowledge of his previous relationship with Lydia Glasher, Grandcourt's former mistress and the mother of his children. Whereas the sensation novel gratifies its readers by turning female fantasies of rebellion and persecution into actual events, Eliot does so by making the utterance of fantasy, its transition from private secret to public discourse, a cataclysmic moment. Similarly, she maps the sensation novel's logic of crime and secrets onto the psyche; just as the detective safeguards the family by solving its mysteries, a sympathetic listener like Daniel Deronda, who is a detective for the soul, cures Gwendolen's psyche of its torments by uncovering her secrets.

The ties between the sensation novel and George Eliot's work are thus stronger than she might have been willing to admit. There is of course a significant difference between her desire to promote sympathy and the sensation novelists' production of excitement and suspense. Rather than seeking to entertain her readers by encouraging rebellious fantasy or soothing hidden fears and anxieties, Eliot wants to educate them to put their affects to productive social and moral use. Both kinds of fiction, however, depend on the production of affect to achieve their power. Eliot's relation to the sensation novel is similar to that of twentieth-century critics who recognize the progressive potential of mass culture; she seeks to capitalize on the affective power of narrative and turn it to purposes other than idle amusement and escape. Fredric Jameson's observation that modernist constructions of mass culture and high culture must be understood as dialectically related could be applied to an earlier period; the aims of Victorian novelists with a serious social mission were formulated in response to the mass production and consumption of popular fiction.[4] The bulk of Eliot's novels—*Romola* (1862–1863), *Felix Holt* (1866), *Middlemarch* (1871–1872), and *Daniel Deronda* (1876)—were published in the wake of the sensation novel's popularity, and "Silly Novels by Lady Novelists" suggests that Eliot had a vested interest in ensuring that such fiction not be considered the best that women writers could produce. Moreover, in her novels, one of the symptoms of her female characters' lack of education and moral sympathy is often their susceptibility to the romantic notions promoted by popular fiction; Gwendolen, for example, "rejoiced to feel herself exceptional; but her horizon was that of the genteel romance where the heroine's soul poured out in her journal is full of vague power, originality, and general rebellion, while her life moves strictly in the sphere of fashion" (83).

Despite her attempts to distance herself from popular fiction writers, Eliot's ideology of affect is not fundamentally different from that of the sensation novelists. Her ethics of sympathy hinges on the representation of feelings as a natural force or spontaneous psychic energy; the foundation of ethical behavior is emotional investment in objects or persons outside the self. The intense drama of Gwendolen's mental life is crucial to Eliot's project of demonstrating that political change consists of "social regeneration through a reshaping of thought and feeling."[5] The self, conceived of as a repository of often unconscious feelings, is the locus of transformation. In Eliot's moral universe, the original sin is narcissism or egoism, that is, an inability to have feelings about, or to cathect on, anything other than the self. Moral reformation of the egoist consists in the redirection of the natural affections; whether attached to another person, a work of art, or even a spot of ground, once focused outside the self, emotional investments provide the foundation for political goals or collective action. Thus, although the object to which it is attached can change, affect itself is always natural.

Read from the vantage of a theory that affect is socially constructed, Eliot's politics of sympathy can be located within the context of a nineteenth-century discourse that constructs the expression of feeling as fundamental to individual subjectivity. When the affective is naturalized, the political is often personalized, and private intersubjective relations take the place of public and collective ones. Terry Eagleton, for example, argues that Eliot's tendency to substitute ethics for politics "is a mystification inherent in the very forms of realist fiction, which by casting objective social relations into interpersonal terms, constantly holds open the possibility of reducing the one to the other."[6] George Eliot's novels are central to a Victorian tradition that claims for literature or high culture a special role in laying the groundwork for political change because it has the capacity to develop and educate feelings. When Daniel suggests to Gwendolen that she "turn [her] fear into a safeguard," he is arguing that affect, even when its origin is unconscious, can itself be a source of moral behavior rather than a force requiring external restraint. This containment strategy resembles the sensation novel's tendency to cast social problems as emotional ones in order to construct emotional solutions. Although ostensibly more self-conscious and constructive in its goals, Eliot's narrative about psychological and moral development performs the same cultural work as the sensation novel, constructing a discourse of affect as central to individual subjectivity and political action.

Eliot's politics of affect is further complicated by the role of gender difference in her depiction of the regenerative power of the emotions. The expression of affect in part provides the ground for an ethics of individual and psychic action because Eliot, like Mrs. Henry Wood, represents the social position of women in terms of the repression or internalization of affect. Gwendolen's silence is not just the punishment deserved by an erring egoist, but the sign of a woman so powerless to act that she can only respond to her situation psychologically. The novel's psychological drama constitutes a form of feminist politics; by articulating Gwendolen's hidden inner life, the narrative provides access to a character who would otherwise be invisible or insignificant. The narrator, for example, defends the importance of a narrative about female consciousness as follows:

Could there be a slenderer, more insignificant thread in human history than this consciousness of a girl, busy with her small

ences of the way in which she could make her life pleasant? . . .
What in the midst of that mighty drama are girls and their blind
visions? They are the Yea or Nay of that good for which men are
enduring and fighting. In these delicate vessels is borne onward
through the ages the treasure of human affections. (159–160)

The narrator attempts to mediate between Gwendolen and the "mighty
drama" of world historical events by telling the story of her inner life. The
difficulty of such mediation, a challenge that Eliot consistently takes up in
her fiction, is symptomatic of the marginal position of women in history. By
suggesting that the story of a girl's mind may be as important as the history
of wars, the narrator offers a feminist critique of what counts as history.
Different narrative strategies must be adopted in order to write a history that includes women or accounts for their exclusion. The metaphor of
the "vessel" suggests that the narrator must turn inward to the mind in order
to depict the "affections" that it is women's role to preserve. A narrative
about the psyche and emotions expands the domain of culture and politics
to include the private, feminine sphere. However, psychological realism
and its accompanying ethics of sympathy may only remain symptomatic of
the problem of women's place in history, by taking for granted the conditions that make women's lives primarily interior.

At the heart, then, of George Eliot's lofty and ambitious ethical mission
lies a figure familiar to readers of the sensation novel: the mysterious and
suffering middle-class woman. Like Lady Audley, Anne Catherick, Laura Fairlie, and Isabel Vane, Gwendolen Harleth is the locus of a mystery around
which turns a sensational narrative. The opening sentence of the novel
poses the secret to be uncovered: "Was she beautiful or not beautiful? and
what was the secret of form or expression which gave the dynamic quality
to her glance?" (35). In this case, the voyeuristic desire to uncover the mystery of Gwendolen's appearance becomes an ethical project; Eliot, the high-
culture novelist, substitutes for the more superficial or trivial question that
might entertain the sensation novel reader, an ostensibly more serious
question about the inner self: "Was the good or evil genius dominant in
those beams?" Like the authors of the sensation novel, Eliot investigates her
heroine's deceptive appearance and is both sympathetic and judgmental,
although the moral evaluation of the woman turns on whether she is ego-
tistical, not on whether she is criminal, insane, or fallen.

Furthermore, like *East Lynne*'s suffering heroine, Gwendolen provides the vehicle for a melodramatic spectacle because her pain is psychic, and hence invisible. Eliot relies on the repressive hypothesis as much as do the sensation novelists. The exposure of Gwendolen's utterly invisible emotional life becomes a test of her narrative skill and Daniel's moral sensitivity. If the sensation novel can only devise sensational, and by implication unrealistic, solutions for its heroines' distress, Eliot provides hers with rescue in the form of a sympathetic listener. Isabel Vane's misery is accessible only to the reader, who watches helplessly as she suffers alone and misunderstood. Eliot provides Gwendolen with a flesh-and-blood savior, but the help he offers is similar to that which melodrama encourages its readers to imagine. He enables Gwendolen to express her hidden feelings, offering an affective solution not a social one. Endorsed by the narrator as a model of virtue, Daniel's presence marks the difference between the mass-culture sensation novel and a high-culture novel about the politics of sympathy. Daniel, however, bears a striking resemblance to the power-seeking detectives and sensitive men of *Lady Audley's Secret* and *The Woman in White*. In order to assess the politics of sympathy, it is necessary to scrutinize the power and the limits of Gwendolen's sympathetic mentor figure and to consider whether his therapeutic aid to Gwendolen is a poor substitute for the broader social transformation needed to alleviate her problems.

Whether she succeeds in realizing them or not, Eliot's political ambitions are certainly far grander and more explicit than those of the sensation novelists. She further raises the stakes of the politics of affect by envisioning the possibility that the sympathy Daniel offers to Gwendolen might also be extended to the more collective political agenda of Zionism. However, the famous controversy about the failure of this half of the novel's plot suggests that Eliot's enthusiastic investment in Daniel and his Zionism has not been shared by many of her readers. In other words, she fails to make Daniel or Zionism affectively compelling, or sensational. Whether or not she converts us to the politics of sympathy, Gwendolen ultimately wins the sensationalist sweepstakes in the novel. The discrepancy between the two plots might prompt skepticism about the claim that the sensations generated by beautiful, mysterious, and suffering women or mass culture could ever be transferred to more deserving people or more abstract goals. I will explore how Daniel's capacity for sympathy relates to his endorsement of Zionism, a politics with suspicious ties to ideologies of nationalism and imperialism. But before examining more overtly political forms of affect, I want to explore the sensational mystery of the suffering Gwendolen Harleth. For Daniel's rescue mission is problematized from the outset by the less than natural way in which Gewndolen's affects and their repression are created by Grandcourt's insidious triumph over her psyche.

Does Gwendolen Get Her Choice?: Marriage as Emotional Exploitation

Grandcourt is a difficult villain to pin down. Likened to a tyrant, an imperialist, a torturer, and a sadist, he wields power in ways more subtle than these metaphors imply. The text's extravagant language struggles to render concrete a form of domination whose means and effects are frequently invisible. How does one see the violence imposed by an "empire of fear"? By suggesting that marriage can be like colonialism and that emotional persecution can be a form of tyranny, Eliot links and equates oppression in the domestic sphere with its more public manifestations. For example, Grandcourt's ties to conventional politics are described as follows: "Grandcourt's importance as a subject of this realm was of the grandly passive kind which consists in the inheritance of land. Political and social movements touched him only through the wire of his rental. . . . But Grandcourt within his own sphere of interest showed some of the qualities which have entered into triumphal diplomacy of the widest continental sort" (644–645).[7] Grandcourt's domination of Gwendolen is not merely a pale substitute for other, more overtly political forms of power. His control of the domestic sphere is no less important than England's imperialist ventures around the globe. The leisure afforded him by his social privilege allows him to tend to the business of keeping his wife in check. He need not be aware of political movements in his everyday life because his social and economic position is secure, the result of his "passive" inheritance of property. Thus, he can direct all his energies to the personal domain, the only arena where he may not be able to take his authority for granted. His domination of Gwendolen is not just the analogue of imperialism but its extension; patriarchal power must exert itself over wives, as well as the lower classes and the colonized, in order to secure its authority. Like contemporary feminists who insist on the political significance of domestic violence, Eliot connects Grandcourt's "own sphere of interest," the domestic realm, with other dimensions of the social formation, establishing links between the power of the husband and the power of the imperialist.

Yet, although Grandcourt's control over Gwendolen reveals his potential skills as a politician, it also differs significantly from more overt forms of political domination. The following analogy, by dramatizing his brutality as a literal gesture, runs the risk of obscuring its intangibility: "If this white-handed man with the perpendicular profile had been sent to govern a difficult colony, he might have won reputation among his contemporaries. He had certainly ability, would have understood that it was safer to exterminate than to cajole superseded proprietors, and would not have flinched from making things safe that way"(655).

Grandcourt's success in governing Gwendolen consists in never having either to "exterminate" or to "cajole" her. The narrative interest generated by their unhappy marriage lies in the invisibility of both domination and its painful effects. The narrative shuttles back and forth between the picture of civilized domesticity they present to the world and Gwendolen's private misery. There are no behind-the-scenes explosions, orders, or complaints; Grandcourt can tyrannize Gwendolen simply by making her play the part of the contented wife. "Their behavior to each other scandalized no observer. . . . Their companionship consisted chiefly in a well-bred silence" (735). Grandcourt's power resides in this "well-bred silence"; he dominates by imposing silence and thus renders domination itself silent. In order to see his mastery, one must look to the spectacle of normalcy he and Gwendolen present to the world, a spectacle that is both mask and sign of domination.

But there is an inside story, the narrative of Gwendolen's silenced psyche. Grandcourt's tyranny is invisible because its object is the mind rather than the body or some tangible object. Graphic metaphors of physical violence render concrete his brutal effect on Gwendolen. "That white hand of his . . . was capable, she fancied, of clinging round her neck and threatening to throttle her" (481); Grandcourt was "conscious of using pincers on that white creature" (649); "His words had the power of thumbscrews and the cold touch of the rack" (745). The rhetoric of sadism emphasizes the reality of the psychic world; Grandcourt's violence need not be physical to produce a pain as strongly felt as bodily pain. Yet, power over the mind seems crucially different from power over the body. Grandcourt's effect on Gwendolen is incommensurate with his actual behavior; if words alone have "the power of thumbscrews," he can inflict pain without appearing to do so. His hidden control is subtler and more effective than that produced by overt force. It is not that psychological torture has become so pronounced that it is like physical violence; Grandcourt has instead refined his sadism to the point where it transcends the physical. He need never be so crude as literally to beat his wife; instead she bows to "the quiet massive pressure of his rule." The key term here is "quiet"; Grandcourt prefers to master Gwendolen's actions indirectly by confining her consciousness because he can do so without ever openly declaring his intentions.[8] The Grandcourts' marriage provides the perfect vehicle for a novelist intent on depicting psychological interiority to explain personal relations because the struggle between them is completely invisible from the outside.

Because the narrative of Gwendolen's interiority serves not simply as evidence of her pain but as evidence of Grandcourt's power, it becomes difficult to distinguish her pain from his power. Not only is Grandcourt's mastery silent, but it functions by fostering, rather than eliminating, Gwendolen's desire to rebel. "Everybody must do what was expected of them whatever might be their private protest—the protest (kept strictly private) adding to the piquancy of despotism" (736). Gwendolen's "private protest" is no deterrent to Grandcourt; he actively seeks both to aggravate it and to ensure that it has no public outlet. The pathos of Gwendolen's position is generated not just by her resentment of her husband, but by her recognition that this feeling is useless as a catalyst for resistance. "Of what use was rebellion within her? She could say nothing that would not hurt her worse than submission" (481). Grandcourt is able to make her resistance and her mental pain the sign of his power. "What he required was that she should be as fully aware as she would have been of a locked hand-cuff, that her inclination was helpless to decide anything in contradiction with his resolve" (645). Grandcourt colonizes even Gwendolen's freedom to think what she likes, a freedom that only imprisons her more firmly because it makes her painfully aware that she is unable to act. The more feelings that fill the space inside the "hand-cuff" around her mental life, including the "inclination" to act "in contradiction with [Grandcourt's] resolve," the greater his sense of power becomes.

Grandcourt dominates his wife by converting the feelings that would seem most unquestionably to constitute her identity into a sign of his own power. Gwendolen's interiority is no longer her own; she feels constantly watched as she tries desperately to hide her unhappiness. Grandcourt's persecution is so successful because he turns her mind against itself, rather than overtly making demands of her. The process is "a sort of discipline for the refractory which, as little as possible like conversion, bends half the self with a terrible strain, and exasperates the unwillingness of the other half" (656). Gwendolen supplies her own instruments of torture, as her mind divides into two impulses that work against one another. Grandcourt actually enjoys "exasperating" her "unwillingness" since his satisfaction in preventing her rebellion increases in direct proportion to the strength of her desire to do so; her resistance fuels his victory instead of threatening it. Both halves of Gwendolen's life, her "practical submission" and her "constructive rebellion" serve to strengthen his sense of authority. Her mental resistance to Grandcourt signifies no form of autonomy or difference from his purposes; interior life only intensifies her subjection instead of becoming a region in which she can preserve some measure of independence.

Rather than perverting the institution of marriage, Grandcourt's sadism exposes the power relations inherent in the contract; marriage is not a public declaration of mutual affection but an institution that legalizes the husband's right to control his wife. Grandcourt capitalizes on the private nature of bourgeois marriage and the ideological construction of marriage as a psychosexual and affective bond rather than an economic or material exchange, an ideology firmly consolidated in the nineteenth century. Taking advantage of the hidden potential of the marriage contract, Grandcourt extends the power it grants him to include Gwendolen's mind as a domain for control and to maintain the strict secrecy of his domination. Their marriage presents to public view a perfectly conventional bond, a fair exchange. The absence of any love between them makes clear the economic motives that underlie property marriage. Gwendolen marries for financial security, Grandcourt in order to have a wife whom he can display like a piece of property. His financial power is definitively established by his ability to exclude Gwendolen from the terms of his will. The laws of primogeniture take precedence over affection for a wife; Grandcourt is free to guarantee the transfer of his property to his eldest son even if this means that he fails to provide adequately for his wife. Gwendolen completely submits to the terms of the will because of her guilt about displacing Lydia Glasher. In doing so, she assents not merely to her position as a vehicle for the transfer of property from one generation to the next but to her exclusion from this process; her sense of justice takes the form of refusing to disenfranchise Grandcourt's eldest son from his inheritance, either by giving birth to a son of her own or later by taking the pittance Grandcourt has bequeathed to her. It is peculiar that a marriage arranged so cold-bloodedly should be so bankrupt as a form of economic exchange; Gwendolen produces no heir and receives very little of the financial gain that might be expected to accrue to her. However, the relative insignificance of material considerations in their marriage enables the relationship to become a psychological exchange, and any dividends it produces are in this form of currency. Their financial exchange is supplemented by a complex of psychological responses and interactions, for which the economic seems merely a prop. Grandcourt expects Gwendolen to be an "object on which to exert his will," and he takes advantage of his economic power simply as one of the means at his disposal to torture Gwendolen. Whatever her economic motives, Gwendolen also hopes to be able to wield the power to "do as she likes" with Grandcourt. And her response to Lydia Glasher seems out of proportion to the guilt she might be expected to feel about displacing her economically.

This psychological supplement to Grandcourt's economic power makes *Daniel Deronda* a suggestive proof text for debates about the relative priority of capitalism and patriarchy in determining family structures. It has been a continuing problem for Marxist feminists to explain why sexual division within marriage takes place over and above the need to guarantee paternity and inheritance and to reproduce the labor force.[9] A traditional materialist analysis would seek to explain men's domination over women as ultimately determined by the economic mode of production, in this case capitalism. On this model, the ideology of romance, which the bourgeois novel reproduces, is a form of mystification or false consciousness, smoothing over, and often disguising, the property relations that underlie marriages. As Friedrich Engels puts it: "[Monogamy] was not in any way the fruit of individual sex love, with which it had nothing whatever to do; marriages remained as before marriages of convenience."[10] Like other nineteenth-century novels that construct a discourse of desire and psychology in order to explain the dynamics of affective bonding, *Daniel Deronda* suggests that marriage is about more than just property exchange. Unlike other novels, however, it suggests that what exceeds material determination is not love, but power. Within the private confines of the family, the intersubjective relations between husband and wife provide yet another occasion for the unequal distribution of power, and the Grandcourts' marriage extends oppression rather than covering it over. Yet this continuity between the economic and affective registers is only possible because Grandcourt carefully maintains the boundaries between them, consigning his psychological domination to secrecy.

Although Gwendolen's emotional distress seems more pronounced than her economic subjugation, she vainly seeks to explain her predicament in terms of the economic structure of marriage. The rules of property marriage do not legislate the psychological dynamics between a couple, leaving Grandcourt the opportunity to guarantee his power through a form of sexual domination. Gwendolen can only appeal to a marriage contract that makes no provisions for emotional grievances. "Her capability of rectitude told her again and again that she had no right to complain of her contract, or to withdraw from it" (665). She has received the property and social position that are the only things guaranteed to her by the marriage contract. But the language of contract also provides the terms for the extension of the market economy to the mind. Gwendolen sells much more of herself than she had bargained for:

> But now enter into the soul of this young creature as she found herself, with the blue Mediterranean dividing her from the world, on the tiny plank-island of a yacht, the domain of the husband to whom she felt that she had sold herself, and had been paid the strict price—nay, paid more than she had dared to ask in the handsome maintenance of her mother:—the husband to whom she had sold her truthfulness and sense of justice, so that he held them throttled into silence, collared and dragged behind him to witness what he would, without remonstrance. (733)

Gwendolen gives over to Grandcourt's control the psychological life that has become a new arena within which he can secure her domestic slavery. This transaction is facilitated by the privacy of marital relations; together the Grandcourts are "divided from the world on the tiny plank-island of a yacht." Within this separate "domain," Grandcourt is free to wield his power without interference. But in suggesting that Gwendolen "felt that she had sold herself," what "self" is the narrator referring to? Grandcourt's half of the bargain is clearly economic; he gives her a "strict price," providing financial security not only for her but for her family. Gwendolen's contributions to the marriage are less material; like other middle-class wives, she grants to her husband the right to possess her sexually, or, less crudely, to use her glamorous appearance as the sign of his wealth and power, and she is presumably responsible for managing her husband's domestic affairs, although the text reveals very little about Gwendolen's performance of this labor. Hinting that Grandcourt's possession of his wife constitutes a form of slavery, the narrator goes further, though, emphasizing that he also lays claim to the "truthfulness" and "sense of justice" that are part of her inner life. In other words, Gwendolen sells that part of her "self" which would ordinarily be conceived of as remaining outside the system of exchange as an inalienable part of self. The Grandcourt's marriage creates a slippage between economic and psychological property in which the latter becomes an object of exchange partly because the transaction is hidden, recognized only by its participants.[11]

The exchange that occurs in Gwendolen's marriage resembles the "mystery" of surplus value that Marx describes in *Capital;* the laborer receives the fair exchange value for his labor time but proceeds to work the extra hours that create surplus value. Marx's analysis is instructive because it points out that a fair contract does not preclude exploitation. The capitalist's extraction of surplus value from the worker's surplus labor is "a piece of good luck for the buyer, but by no means an injustice towards the seller."[12] Gwendolen's mind become the surplus value that Grandcourt extracts in marrying her, that which, like the capitalist's profit, accrues to him without his having to pay for it. What is so excruciatingly painful about her subjugation is that she can find no tangible evidence of her exploitation; like the laborer, she cannot appeal to her contract for the grounds to complain. Grandcourt's domination works so well because Gwendolen freely assents to it; she condemns herself for her choice, for losing what she sees as a fair fight, rather than assigning responsibility to Grandcourt or to a social institution whose nature it is to deprive her of any real power. She enters into contract with Grandcourt partly because she operates on the laissez-faire principle of "doing as she likes," and she must acknowledge his equal right to do the same; her autonomy leads to her loss of autonomy. Their marriage suggests that the self, including even apparently private thoughts and feelings, is not outside the system of exchange, but an entity that can be expropriated from its ostensible "owner." But this possibility of selling the self creates a problem because it becomes difficult to assert that Gwendolen is being oppressed if the "self" is part of the contract rather than that which is violated by it.

This contradiction between definitions of selfhood and ownership in capitalist ideology is discussed by Walter Benn Michaels in "The Phenomenology of Contract," which explores how a market economy must both forbid slavery and permit the sale of any commodity, including the self. Michaels connects the sexual and economic domains by arguing that masochism and capitalism exhibit the same logic.[13] Just as, under capitalism, the wage-laborer is free to sell his labor under contract, so the masochist is free to sell himself. Michaels argues that capitalism defines the self in economic terms as a form of property that can be owned or sold, and that masochism represents an extension of the right to freedom of contract to include the self. "The right of the individual to own himself must not be infringed, and so the right of the individual to sell himself and to be owned by someone else must not be denied."[14] Sadomasochism produces, not tyrants and slaves, but buyers and sellers, and even selling the self is still a sign of freedom and a confirmation of the identity constructed within the market economy. Michaels suggests that the replacement of slavery with contractual labor does not necessarily free the worker; instead, slavery is sanctioned and disguised by the ideology of the freedom of both worker and employer to enter into a contract. Similarly, in *Daniel Deronda,* Gwendolen sells her psychological life under the guise of voluntarily choosing to marry Grandcourt. This contradiction between freedom and selfhood, a contradiction produced by defining selfhood as freedom, might lead one to ask whether, as the logic of contract stipulates, "any voluntary exchange is equitable." Marx questions the notion of the autonomous subject by suggesting that the laborer voluntarily enters into a contract, but is limited by existing social and economic conditions in what he must accept as fair exchange. If he must sell to the highest bidder in order to live, and the highest bidder still exploits him, he has freedom only within given limits. Similarly, Gwendolen voluntarily marries Grandcourt but only from a position of such severe limitation that she must accept his domination. She is held to the terms of a contract that is loaded against her from the outset, a contract not just of her and Grandcourt's making but one that constitutes the institution of marriage.

Rather than being the source of Gwendolen's autonomy or identity, her psychological life becomes one more of Grandcourt's possessions, and any claims she might have to selfhood seem very slim indeed. The episodes in chapter 48 reveal Gwendolen struggling not just to act, but even to think and feel, privately or independently, with all attempts at rebellion ultimately futile. She finds it difficult, for example, to resist Grandcourt's insinuations that Daniel's connection with Mirah is more than just charitable: " 'It is not true! What does it matter whether he believes it or not?' This was what she repeated to herself—but this was not her faith come back again; it was only the desperate cry of faith, finding suffocation intolerable" (650). Her efforts to think independently of Grandcourt merely result in desperate incantations produced within the "suffocating" atmosphere of her husband's opinions. She impulsively decides to visit Mirah in order to receive confirmation of Grandcourt's error. In this moment of combined desperation and rebellion, her entrapment takes the form of a kind of autism:

> She . . . walked about the large drawing room like an imprisoned
> dumb creature, not recognising herself in the glass panels, not not-
> ing any object around her in the painted gilded prison. Her hus-
> band would probably find out where she had been, and punish her
> in some way or other—no matter—she could neither desire nor
> fear anything just now but the assurance that she had not been de-
> luding herself in her trust. (651)

Even as she attempts to defy him, Gwendolen is aware of Grandcourt's constant surveillance and of the likelihood that her efforts will be useless. Inside the prison of her husband's control, Gwendolen ceases to have an
identity, neither "recognising herself" nor other objects, incapable of
speech or unimpeded movement. Even though she resists Grandcourt
emotionally, this resistance is so thoroughly contained by him that it too
becomes part of his domain. The passage is ambiguous about whether her
self disappears because Grandcourt denies her any privacy or because her
rebellious introspection locks her in a world of her own making. Submission and rebellion seem to produce the same result—the shrinking of her
psyche as the domain of selfhood.

Later in the chapter, when Gwendolen discovers that Grandcourt has
known all along that she had met with Lydia Glasher, she attempts to cease
thinking altogether. She feels completely violated and humiliated, imagin-
ing his "cold exultation in knowing her fancied secret." Since she seems to
have no mental privacy, she decides to resist simply by showing no sign of
it, following Grandcourt's desires to the letter. Her pride keeps her from
complaining and the activity of the mind that might seem to provide relief
from him leads nowhere. Yet she cannot entirely stop thinking and remains
tortured by "thought" that "is as penetrative as air." Gwendolen's mental life
becomes her own punishment, not something to indulge in privately but
something that plagues her. "And without shutting herself up in any soli-
tude, Gwendolen seemed at the end of nine or ten hours to have gone
through a labyrinth of reflection, in which already the same succession of
prospects had been repeated, the same fallacious outlets rejected, the same
shrinking from the necessities of every course" (664). Gwendolen's "reflection" merely produces a "labyrinth," a self-contained set of thoughts from
which no action can emerge. She is condemned to think even though her
mental life can produce nothing. The narrator's attempt to probe the depths
of Gwendolen's psyche in order to describe her character only reveals a
domain that has been created and colonized by Grandcourt. Grandcourt

confines Gwendolen to psychological activity, which is intensified because it has no outlet. Psychological life does not exist outside the realm of exploitation or economic exchange; rather this realm is the currency of domination. Her mental life is consistently evacuated as a place of independent thought, and finally becomes perpetually marked by Grandcourt's control. Eventually her rebellion can only take the form of unconscious fantasies of murder and destruction. Yet the narrative offers little access to this dimension of Gwendolen's psyche; it is only during her confession to Deronda that we finally hear about the intensity of her fantasies. But it is difficult to see how her affective life can be the object of Daniel's sympathy when it is so entirely of Grandcourt's making, so little an "equivalent center of self." And, indeed, closer scrutiny of Daniel's attempted rescue of Gwendolen will reveal that resistance to Grandcourt's "empire of fear" proves difficult when it takes the form of merely articulating the feelings that he sadistically renders so silent.

Sympathy as Benevolent Sadism

Taken in itself, the narrative of the Grandcourts' marriage might seem to offer a powerful critical analysis of how economic and affective structures interact in bourgeois marriage to ensure the subjection of women. However, this plot bears a tangled relation to the novel's processes of representation and to the story of Gwendolen and Daniel's relationship. Although the Grandcourts' marriage reveals how the psyche serves as an object of domination, the novel must separate power and the psyche in order to propose that the narrator reveals Gwendolen's interiority more truthfully than Grandcourt does, that Daniel's sympathy is not a way of appropriating another's self, and that Gwendolen can turn to her inner life as a resource for moral transformation (in the words of the epigraph: "Let thy chief terror be of thine own soul").

This project is a vexed one, given the unstated complicity between Grandcourt and the narrator. The bifurcation of Gwendolen's psyche that her husband produces gives rise to the "wonderfully mixed nature" that makes her an interesting character to the narrator. Grandcourt's control requires that he be able to infer her psychological state without any overt evidence of it. Eliot refers repeatedly to his capacity for "divination" of Gwendolen's mental resistance (see 616, 656, 670, 732). Yet, this capacity for "divination" also characterizes the narrator's power to read the invisible, and the narrative must go to some lengths to distinguish his knowledge from Grandcourt's. It does so by continually stressing the inaccessibility of Gwendolen's thoughts and feelings to the undiscriminating observer and by emphasizing the disparity between her psychology and her behavior: "The embitterment of hatred is often as unaccountable to onlookers as the growth of devoted love, and it not only seems but is really out of direct relation with any outward causes to be alleged" (736). Yet, the narrator goes on to account for the "unaccountable" in part by setting his own privileged perspective against Grandcourt's ignorance of his wife's feelings: "Had Grandcourt the least conception of what was going on in the breast of this wife?" "How, then, could Grandcourt divine what was going on in Gwendolen's breast?" These questions are used as points of departure for the narrator's own speculations about Gwendolen's inner life as he supplies the answers unavailable to Grandcourt. The narrator can invite the reader to "enter into the soul of this young creature," including us in his understanding of both Grandcourt ("Grandcourt might have pleaded," "He knew quite well") and Gwendolen ("Gwendolen, we know, was thoroughly aware"). Such passages display quite prominently Eliot's characteristic narrative strategy of inhabiting multiple consciousnesses from within and passing judgment from without. According to the narrator, Grandcourt misreads the source of Gwendolen's resistance even as he finds a way to contain it: "He had correctly divined one half of Gwendolen's dread—all that related to her personal pride, and her perception that his will must conquer hers; but the remorseful half, even if he had known of her broken promise, was as much out of his imagination as the other side of the moon" (658). Attributing Grandcourt's epistemological shortcomings to a moral deficiency, the narrator claims that "want of sympathy condemns us to a corresponding stupidity" (658). Grandcourt's "stupidity" seems to be caused by his exercise of power; he cannot understand Gwendolen's "mixed passions" as long as he mobilizes her pride only to conquer her. The narrator's dissociation of himself and Grandcourt is predicated on the claim that true sympathy or understanding does not involve the use of power. The novel thus doubly capitalizes on Grandcourt's persecution of Gwendolen, depicting the psyche that he constitutes as hidden and then casting out his behavior as a negative example of how to probe another's mental life.

Not only the narrator but Daniel is aligned with Grandcourt in ways that make it difficult to reject the model of power Grandcourt represents. Although Daniel seems to offer an escape route from Grandcourt's tyranny, he still functions as a powerful authority for Gwendolen. Gwendolen's relations to the two men in her life cannot be considered independently of one another; they exist in triangular relation, with Daniel defined as the outlet from the marriage. "The will to be silent in every other direction . . . had thrown the more impetuosity into her confidences towards Deronda" (608). Her encounters with Deronda become the secret that sparks Grandcourt to action in order to curb her. The novel charts two mutually reinforcing trends—Gwendolen's complete submission to her husband, who strikes her "dumb," and the increasing intensity and honesty of her conversations with Daniel. Her meetings with him take on the structure of an illicit affair; the two of them furtively snatch moments together under the watchful eyes of Grandcourt, who responds with something very similar to jealousy. Their relationship can only exist in the context of Gwendolen's marriage; one of the reasons she cannot stand to leave her husband is that she would no longer be free to associate with Daniel without creating a scandal. Daniel's interest in Gwendolen is partially due to his erotic attraction to her, but this attraction must always be converted into sympathy. Their encounters are scenes of instruction, with Daniel playing the roles of confessor, analyst, and teacher. Although Gwendolen's escape from her marriage might seem to run counter to the sensation novel's form of symbolic resolution, since rather than having an affair she simply wants someone to talk to, her relationship with Daniel maintains all the affect and significance of a sexual liaison. The plot, for example, would have to be drastically transformed if Gwendolen were to speak to a woman friend rather than Daniel. As confessor, Daniel gets to hear what no one else does, the secrets of Gwendolen's inner life. Their intimacy takes the form of private conversation rather than physical contact, but, like an affair, is marked by the tension of illicitness and revelation. Still, the intensity of Gwendolen's outbursts with Daniel depends on Grandcourt's repression; he defines their relation as both prohibited and revealing.

Not only is Daniel's relation to Gwendolen dependent on Grandcourt's sadistic power, it resembles the marriage more closely than might be expected. Daniel's sympathy, rather than liberating Gwendolen from the constraints of life with Grandcourt, as an affair might, confronts her with new limits. "Always among the images that drove her back to submission was Deronda" (665). Even as confessor, as someone to whom Gwendolen can reveal her inner life, Daniel becomes an authority from whom she is afraid to hide anything. "He seemed to her a terrible-browed angel from whom she could not think of concealing any deed so as to win an ignorant regard from him: it belonged to the nature of their relation that she should be truthful, for his power over her had begun in the raising of a

to speak is to become the opposite of sympathetic, if words demonstrate an "insensibility to another's hardship" or a "violation of awe." At the same time, however, Daniel's passivity and his epistemological difficulty in the face of Gwendolen's suffering seem to be given moral value as the response that conveys the greatest respect for another's pain. His helplessness mirrors hers, so that he manifests his sympathy by participating in her suffering rather than offering a cure for it. But he also displays tremendous anxiety about the uselessness of his perceptions, however sensitive they might be.

The passage charts various ways in which Daniel reassures himself against his own weakness. Once Gwendolen's private suffering comes to stand for the "mysteries of *our* human lot" (emphasis mine), he seems both most inundated by her consciousness and strangely soothed. Suddenly, they have some common ground—there is a universal "human lot" that connects them. Daniel's affective experience is represented in the language of the sublime, as indicated by the classical Longinian reference to "the poor ship with its many-lived anguish beaten by the inescapable storm." As Thomas Weiskel describes it, using psychoanalytic categories, the sublime experience begins with an anxiety of incorporation, in which the self is overwhelmed by an excess from without. This anxiety is eased by locating what was outside within the self.[15] Like the Romantic poets, especially Wordsworth, who are her precursors, Eliot depicts a male spectator whose perception of a woman's suffering inspires lofty meditations on self and soul. Daniel takes Gwendolen's suffering into himself. His own self shrinks in its confrontation with the vastness of her psyche (now become a universal psyche), but the payoff is his ability to comprehend or participate in her pain. He can now acknowledge the complexity of her feelings in a way that causes his anxiety about her otherness to fade. This process is accomplished in part by his abstraction from the specific details of her life; the particularity of her marriage to Grandcourt is effaced by the presumably more significant perception of the "mysteries of our human lot." In other words, Daniel is reassured and relieved from the burden of acting because he can ignore the politics implicit in Gwendolen's domestic distress and focus instead on a universal humanness. And rather than appearing to be irresponsible or cruel, he seems sensitive.

The next sentences demonstrate a further defense against weakness, one that transforms his earlier fears about the dangers of speech. He begins to recover his sense of power once he contemplates being able to say something to Gwendolen. For both of them the inability to speak only increases the desire to speak; despite his muteness Daniel feels "words that rushed into his mind" and feels "himself holding a crowd of words imprisoned within his lips." Once again repression increases the intensity of the inner life rather than prohibiting it. This welter of inner speech finally issues forth for Daniel in a single thought—the advice to Gwendolen that she confess all to her husband. He transfers onto her his desire to speak, hoping that she can do what he cannot, and he also transfers her back to Grandcourt. Furthermore, what had earlier been a problematic gap between speech and thought now helps to reassure him, since he "carries in his mind a vision of reasons" that cannot be fully expressed in the "brief sentences" he imagines uttering. Daniel's desire to have Gwendolen confess to Grandcourt amounts to a request that she insert herself anew in the structure of power that is her marriage, by allowing Grandcourt rather than him to function as her authority and confessor. The use of the term "husband" in place of the name "Grandcourt" emphasizes his structural position as male authority; Daniel wants to get out of the triangle in which he is enmeshed.

Grandcourt's interruption of the scene reinforces the triangular structure of Gwendolen's relations with the two men. His entrance saves Daniel from the possibility of his advice being inadequate, and Grandcourt seems to collaborate with him in failing to alleviate Gwendolen's pain. His abrupt foreclosure of all further discussion seems to reveal the futility of Daniel's advice, but blame for Gwendolen's repression reverts back to him. At this moment, the reader finally comes to occupy Grandcourt's position as he observes the tableau of Gwendolen and Daniel in the fixed positions of victim and confessor. "What he saw was Gwendolen's face of anguish framed black like a nun's, and Deronda standing three yards from her with a look of sorrow such as he might have bent on the last struggle of life in a beloved object" (673). The fusion of Gwendolen and Daniel in mutual suffering ends as they freeze into two distinct and irreconcilable positions. Gwendolen is the sufferer and Daniel the confessor, and the distance between them, even if literally only three yards, seems unbridgeable. Grandcourt's position resembles Daniel's when he feels cut off from a "a vessel in peril of wreck." Such images operate to intensify the separation of beholder and beheld, which, although it increases the beholder's sense of helplessness, also acts to preserve him from having to do anything. If Gwendolen is experiencing "the last struggle of life" then she is beyond salvation, and Daniel can only suffer along with her. Grandcourt's entrance produces a dramatic and conclusive "fall of the curtain," allowing Daniel to escape from helping Gwendolen without seeming to abandon her.

The Sensitive Man

Throughout the novel, Daniel's encounters with Mirah and Gwendolen are similar to this one; he is overwhelmed by the complexity of their suffering and at the same time feels unable to help them. Both of these emotions are depicted in the rhetoric of the sublime. When he literally rescues Mirah from drowning, for example, Daniel feels an "awe in the presence of inexorable calamity" similar to his perception of Gwendolen in the episode just discussed. Like Gwendolen, Mirah is presented as a specifically female subject, "a pale image of unhappy girlhood," whose interest lies in her hidden psychological life:

> He fell again and again to speculating on the probable romance that lay behind that loneliness and look of desolation. . . . His mind glanced over the girl-tragedies that are going on in the world, hidden, unheeded, as if they were but tragedies of the copse or hedgerow, where the helpless drag wounded wings forsakenly and streak the shadowed moss with the red moment-hand of their own death. (228)

The power of his sympathy is grounded in his ability to read the invisible and the miniscule; girls' lives "lie behind" what can be seen from their appearance, and they can seem as insignificant as the "streak" on the "shadowed moss." His experience of the sublime in confrontation with her life demonstrates both the importance of her mind and the sensitivity of his. Daniel's perception parallels the narrator's claim that the "insignificant thread" of the "consciousness of a girl" does matter to history. The language of narrative in the passage ("romance," "girl-tragedies") suggests that Daniel's sympathy is aligned with and carries out the narrator's project of exploring and affirming the status of female subjects. The failure of Daniel's sympathy would have to be read as a failure of the novel's project as well.

   The prominent place of gender in Daniel's speculation about Mirah's secret life suggests that mass-culture forms, such as the sensation novel and the domestic melodrama, may influence Eliot and Daniel as much as the depiction of the sublime in the high-culture texts of the Romantic poets (who were themselves, of course, influenced by eighteenth-century popular forms). Rendering women's lives visible depends on constructing a sensational narrative; Daniel imagines "a probable romance" or a "girl-tragedy" to be the explanation for Mirah's pain. Just as Mrs. Henry Wood depicts Isabel Vane's silent suffering in *East Lynne,* so George Eliot seeks to articulate the otherwise unacknowledged pain and distress of her female hero-ines. The difference between the two narratives is that Eliot's women are rescued by a sympathetic male listener, rather than a morally suspect sedu-cer, such as Sir Francis Levison in *East Lynne*. But the novels are more simi-lar than Eliot might have liked to admit, given that Daniel's sympathy is as erotically charged and as dangerous as Levison's more overt seduction. Furthermore, the politics of affect implicit in the melodrama that Wood con-structs around Isabel's silence is very like the affective charge generated by Eliot's account of Gwendolen's suffering. Just as *East Lynne* encourages its readers to imagine that Isabel's expression of affect and breaking of silence would bring her relief, so Eliot encourages her readers to find Gwendolen's and Mirah's confessions to Daniel the sign of a moral and social transfor-mation grounded in sympathy. And the fact that *East Lynne's* politics of affect is suspicious, providing as it does a containment strategy against more dras-tic social change, suggests that *Daniel Deronda's* melodrama might be equally problematic. Reading *Daniel Deronda* in conjunction with *East Lynne* and other popular fiction exposes both Eliot's debt to mass culture and her inability to distance herself from its successes and failures. Cer-tainly she attempts to imagine a more tangible means of expression for her female characters by creating an ideal (for some, overly ideal) sensitive male. But her utopian vision fails in so far as Daniel is in fact just as oppres-sive finally as Sir Francis Levison, although perhaps no less attractive. That her depiction of Gwendolen and Daniel's relationship depends implicitly on its gender division makes it difficult for it not to carry with it the cultural meanings assigned to that gender difference, including the domination of women by men. This same problem will emerge most clearly in Freudian analysis, where as long as the analyst is male and the patient female, the relationship can only replicate the patriarchal relations outside of the ana-lytic encounter.

The analogy between Gwendolen and Daniel's relationship and the psychoanalytic encounter suggests the necessity of considering how trans-ference and countertransference figure in their interactions. In his sympa-thetic encounters with women, Daniel's experience of the sublime or of melodramatic affect has as much to do with his own position as it does with the problems of understanding female subjectivity. During the encounter described in chapter 48, he is first aligned with Gwendolen's position, when he attempts to identify with her, and then with Grandcourt's position, when he transfers Gwendolen back to her husband's authority. His instability can be attributed to his uncertain status within a social formation based on patriarchal privilege. Moreover, the instability of his socioeconomic identity is also represented as an ambiguous gender identity; his indecision about his life and his susceptibility to feeling, for example, mark him as feminine. Throughout the novel, Daniel's sympathethic encounters with women reveal his desire both to rescue them and to identify with them. Identifying with women makes him like them, whereas rescuing them makes him, unlike them, the patriarchal savior. Sympathizing with them allows him ambiguously to do both, because sympathy is predicated on identification and the power of a kind of voyeuristic distance. This double role, and the weakness and passivity it creates, acts as a cover for a more troubling anxiety that Daniel has about his origins. As the final revelations about his past reveal more clearly, his sympathy for others is grounded in his fears about the loss of his mother, whom he associates with the women who capture his attention. Her identity, about which he knows nothing, operates as a blank onto which he can project his imaginative vision of other women's suffering. In his first encounter with Mirah, for example, the relation between her and his mother is made explicit: "The agitating impression this forsaken girl was making on him stirred a fibre that lay close to his deepest interest in the fates of women—'perhaps my mother was like this one' " (231). Daniel gains a sense of power both from understanding Mirah and from helping her, but she also serves as an image of his own suffering since he too feels alone and excluded. She is an "impersonation of the misery he was unconsciously giving voice to" (227). At such moments he seems to be in the position both of rescuer and of victim, hoping to save the woman who stands in for his needy mother but terrified that she might be beyond salvation or that she might reject him, in which case she rather than he would be the powerful one.

Hertz's and Weiskel's studies of the sublime help to unravel the ways that Daniel's sympathetic investment in the fates of women is more than just an epistemological or ethical problem.[16] Salient for my purposes here is their identification of the anxiety provoked by the sublime as a cover for other forms of anxiety. In psychoanalytic terms, these two types of anxiety can be labeled the pre-Oedipal and the Oedipal; the more clearly defined positions of the Oedipal triangle act as a reassurance against the more diffuse positions that operate in pre-Oedipal scenarios. Thus, for example, Daniel's alternation between positions of weakness and strength is a strategy for managing his fears about the indeterminacy of his identity. By figuring himself in the position of rescuer, he can ward off the possibility of feeling helpless or of being confronted by an overwhelming maternal power. By identifying with another's suffering, he can play out fears about the tragedy that might lie at the origin of his own life.[17]

Just as Gwendolen's inner life is a function of her position as a woman, so Daniel's sympathy, the predominant sign of his interiority, is a function of his displaced social position. The marginalization that women experience serves as an image of the marginalization he experiences as a man without a secure economic or social inheritance. But his affinity with women is not exactly the result of sharing their experience; Daniel's feminization, his ability psychically to cross gender lines, ultimately operates in the service of his insertion into the patriarchy. He sympathizes with women who can stand as figures for the mother he must know, rescue, and control before he can determine his own destiny. His sympathy is crucially tied to his lack of a vocation, and thus is subject to transformation once he commits himself to Zionism. In so far as his ability to identify with women depends on his passivity, and his desire to save them is a form of control, his sympathy seems to have little to do with understanding or improving the position of women. His sympathy always remains the response of a man projecting onto women his relations to the patriarchy, even when it looks like the work of a man who is sensitive enough to turn himself into a woman. Once he embraces his Jewishness, he can also adopt a more stable male identity. Like the white mothers who identify with black slave women in *Uncle Tom's Cabin,* Daniel's identification with women provides a clear image of his own suffering but is blind to what are in fact fundamental differences in social privilege between him and the women with whom he sympathizes. Although the instability of Daniel's position in these scenes of rescue can be read simply as the sign of the failure of sympathy, this ambiguity also allows the novel to have it both ways and to promote sympathy as a process that merges weakness and power; Daniel can participate in suffering but be outside it enough to meliorate it. His sympathy is the glue that holds the structure of the novel together, allowing him to move between Gwendolen's domestic world and Mordecai's political world. By making Daniel both male and female, both rescuer and victim, the novel can connect the psychosexual domain with the social and the political sphere. As the hinge between Gwendolen's and Mordecai's worlds, Daniel must be depicted in terms that erase the distinctions between these spheres. George Eliot's politics of affect thus constructs sympathy as a mechanism by which the private world of intersubjective communications is itself fully politicized, and the model for more public forms of political action.

Daniel's power in sympathetic encounters might also be described as a form of masochism, a process through which his pain becomes a means of offering solace. In other words, sympathy becomes a form of power because it is a mechanism for converting pain into pleasure. Leo Bersani, for example, suggests that "'sympathy' always includes a trace of sexual pleasure, and . . . this pleasure is, inescapably masochistic. If this is the case, there is a certain risk in all sympathetic projections: the pleasure that accompanies them promotes a secret attachment to scenes of suffering or violence."[18] During one meeting with Gwendolen, for example, Daniel conceives of himself in the following terms: "He was under the baffling difficulty of discerning, that what he had been urging on her [Gwendolen] was thrown into the pallid distance of mere thought before the outburst of her habitual emotion. It is as if he saw her drowning while his limbs were bound" (509). His authority to advise Gwendolen suddenly places him in a position of physical helplessness that graphically isolates him from her. He suffers as much as she does, depicted as the masochist with "bound limbs." What is peculiar is that this moment of mutual suffering becomes the turning point that gives Gwendolen a sense of strength. Only moments before Daniel had been calmly issuing advice to her, "seizing a faint chance of rescuing her from some indefinite danger." She assents but with a gesture that indicates "deprecation of the notion that it was easy to obey that advice," afraid that "turning her fear into a safeguard" will only lead to horrible consequences. Her "outburst of emotion" is arrested when she finally looks at Daniel, whose appearance is described above. His suffering begins to give her strength: "The pained compassion which was spread over his features as he watched her, affected her with a compunction unlike any she had felt before" and she suddenly agrees that "he can help her." The scene is a confusing see-saw of intersubjective communication, moving back and forth between Gwendolen and Daniel to the point where it is hard to know who is suffering and who is advising, who is watching and who is being watched, and whose pain and helplessness is greater. It seems odd that Daniel should relieve Gwendolen not by counseling her but by providing her with an image of how her own suffering affects him. His helplessness diminishes her own sense of futility, so that sympathy works by drawing some dividend from incapacity. Daniel's sympathy need not seem inadequate if its very inadequacy becomes the vehicle of its success. His power resides in his ability to submit to Gwendolen's suffering. Masochism converts itself from being a sign of his incapacity to being the source of his power, but a power that never has to appear overtly as such.

Sympathy and Nationalism

Daniel's ambiguous role in Gwendolen's development raises questions about how Eliot's politics of affect functions in the context of the other half of the novel, the story of Daniel's discovery of his Jewish identity and his growing commitment to Zionism. A formal response to the problem of connecting private and political relations, the novel's double plot links Gwendolen's affective life and her relations with Grandcourt and Daniel to a larger social context. Daniel stands as the hinge between the two plots; torn between Gwendolen's demands for comfort and Mordecai's demands that he pursue the cause of Zionism, he finally chooses the latter. Terry Eagleton has suggested that Daniel leaves English society for a utopian political project and that his "redemptive influence" on Gwendolen enables Eliot to suggest that the impulses underlying his Zionism might also transform bourgeois society.[19] Not only, however, is his rescue of Gwendolen far from successful, but his enthusiasm for Zionism is rather less utopian than Eagleton suggests. It is significant that the suffering middle-class woman should be the figure for Daniel's link to bourgeois capitalist society. The novel's double plot reflects a split between public and private spheres and opens up two different conceptions of politics: Daniel's Zionism represents politics conceived in conventional terms as taking place in the public realm of religious, national, or state institutions; his relations with Gwendolen suggest a politics concerned with the private domain of marital, familial, or interpersonal relations. Given that Daniel leaves Gwendolen for Mirah and Zion, this latter project finally seems even more intractable than the plight of the Jews. The novel wants to promote a continuity between the two plots in order to expand the domain of politics, but Daniel and Gwendolen's final separation suggests that a politics based on sympathy and intersubjective relations may not be viable.

Whereas Eagleton suggests that Daniel's larger political mission serves as a model for how English middle-class society might be improved, I would argue that Daniel's relations with Gwendolen serve as the model for the relations with Mordecai and his mother that he must resolve in order to confront the problem of understanding Judaism. George Eliot uses the double plot in order to show how the affects generated in the domestic realm provide the ground for Daniel's emotional connection to Mordecai, and more broadly, to Zionism. Zionism is thus figured as the collective aggregate of the affective bonds that unite individuals within, for example, marriage or the family.

Daniel is ultimately able to embrace Zionism only after he meets his long-lost mother, the Princess Halm-Eberstein, and discovers that he was born a Jew. His encounters with her indicate most clearly that his sympathy, which is supposed to reach out to Gwendolen and Mordecai alike, does not necessarily mediate between the personal histories of women and the public history of Jewish oppression. If his sympathy aspires to cross gender boundaries and if his mother is the ultimate referent of his moments of identification with women, it is significant that she is the one person who refuses him the possibility of identifying with the female position. When they finally meet, and she tells him her story, he says to her, "I enter into the painfulness of your struggle. I can imagine the hardship of an enforced renunciation." He claims the ability actually to "enter" her mind, to be able to form images of her inner life. She replies: "You are not a woman. You may try—but you can never imagine what it is to have a man's force of genius in you, and yet to suffer the slavery of being a girl" (694). Although she describes herself as being of mixed gender, she draws a line between herself and Daniel. His social disenfranchisement may place him in a female position, but this is not the same as "the slavery of being a girl." Her use of this locution recalls Gwendolen's situation and raises doubts about Daniel's ability to imagine her position as well. The princess's response to Daniel reveals more sharply the gender politics implicit in his supposedly benevolent concern for women, suggesting that men's sympathy for women is in fact a mechanism for controlling them. Whether priest, psychoanalyst, friend, or husband, the man who listens to a woman's problems may simply replicate the power structures he seeks to escape, or do as much harm as those whose forms of domination are more overt.

Rather than preventing him from understanding his heritage, the princess's "check" to Daniel's sympathies is precisely what he needs in order to assume his Jewish identity. If, as Neil Hertz suggests, Daniel's encounter with his mother marks the point at which he "puts a pre-Oedipal mother aside [and] . . . enters the symbolic order and takes his place under the sign of his Jewish grandfather," it also represents a swerve away from his affinity with women.[20] He accedes to patriarchal power by renouncing the destiny his mother had chosen for him, and thus implicitly ignoring her complaints about the position of women within Jewish culture. He no longer shares a marginal identity with the woman to whose story he listens, but is instead about to become heir to the tradition she rejects. He need not sympathize with her to acquire an identity, since he can now turn to men like Mordecai and Kalonymos (who literally transfers to him his grandfather's property) to establish his links with a social tradition. His failure to establish relations with his mother also suggests that in embracing his Jewish identity he must exclude other choices and that his sympathy can no longer encompass everyone. In refusing to sympathize with his mother's feminist complaints about the patriarchal nature of Jewish tradition, he implicitly chooses against the task of creating a social structure that is more hospitable to women.

Part of the cost of that choice, both ideologically and practically, is another woman, Gwendolen. That Daniel's and Gwendolen's destinies diverge at the end of the novel further suggests that the politics of affect implicit in his sympathy for her, rather than forming the basis for his Zionism, becomes that which he gives up when he leaves her. His need to diminish their relations, a process made convenient by his departure for Palestine, is a further reminder that his sympathy for her has always been connected to sexual attraction. Sympathetic relations in *Daniel Deronda* don't transcend the socially determined structures available for relations between men and women; once marriage is foreclosed their relationship would have to become the transgressive romance that Grandcourt made it out to be. Daniel's choice of Mirah further suggests that rescue of a woman can only occur in the form of marriage. Desire merges with and consolidates sympathy; Daniel's mother, for example, suspects that his attraction to a woman must lie behind his commitment to the nationalist cause. The possibility that sympathetic relations between members of the opposite sex need not be sexualized remains unexplored in the novel. The intense affective bond created by sympathy thus remains closer to more conventional erotic or romantic bonds than one might expect from a narrative that seems to be trying to avoid the melodrama of romance. Like *East Lynne, Daniel Deronda* fails to imagine affective relations that are not based on the private and individual bonds of heterosexual romance or parenting.

Daniel's intensely charged homosocial friendship with Mordecai, and his marriage to Mirah, represent not just personal ties but the means by which he gains access to a whole culture. Choosing Mirah is also choosing Mordecai; she becomes the vehicle that cements Daniel's bond with her brother. Their marriage reinforces the structure by which women become objects of exchange for relations between men. When Daniel reveals to Mirah and Mordecai that he is in fact a Jew, the moment is described as follows: "The two men clasped hands with a movement that seemed part of the flash from Mordecai's eyes, and passed through Mirah like an electric shock" (816). Mirah is the medium by which the "marriage of . . . souls" between Daniel and Mordecai takes place. If Daniel and Mirah's bond represents an alternative to the self-contained privacy of bourgeois marriage because it leads to a larger political project, it does so only by virtue of subsuming heterosexual relations to relations between men.

Daniel's homoerotic bond with Mordecai is both like and unlike his emotional ties to women.[21] When Mordecai discovers him on the river in fulfillment of his dream of an heir, they are likened to "two undeclared lovers." Yet the eroticism of this bond is barely perceptible because it takes place within a social context that allows them a great deal of intimacy that need not be overtly sexualized. The narrator suggests that Daniel's relations with Mordecai are an extension of his sympathetic relations with women: "The more exquisite quality of Deronda's nature—that keenly perceptive sympathetic emotiveness which ran along with his speculative tendency—was never more thoroughly tested" (553). However, once the sympathetic bonds are same-sex ones, the problems created by their erotic quality seem to disappear. Daniel can be receptive to the power of Mordecai's "peremptory claim" on him without being helpless or overwhelmed as he often was by Gwendolen. Submission and power are less problematically combined in their relations; by submitting to Mordecai's will, Daniel ultimately inherits his position of authority. The two men balance one another in an exchange of needs and skills, submission and control. The transmission of Jewish heritage from one to the other makes possible a fusion of souls, which even when eroticized, seems entirely traditional and conventional. The sympathy between Mordecai and Daniel differs from the bond between Gwendolen and Daniel, but the narrative obscures the difference.

Daniel Deronda's contradictory representation of these important emotional bonds as simultaneously erotic and nonerotic, and like and unlike one another, reveals the tensions in its politics of affect. Eliot's claim for the collective political potential of private affective bonds depends on the assumption that the natural emotional attachment that Gwendolen and Daniel feel for each other can be transferred from the individual to the public domain. The novel thus suggests a continuity between their relationship and the sympathetic bond between Mordecai and Daniel, which represents the emotional ties that link individuals to a collective entity, the state, and to the abstract concept of national identity. Benedict Anderson has suggested that nationalism as a nineteenth-century ideology consisted of the construction of "imagined communities," precisely the kind of affective work Eliot seeks to make the ground of politics.[22] That there might not be a continuity between erotic and nonerotic affects or between individual and collective ties is suggested, however, by *Daniel Deronda*'s ambivalence about whether or not the relations between Daniel and Gwendolen and between Daniel and Mordecai are erotic. By having it both ways, Eliot avoids the need to explain how an erotic impulse can transform itself into a noneroticone. Critics have also noted Eliot's ambivalence on the question of whether Daniel's allegiance to Zionist ideals is socially constructed, the product of his rapport with Mordecai, or natural, the product of his birth as a Jew. The two contradictions are linked and point to the problematic foundation of nationalism in nineteenth-century discourses about race and ethnicity. Embedded in claims that the emotional ties that link those who share a cultural identity are natural, nationalist ideology disavows its constructedness.

Although for Eliot Zionism represents a utopian antidote to the absence of community in Victorian capitalist culture, it bears uncomfortable similarities to the Victorian ideologies of nationalism and imperialism from which it borrows. Nineteenth-century Zionism emerged out of the same discourses of nationalism that constructed a notion of Englishness in order to underwrite colonialist and imperialist enterprises. Eliot's sympathies for Zionism are thus less oppositional than would appear from her representation of the Jews as a disenfranchised group. Like other nationalist ideologies, Zionism, for example, asserts collectivity through the construction and exclusion of other social groups. Edward Said points out that Eliot's representation of the "utopian" domain of the Middle East as an unpopulated and open space conveniently erases the Arab presence.[23] As continues to be the case, sympathy for the Zionist project on the part of European or Euro-American Christians can serve as a means of providing the illusion of sympathy for the other, while also conveniently making it possible to ignore other groups considered alien to the Judeo-Christian tradition. The reader's sympathy for other cultures may not really be put to the test by the figure of Daniel Deronda as Jew, since although he is finally one of "them," he is English throughout most of the novel. In fact, to the extent that the "Daniel Deronda half" of the novel has been seen as lacking, we could say that Eliot fails to make either Mordecai as an individual or Zionism as a collective ideal emotionally compelling to her readers.

The attempt to forge nationalist unity is problematic, especially if that unity is seen as natural rather than contingent. In asserting a shared collective identity, nationalism can erase differences of gender, sexuality, or class. The appeal to natural affective bonds as a ground for action is thus as problematic in the public sphere as it is in the private. Eliot's novel serves as a caution against assuming that the transfer or dispersal of affect from the private space of the family to the public domain of the nation is a possible antidote to privatization. Zionism is simply the family and the home writ large, which is partly its attraction to Eliot. Nationalisms forged around a nostalgic fantasy of home and shared identity may be ultimately both politically regressive and falsely grounded.

Although Eliot presents Zionist nationalism as a means by which the politics of affect can become both public and collective, the endorsement of this version of affective politics ultimately makes its transformative potential within the private sphere dubious. Daniel's renunciation of Gwendolen in favor of Mirah, Mordecai, and Zionism ultimately reestablishes a familiar and gendered hierarchy, in which masculine public performance is privileged over feminine, domestic, and private relations. When Daniel prepares to meet his mother, for example, he characterizes the interlacing of his fate with Gwendolen's in the following way: "Strangely (and now it seemed sadly) their two lots had come in contact, hers narrowly personal, his charged with far-reaching sensibilities, perhaps with durable purposes, which were hardly more present to her than the reasons why men migrate are present to the birds that come as usual for the crumbs and find them no more" (684). The narrative's earlier claim that the lives of women are of world historical importance is withdrawn here. Gwendolen's lot is "narrowly personal," whereas Daniel's future is invested with the dispersed affective energy of "far-reaching sensibilities." The contact between them is about to be severed; soon Gwendolen will find no more "crumbs" of advice dispensed from on high by her benevolent mentor. She is the ignorant creature (a "bird" rather than a woman) compared with whom Daniel's larger ambitions can only look more important. His renunciation of his ties to her seems to establish the gravity and superiority of his new mission, but the patronizing tone of the passage reveals that he is abandoning her. Eliot withdraws from her earlier more radical implication that saving Gwendolen might in fact be a more ambitious project than founding a Jewish nation.

Unlike so many Victorian novels in which the domestic arena provides a utopian escape from the troubled world of politics, *Daniel Deronda* uses a public project in order to avoid the difficulties created by private, domestic relations. Whereas the conventions of bourgeois marriage that determine Gwendolen's situation remain untransformed, Daniel's Zionist ambitions are presented in such a vague and utopian way that his future can be more optimistically imagined. One might wonder, for example, what the position of women would be in the new Zionist state Daniel hopes to form.

Addressing the political exigencies of Gwendolen's female troubles would require change at the level of the everyday experience of affective and domestic life and involve a drastic revision of what constitutes "political" transformation. To cast Daniel's pursuit of his vocation as "far-reaching" is to reinforce the gendered division between private and public spheres, measuring the importance of political action in terms of its geographic scope, and implicitly legitimating the impulses behind imperialism. Even progressive nationalist political agendas, to the extent that they depend on the seizure or establishment of state power, run the risk of merely reestablishing traditional power structures if they ignore gender relations and the domestic sphere. To the extent that Mordecai's and Gwendolen's spheres represent mutually exclusive choices for Daniel, the novel fails as a construction of a politics of affect because it fails to challenge the gendered distinction between the public and private spheres.

Daniel Deronda's failure to propose a political solution to Gwendolen's problem might demonstrate Eliot's awareness of the complexity of doing so, if it weren't that the narrative works to legitimate her final isolation as morally valuable. Daniel's departure is in part justified by the claim that Gwendolen can save herself without needing a mentor or a specific authority for guidance. In counseling her to "turn [her] fear into a safeguard," Daniel suggests that she turn to herself rather than to him for help. The epigraph to chapter 69, in which he takes leave of Gwendolen, suggests how she can receive direction without appealing to a particular person:

> The human nature unto which I felt
> That I belonged, and reverenced with love,
> Was not a punctual presence, but a spirit
> Diffused through time and space, with aid derived
> Of evidence from monuments, erect,
> Prostrate, or leaning towards their common rest
> In earth, the widely scattered wreck sublime
> Of vanished nations.

Gwendolen's "punctual presence," Daniel, is renounced in favor of a more "diffuse" spirit. His departure is represented as a positive event, since it allows Gwendolen to administer his advice to herself, by finding strength within. She must connect her own life with the larger movement of history, which makes itself felt by "evidence" of "the widely scattered wreck sublime of vanished nations." Weiskel's suggestion that the experience of the sublime allows the individual subject to identify an external law with its own power is applicable here.[24] Gwendolen has also become the bourgeois subject that Foucault describes, disciplined to regulate herself without the forcible intervention of any external power.

When Daniel tells Gwendolen that he is a Jew, she experiences a sublime moment that reveals her potential to come to self-knowledge through submission: "She was for the first time feeling the pressure of a vast mysterious movement, for the first time being dislodged from her supremacy in her own world, and getting a sense that her horizon was but a dipping onward of an existence with which her own was revolving" (876). What might seem like an important turn away from narcissistic egoism takes on a different connotation when read as the experience of a woman acknowledging that her own existence is unimportant in relation to her male mentor's vaster ambitions. Weiskel connects the process of self-regulation produced by the sublime with the Oedipus complex, a link that suggests that Gwendolen's new consciousness involves a submission to patriarchal authority. Because she is a woman, her insertion into patriarchal structures differs from Daniel's. Rather than entering into history as Daniel does, by becoming a Zionist leader, Gwendolen is to let history enter her, feeling herself a mere "speck" rather than an agent of change. The notion of self proposed in the passage links Gwendolen's psyche and the course of world events, just as the narrator's much earlier account of the importance of young girls' lives did. At that moment, however, a discourse about interiority seemed required by the invisibility of Gwendolen's feelings and her isolation from the world. Now that which once seemed most private and inaccessible—her pain, dread, and suffering—joins her to the rest of society, as she comes to participate in a generalized human "existence." The distinction that founded Eliot's narrative form is supposed to disappear once Gwendolen overcomes an isolation that is now merely the result of her own ignorance, rather than the product of her social construction as a woman. But the community Gwendolen experiences is quite literally only an "imagined" one, leaving her without any substantial affective bonds outside her family.

Daniel Deronda ultimately records a split between the private and public spheres, and its politics of sympathy and the expression of affect not only fails to fulfill its radical promise but underwrites the power differences constructed by ideologies of gender, imperialism, and nationalism. Unable finally to propose a political vision that would address the domestic problems responsible for Gwendolen's fate, the novel leaves Daniel to a traditional form of politics and Gwendolen to private moral reformation. Psychological realism chronicles but cannot cure the psychic pain that, in Gwendolen's case, is the product of bourgeois marriage and patriarchal power. Daniel's sympathy merely reinforces the distribution of power that marks her subordination to Grandcourt. Daniel's own development is further evidence that affective life is not natural but constructed, since his capacity for sympathy depends on his social displacement. Daniel, however, finally accedes to patriarchal authority; Gwendolen is left to her own psychological devices. She internalizes the role Daniel once played for her, but remains torn between the terror of her unconscious and the injunctions of the superego. "Through the day and half the night she fell into fits of shrieking, but cried in the midst of them to her mother, 'Don't be afraid. I shall live. I mean to live' " (879). Plagued by nightmares and an interiority that registers her condition but does not alleviate it, Gwendolen finds her only solace in the grim voluntarist determination to "be better" in some unspecified future.

Eliot draws on the feminist politics implicit in the sensation novel's emphasis on the radical potential of the expression of affect in order to construct the more invisible melodrama of sympathy. But her silenced women and her sympathetic men produce a relation of power that is marked by gender division within the sphere of interpersonal relations, and, when expanded to the public sphere in the form of Zionism, creates a form of community that excludes women and non-Western ethnicities. As a model for how the affective power of primary relations might be transformed into a political agenda, Eliot's novels are wanting, and her failure suggests that the problems with a politics of affect may be that the affective experiences that progressive critics envision being put to other purposes might be too tightly bound to capitalism and bourgeois culture to be extricated from them.

It is with this problem in mind that I turn to another Victorian text, but one that is nonfictional and more overtly radical than any of the works thus far discussed—Karl Marx's *Capital.* Just as Eliot seeks to produce sympathy for those who are suffering, Marx seeks to arouse his reader's feelings for the plight of the worker in the factory. Comparing the two texts one might be led to conclude that Marx locates a more compelling instance of pain in his focus on the effects of factory production and its underlying economic causes. Gwendolen, after all, despite the fact that she is a woman, is still a bourgeois woman, less powerless than her representation as victim makes her seem. It might be tempting to conclude that Marx's account of the worker's exploitation exposes more dramatic and real forms of suffering, compared to which Gwendolen's psychic pain seems somewhat trivial. Closer examination of *Capital* reveals, however, that sympathy is not a political strategy whose problems can be avoided simply by finding the right oppressed group.

Seven

Marx's *Capital* and the Mystery of the Commodity

"In Highgate Cemetary, Marx Is Safe on a Pedestal": "Events in Eastern Europe over the last few months have focused attention on Marx's gravesite, at Highgate Cemetary in London. The gravesite recently served as a backdrop for photographs of a new line of Cyrillic-lettered sportswear made in Italy."
—*New York Times,* 14 March 1990

Don't make me wait. Come into my house. (Give me body.)
It's hard to keep a good woman down. So I keep comin'.
—Queen Latifah, "Come Into My House"

A discussion of Marx's *Capital* might seem to represent an abrupt departure from the task of reading the politics of affect in the Victorian novel. I contend that *Capital* is a sensation narrative, the story of the social and political violence produced by nineteenth-century industrial capitalism. Rather than focusing on the figure of the suffering or mysterious woman, *Capital* provides a sensational account of the worker in the factory, a worker who for the most part is assumed to be male. The aches and pains of the laboring worker's body provide a sensational figure for capitalist exploitation. At issue for me are the extent to which *Capital* creates a melodramatic or sentimental spectacle of the worker and whether the use of sensational narrative strategies compromises Marx's project.

There are, of course, also important differences between *Capital* and the sensation novel. The apparent discontinuities are symptomatic of the difficulty of linking the middle-class woman in the home with the working-class man in the factory, or of linking fictional texts and literary studies with nonfictional texts and the social sciences. Juxtaposing the texts provides a way to gauge what is absent from each. First published in 1867 after Marx had done extensive research in England, *Capital* emerges out of the same historical context that produced the sensation novel, but it has a very different story to tell about Victorian culture. Marx's desire to reveal the exploitation of the worker by explaining the mechanics of capitalism would seem to represent a far more ambitious project than that of the sensation novelists. Furthermore, the apparent scientificity of his discourse, which combines abstract philosophical speculation and empirical data, suggests that Marx would be more likely than the sensation novelists to provide an accurate and politically radical vision of Victorian England. It would be possible to read *Capital* as the master-narrative about the social divisions and tensions of which the sensation novel is a merely a symptom. The affective suffering of the bourgeois women depicted in the sensation novel and the affective pleasures of its readers could then be traced to their origins in the capitalist mode of production. The emotional pleasures and pains of middle-class men and women might seem like mere bourgeois self-indulgence when placed next to Marx's horrifying stories about work in the factory and the physical suffering of the working classes. The cultural critic armed with a Marxist framework could then turn to the task of showing how the novel's fictional representations work to obscure the class conflicts and economic processes that *Capital* uncovers and to secure the ideological hegemony that enables such forgetting.

On the other hand, challenges to economic determinism, models of base and superstructure, the truth claims of social scientific discourse, and the gender-blindness of class analysis provide an opening for the sensation novel to say something to *Capital*. Read as a text or representation, Marx's work can be seen as one more story about Victorian culture, as much the product and producer of symptomatic absences, symbolic resolution, and ideology as the sensation novel. Furthermore, *Capital*'s use of sensationalism makes it impossible to conclude that it provides a truer account of nineteenth-century culture simply because it is a realist narrative. I am interested in reading *Capital* in order to explore how sensationalism can be used for overtly political ends and in order to consider alternatives to the sensation novel, which often fails to mobilize affective experience in order to produce social transformations. The differences between *Capital* and the sensation novel cannot be easily characterized as the difference between realism and sensationalism, radical politics and conservative politics, or analysis of economic base and analysis of the superstructural domain of affect. An analysis of *Capital* suggests that it is difficult for political discourse to escape from sensationalism but also that sensationalism does not necessarily lead to reactionary politics. If Marx uses sensationalist strategies, then alternatives to mass culture's politics of affect might be hard to specify. Rather than disabling political analysis or action, however, this observation can serve as a point of departure for considering how progressive politics can incorporate mass culture, sensationalism, and affective experience, rather than dismissing them.

Capital engages with the politics of affect and sensation because it invites the following question: What happens when the body in pain, or more specifically, the male worker's body in pain, is offered up as a *visible* and tangible site of exploitation or oppression? I emphasize the word "visible" because even when such representations are textual, they very often depend on the presentation of a spectacle or scene of suffering. The collapsing of seeing and reading is a reminder that what is at stake are *representations* of reality, rather than reality itself. However, representations can offer *reality effects,* often by effacing the signs of their production and appearing to be mimetically real or to possess immediate and transparent meanings. The question then concerns the politics of documentary realism, a form often used for progressive political purposes in order to remind us of or *expose* us to hidden truths. The presentation of brute facts or empirical evidence can serve enormously important purposes, but the lessons of poststructuralism have also made it necessary to question documentary's presumptions to transparency. In the twentieth century, visual forms such as the photograph, the film, and the video have become the most powerful forms of documentary, displacing the use of words with their apparent capacity to provide direct and immediate information. But the nineteenth-century was the point at which the camera emerged to record experience, and its impact was significant enough for Marx to describe ideology as a *camera osbcura*.[1] Leaving aside for the moment debates about whether to understand ideology as false consciousness or as "the imaginary relations of individuals to their real conditions of existence," we might consider how the metaphor suggests that Marx considers his project to consist not of presenting the reality *behind* the image but of presenting the image right side up.[2] In other words, he is seeking not to replace images with a reality, but to provide an alternate set of images that perform a political task more adequately.

It might seem contradictory to claim that *Capital* is both documentary and sensationalist. Documentary's political effects often depend on its claim to present the truth without exaggeration or adornment. To call a documentary sensationalist is to imply that it is not factual. At the same time, however, documenting social violence by representing the body in pain consists of "sensationalizing" or presenting in the flesh what might otherwise be abstract or invisible social processes. Furthermore, the impact on the audience depends on making suffering affectively powerful or sensational. Documentary often, however, denies its use of sensationalism when it claims to be natural, truthful, or realist. Only if documentary is understood to be a construction of reality can its links to sensationalism be made manifest. I am interested in *Capital's* status as a documentary text, and in the extent to which it acknowledges its sensationalism and its construction of reality. I will eventually argue that *Capital* offers a critique of documentary realism and an alternative form of cultural politics, one that includes the discursive project of renaming capitalism as the production of surplus value.

The Male Body in Pain

In order to clarify and complicate what is at stake in *Capital's* sensational documentation of the worker in the factory, I want to turn to some more contemporary representations of male bodies in pain. The use of this nineteenth-century political and cultural strategy as a form of oppositional discourse is a matter of continued urgency. Documentary's use of sensationalism may go unnoticed when male subjects are at stake because their suffering may be culturally legitimate in a way that women's suffering is not. Thus, what seems melodramatic or sentimental in women's lives may seem natural in men's lives. Furthermore, the emotional power of women's genres, such as the sensation novel and domestic fiction, goes unnoticed in male genres, such as the war story, the crime story, or the western.

Oliver Stone's war stories, *Platoon* and *Born on the Fourth of July,* which are about the Vietnam War, and *Salvador,* about death squads and guerrilla opposition in El Salvador, are contemporary examples of the sensational use of the male body in pain. They constitute only one instance of a much larger phenomenon, but they appear to manifest a liberal politics, critical of U.S. involvement in Vietnam and in El Salvador. Furthermore, they offer an example of how promoting a political position about war turns on the presentation of dead and injured male bodies as evidence of war's capacity to produce violence. Stone's films, like Marx's *Capital,* demonstrate the difficulty of separating realism from sensationalism, especially when the body in pain is being represented. The tactic is to render suffering so palpable because so visible that the viewer will be convinced that an injustice is being done. Just as Harriet Beecher Stowe generates abolitionist sentiment in *Uncle Tom's Cabin* by dramatizing slavery's effect on individual lives, Stone focuses on the individual soldier's personal experience of combat in order to generate antiwar sentiment. And like Elaine Scarry, Stone sees war primarily as a question of bodily injury.[3] War is bad because people get hurt, because bodies get wounded, because soldiers die. However, it might be cause for suspicion that those bodies are white male American bodies, as *Born on the Fourth of July's* castration obsession renders clear. The paralyzed Ron Kovic (played by Tom Cruise) learns that war and America are bad because he goes to Vietnam and loses his dick. But he doesn't literally lose it; rather, he loses the masculinity signified by the ability to fuck and to piss standing up. War is bad because nice American white boys lose their dicks. Or war is bad because movie stars like Tom Cruise, pin-up idols who star in movies like *Top Gun,* lose their dicks *and* their good looks.

Stone's representational strategy depends on his belief in the power of vision: misperceptions about war can be corrected by bringing the body's wounds, and hence war's horrors, into focus. In Stone's film *Salvador,* photographer John Cassady says to journalist Rick Boyle, as they walk through El Playon, the dumping ground for the bodies of those "disappeared" by the Salvadoran death squads, "You gotta get close to get the truth. If you get too close you die." But although the journalists may get close enough to retch from the stench of decaying bodies, the close-up shots they send back to the United States are a *representation* of a complex political situation, of which dead bodies are only one dimension. Not visible in the picture, for example, is the U.S. support that sustains an oppressive government. The difficulty of "getting close to the truth" is literalized by the journalists as a question of making the body visible; they risk their lives in order to photograph the victims of the death squads. The dramatic force of their photographs and stories depends on the audience's assumptions about the journalist's heroic willingness to expose themselves to such horrors. Equating war or social conflict with bodily pain or death naturalizes its causes and effects and exploits the sensational (in both senses) power of the audience's fear of injury, danger, and death in order to transform their sensibilities. Effective as this strategy might be in its emotional appeal, it effaces the structural and historical causes of war and displaces attention away from geopolitical relations and U.S. economic and cultural imperialism in order to focus on war's power to destroy life. Like the melodrama of *East Lynne,* the hazards of a strategy that depends on the affective force of the finality of death are that it can produce helpless outrage and a sense that nothing can be done.

Stone's representation of the physical experience of war is also inadequate when the soldier's body disappears from the scene of international conflict. His films can be unthreatening and even celebrated as the real story of Vietnam, a story which focuses on the forgotten vets rather than the war at home, or the relations between Vietnam's internal struggles, U.S. foreign policy, and the history of imperialism.[4] It's safe to tell this story now because the military-industrial complex has already learned its lesson and now engages in low-intensity conflict to avoid running the risk of incurring public outrage because middle-class college-age sons are being sent to obscure foreign countries populated by other races. Instead of sending our boys to Vietnam, we can send Jimmy Carter to Nicaragua to "watch" the elections, fund the contras, and make quick, "clean" forays into Panama with a "minimal" loss of American lives and no discussion of the loss of Panamanian lives. The body has disappeared as the site of warfare, or at least the bodies we care about. Despite George Bush's claim, following the U.S. intervention in the Middle East that "liberated" Kuwait, that "America" had kicked the "Vietnam syndrome," it should be noted that the United States spent enormous amounts to ensure that very few American lives would be lost in combat even if that meant killing large numbers of Iraqi soldiers and civilians and that censorship of the media prevented representations of injured bodies. Yet even such representations might remain insufficient to characterize the nature of U.S. involvement in the geopolitical arena. The geopolitical context that produced Vietnam remains largely unchanged, and a cultural politics that would combat U.S. foreign policy and militarism cannot rely solely on sensational or documentary realism, especially when it concentrates on American soldiers. It's not just that Stone's films are ineffective or arrive too late to do any good; they also point to the difficulty of formulating a progressive politics, given that they pass themselves off as adequate liberal critiques at the very least of U.S. involvement in Vietnam, if not of the United States itself. The real problem remains hidden behind the blood and guts on the screen, even as the audience might think its heart is in the right place. Stone's social critique becomes indistinguishable from his American patriotism. *Platoon,* dedicated to those who fought and were killed in Vietnam, was palatable enough to the media establishment to win the 1986

Academy Award for Best Picture, and the video version begins with a Chrysler Jeep commercial in which Lee Iacocca tells us that films like *Platoon* are part of what makes America great. *Born on the Fourth of July* (the film, not the book, which is significantly different) collapses the difference between antiwar protesters and Vietnam vets by showing Ron Kovic "convert" to an antiwar position that is nothing more than an expression of his abiding love and commitment to his country. The vehicle for this conversion is his verbal assault against his mother, who is held responsible for the Roman Catholic and patriotic ideals that naively sent him to war to be paralyzed. In a fit of drunken anger, he grabs the crucifix from the wall of his family's living room, and holds it with one hand, while in the other hand he waves his catheter, the sign of his absent dick, all the while screaming at his anguished mother the words of rebellion—"penis, penis, penis."

The uses of representations of male bodies are also at issue in the cultural politics that surrounds the AIDS crisis, specifically in debates about the use of images of people with AIDS (PWAs) in order to generate public outrage. In an article called "Visible Lesions," Jan Zita Grover suggests that the representation of the dying PWA contributes to the notion that those with AIDS, as well as those who are HIV positive, are victims.[5] Her comparison of different uses of these images by the media, by activists, and by artists, all of whom appear to be benevolently well-intentioned in their desire to draw attention to the AIDS crisis reveals the ideological codes that inform the supposedly neutral documentation of PWAs. In the media coverage, and in portraits by artists such as Nicholas Nixon and Rosalind Solomon, the PWA is represented as alone, helpless, and debilitated by disease. Countering these images are those which represent the PWA, not as sentenced to death, but as an active individual, capable of living with and fighting the disease, and as a member of a larger social community, not an ostracized or doomed outcast. Such representations enable the possibility of combating the social, if not the biological, causes of AIDS through attention to structures of racism, homophobia, and sexism that manifest themselves in the institutions of the government, the medical establishment, and the media. Much as representations of dying PWAs might focus attention on AIDS, they do so at the risk of exploiting those individuals and naturalizing the causes of the health crisis. Moreover, if they generate only sympathy or pity and not action, they do little to combat the problem. Grover is particularly concerned about art exhibits, such as Nicholas Nixon's show at MOMA, which implicitly depend on aesthetic ideologies of art as transcendent and move away from the local problem of AIDS to confirm an ahistorical humanism.

ACT UP, for example, protested the Nixon exhibit by reminding him and the audience that representation is political, and that the show tended to foreclose historical analysis of the causes of AIDS. Their leaflet at the demonstration demands "No more pictures without context. Stop looking at us: Start listening to us." Activist groups have focused their attention on the government agencies and individuals whose failure to provide adequate social services, information, and funding has contributed to the transmission of the virus and hastened the deaths of those who are HIV positive. An important dimension of this project has been the production of sex-positive images and safe-sex information in order both to prevent transmission without discouraging sexual activity and to counter right-wing efforts to blame the AIDS crisis on sexual promiscuity and drug use.

I mention these examples of male bodies in pain to suggest that a politics of sensation that uses representations of the body to produce emotional responses and political sentiments or actions are by no means unambiguous in their effects. One way to explain this problem is to suggest that representing the body in pain is not unambiguously meaningful and that a political project that assumes that such a representation has an obvious or natural meaning is problematic. Both sensationalism and documentary realism often function with the assumption that context is not necessary, that the image says it all. The problems with representations of the male soldier and the PWA suggest that Marx's text might require scrutiny in terms of what it assumes about the natural meaning of the worker's suffering in the factory. Furthermore, we might also consider *who* is being represented. For the American soldier in Vietnam is assumed to be a victim in a way that may foreclose consideration of other victims, such as the Vietnamese, compared to whom the American soldier may have a complex agency and privilege. A similar problem arises when Marx's melodramatic scenario constructs the worker as the victim of capitalism. We might need to ask who else should be in the picture. Where is the female worker, for example, or the woman in the home whose domestic and affective labor makes possible her husband's appearance in the factory or the production of children who will also be a source of labor power?

Narrative Strategies of Counter-Discourse: *Capital* as Mystery

Although *Capital*'s narrative strategies can be usefully illuminated by comparing it to the realist or social-problem novels of the Victorian period, it also bears a striking resemblance to the sensation novel.[6] *Capital* can be read as a mystery novel strewn with dead bodies. The opening chapter provides a clue, the commodity, which exudes a mysterious aura. A crime has been committed, but we can't see it until we leave the realm of exchange and enter what Marx calls the "hidden abode" of production, the factory. There we might be tempted to conclude, once the overworked, endangered, and exploited bodies of the workers start appearing, that the capitalist did it, and that the worker is the victim. On the other hand, we also learn that the secret behind the capitalist's ability to make a profit from selling commodities is the production of surplus value, and that the worker, not the capitalist, did it. The crime is that the capitalist takes the credit for the job.

Uncovering the secrets of capitalism is a difficult process because the bodies of the workers keep disappearing, to be replaced by objects or commodities. If the worker is a victim, he's a secret victim because his exploitation is hidden by the sensational allure generated by money, capital, and commodities. *Capital* is thus no ordinary mystery novel; it uncovers a nightmarish world in which bodies become things, and things become people, and in which the victim is also the agent. In the course of its search for the secret origins of profit, *Capital* renders the category of agency problematic. The capitalist, for example, is actually only "capital personified," the human recipient of profits that are not of his own making. And the worker who produces surplus value would seem to be complicit in the very process that exploits him. *Capital* is a whodunit that cannot find its resolution by locating a human agent to blame for the violence it uncovers.

Even as Marx uses the structures of the sensational mystery novel, he also implicitly critiques the notions of agency and criminality that the sensation novel promotes. The suffering and misery that capitalism produces cannot be attributed to the malicious intentions or schemes of corrupt capitalists. Marx's text depicts capitalism as a system of social relations that obscures agency and in which the relation between commodities and the processes that create their value cannot be directly seen or felt. The sensation novel, by contrast, provides a more reassuring narrative; it offers up secrets that can be uncovered, criminals who can be arrested, and victims who can be pitied. The peculiarity of the secrets unraveled in *Capital* suggests why the sensation novel became such a popular commodity within the industrial culture it describes. Like *Capital,* the sensation novel expresses the sense of mystery that the invisible and complex social relations of capitalism creates. Unlike *Capital,* however, it locates the source of this mystery in the concrete figures of the criminal or the sensationalized woman, thus easing the anxiety produced by capitalism.

Capital differs from the sensation novel because the solution to its mystery is not a person but a concept. The secret of the commodity's value is uncovered not only by tracing the clues that lead to the worker's body, but also by positing a theory, the theory of surplus value. Surplus value is neither a person nor a thing, and it cannot be seen or felt. It makes its appearance in the form of profit, but the two are not the same, and without the concept of surplus value, the production of capital and the exploitation of the worker cannot be explained. Marx, for example, accuses the bourgeois economists, who invoke the trinity formula to explain how profit is produced, of comparing "lawyer's fees, red beets, and music." The apparently reasonable proposal that land generates rent, capital generates interest, and labor generates wages is actually a jumbled discourse that hides the process by which the capital, which ultimately takes the form of rent, interest, and wages, originates with the production of surplus value. In equating the trinity formula with "lawyer's fees, red beets, and classical music," Marx deploys a discursive and conceptual warfare, explaining how the *language* of classical political economy obscures exploitation, and by virtue of that fact is complicit with it. The failure to distinguish between value and price, or to recognize that capitalist profit is merely the "form of appearance" of surplus value, is a conceptual and discursive error that reproduces capitalist ideology. Choose your words carefully, Marx is saying, if you don't want to be responsible for hiding bodies, or worse yet, killing them. *Capital* is a mystery story in which the secret is a concept that lurks in the definition of terms such as use value, exchange value, surplus value, and primitive accumulation. By substituting abstractions for concrete bodies and objects, Marx suggests that words and concepts provide better information about how capitalism works than do more tangible or visible material objects. *Capital* thus explores the limits of sensationalism, questioning the extent to which sensationalized objects or persons reveal the truth of social relations under capitalism.

The Secret of the Commodity's Value

Marx's investigation of the mysteries of capitalism begins with the commodity. Before the double secret of the worker's laboring body and the production of surplus value can be revealed, Marx must contend with a vast array of objects that shield these truths from view. Thus, *Capital* opens with the observation that "the wealth of societies in which the capitalist mode of production prevails appears as an 'immense collection of commodities'; the individual commodity appears as its elementary form. Our investigation therefore begins with the analysis of the commodity."[7] As the detective or researcher, Marx's goal is to move beyond the appearance of commodities to reveal the underlying social relations that make this collection of objects possible. The phrase "ungeheure Warensammlung" in the German carries the connotation of a "monstrous" collection of commodities, the first instance of the Gothic rhetoric that Marx frequently uses to suggest that personal agency has been replaced by the apparent agency of objects, which, like animated monsters, begin to control human beings.

In the second and third volumes of *Capital,* as he examines the processes of circulation, exchange, and consumption that carry the commodity ever further from the worker who labored to create it, Marx traces how this process and this location are rendered invisible, and the worker's agency displaced onto the capitalist or onto objects. The "secret" of the worker's capacity to produce surplus value is obscured by the apparent emergence of profit from the inherent value of objects or from the fact that they are arbitrarily sold for more than they cost to produce. For Marx:

> Profit is ... a converted form of surplus-value, a form in which its origin and the secret of its existence are obscured and extinguished. Profit is the form in which surplus value presents itself to view, and must be initially stripped by analysis to disclose the latter. In surplus value, the relation between capital and labour is laid bare; in the relation of capital to profit ... the capital appears *as a relation to itself,* a relation in which it, as the original sum of value, is distinguished from a new value which it generated. But the way in which this occurs is cloaked in mystery and appears to originate from hidden qualities inherent in capital itself.[8]

Marx continually seeks to expose the process by which capital is perceived as possessing an inherent capacity to increase itself independently of the worker's production of surplus value. This illusion is at its most extreme, for example, in the case of interest-bearing capital, which appears to demonstrate that money magically generates more money simply by changing hands. In fact, interest is actually a portion of the profits of production, which is paid to the moneylender by the capitalist who borrows from him. Interest-bearing capital is fetishized by the "conception which attributes to the accumulated product of labour, and at that in the fixed form of money, the inherent secret power, as an automaton, of creating surplus value in geometrical progression" (*Capital* III, 399). The image of the "automaton," which recurs throughout the text, indicates how the bizarre spectacle of capitalist moneymaking leads to the anthropomorphization of systems, machines, and commodities. Because the steps by which human labor is transformed into money are invisible, money appears to have to have "secret power" and to be alive with human-like agency.

Marx uses metaphors of vision to describe his analytical procedure; profit must be "stripped by analysis" to "lay bare" the relation between capital and labor, which is "cloaked in mystery." The process of "unveiling" has both a literal and a figurative dimension; Marx is allowing us to see an entity of a concrete kind, the laborer and his work, and also uncovering a conceptual secret. What is "cloaked in mystery" is not only the vision of the worker in the factory, enslaved by the capitalist's control, but also the concept of "surplus value," which can never be tangibly seen or grasped except through its appearance as commodities with prices. Marx engages in both an empirical project, describing the working conditions that are the hidden secret behind the commodity's appearance on the market, and a discursive project, redescribing the nature of profit through the invention of terms such as surplus value. The use of visual metaphors in the latter case is confusing because it gives rise to the impression that "surplus value" can be revealed in the same way that what is behind a veil or cloak can be revealed. The project of *Capital,* however, is to redefine the nature of "vision" in order to challenge the idea that capitalism can be understood simply by looking in the right place. Marx's materialism constitutes a critique of Western metaphysical notions of the relation between "essence" and "appearance." Placing the distinction between "essence" and "appearance" in relation to the distinction between the "invisible" and the "visible," Marx seeks to explain what lies behind appearances without appealing to idealist "essences."

The infamously difficult first chapter of *Capital,* in which Marx begins to define the nature of value, is complicated because he must explain what it means to claim that because value is socially produced it is immaterial and invisible. The value of the commodity seems to be a mystery because we can't look for it in the object as we might look for, or feel, or sense, its other properties. Although value is embodied in objects, it is not a physical property of objects. In shifting attention from objects to a system of social relations, or from commodities to their conditions of production, Marx seems to move from the visible to the invisible and from the material to the immaterial. In order to explain how it is that objects have an exchange-value, that is some measure by which they can be compared with one another in order to determine that, for example, 20 yards of linen = 1 coat, he must first disabuse the reader of the notion that value is a material substance that can be seen or sensed:

> Not an atom of matter enters into the objectivity of commodities as values; in this it is the direct opposite of the coarsely sensuous objectivity of commodities as physical objects. We may twist and turn a single commodity as we wish; it remains impossible to grasp it as a thing possessing value. However, let us remember that commodities possess an objective character as values only in so far as they are all expressions of an identical social substance, human labour, that their objective character as values is therefore purely social. (I, 138)

Marx insists that value is socially produced as a relation between objects rather than being a natural property of objects. This simple lesson runs throughout *Capital* as Marx constantly warns against the error of confusing value with the material embodiments of value. It is Marx's anti-essentialist conception of value that has made it possible to link him to poststructuralist theorists. The conception of value as the product of a system of relations is similar to theories that emphasize the social construction of what appear to be natural essences or the claim that signification operates by means of the differential relations between signs.

Marx's conception of money, for example, is similar to the Saussurean concept of the arbitrariness of the sign. Just as poststructuralist linguistics insists that signs do not have intrinsic or natural meanings, Marx exposes the common assumption that money is intrinsically valuable; instead, money is a material object arbitrarily chosen to mark the value of other objects and to facilitate the process of exchange. In order to make "the mystery of money" [*das Geldrätsel*] disappear, Marx traces the value-form from its "simplest, almost imperceptible outline to the dazzling money-form" ["von seiner einfachsten unscheinbarsten Gestalt bis zur blendenen Geldform"] (I, 139). Money is the universal form of equivalent value, the value that a commodity possesses when it is used to measure another commodity's value. When one commodity represents the equivalent value of another commodity, it does so not by virtue of its specific material qualities or use value but by virtue of its embodiment of abstract human labor. Marx plays with the concrete example of the coat and the linen in order to demonstrate metaphorically that exchange value is not a material property of a commodity:

> From this point of view, the coat is a "bearer of value," although this property never shows through, even when the coat is at its most threadbare. In its value-relation with the linen, the coat counts only under this aspect, counts therefore as embodied value, as the body of value [*Wertkörper*]. Despite its buttoned-up appearance, the linen recognizes in it a splendid kindred soul, the soul of value [*Wertseele*]. (I, 143)

As the "body of value," the coat doesn't have a body, it has a soul. Marx invokes the material properties of the coat—its "buttoned-up appearance" or the possibility that it might be "threadbare"—in order to make clear that the relation between an object and its value is not like the relation between a coat and what it covers. The coat might be arbitrarily chosen to represent the linen's value, but it has a rather more specific function as a metaphor within Marx's text. The interchangeability of the terms "Wertkörper" and "Wertseele" indicates that the object which embodies value is not a "body" in the conventional sense of the term. It is at once material and immaterial, a sign or "bearer of value" [*Werträger*]. The arbitrary relation between value and materiality is especially evident in the case of paper money, whose capacity to represent the value of commodities is not a function of its specific material substance.[9]

In emphasizing the curious paradox by which value is at once embodied and invisible, Marx is concerned not just to correct an error but to explain why the tendency to confuse value with an object's sensuous qualities is so compelling. Central to his diagnosis of the capitalist mode of production is his claim that it encourages commodity fetishism, that is, the illusion that value resides in objects rather than in the social relations between individuals that produces commodities. Commodity fetishism is not merely false consciousness, however; under capitalism, because the spheres of production are separated from the spheres of consumption and exchange, the production process is rendered invisible, and the commodity becomes the only tangible evidence or sign of that process. In order for commodities to present themselves differently to view, the material conditions of industrial production would have to be transformed. Marx's project is thus not merely an epistemological one; one cannot just reinterpret the world, one must change it.

If value is not a thing but a relation between things, by what narrative mechanisms can Marx reveal its secret powers to the reader of *Capital?* On the one hand, he seeks to render the visible invisible, to shift attention from the apparent material reality of objects and commodities to the system of social relations that produces them. The system of social relations cannot be perceived in the way that objects are, much as it might be tempting to take the objects as the source of value. But Marx also wants to make the invisible visible, that is, to reveal the exploitation that capitalism produces so that it does not appear merely as the just legal exchange between the capitalist and the laborer. He does so by chronicling the effects of factory production on the worker's body. Thus, if commodities are material objects whose tangibility is deceptive, the worker's body is, for Marx, an object whose tangibility is effaced by capitalism. Behind the dazzling allure of the commodity and money is the pain of the labor process. The discussions of the working day and the use of machinery in the labor process are replete with lurid descriptions of the deterioration and abuse of the worker's body, which becomes the tangible and visible evidence or sign of capitalist exploitation. Countering the process by which people are reified and things are personified, Marx restores the human dimension to exchange by showing the workers and makes the abstract system of capitalism concrete by giving it a body.

Marx's double strategy of making the invisible visible and the visible invisible could also be characterized in terms of sensationalism. In making the invisible worker's body visible, Marx attempts to sensationalize capitalism, to make its flesh-and-blood violence emotionally vivid for the reader. At the same time, by emphasizing the problem of fetishism, the mistake of thinking that value is visible, tangible, or intrinsic to objects, Marx implicitly argues against the sensationalizing of the commodity. The problem posed by the first part of Marx's strategy is whether it can be distinguished from the process by which commodities are fetishized. If fetishization consists in the substitution of a material object for a system of relations, then Marx might be said to fetishize the abuse of the worker's body as the tangible evidence of capitalist exploitation. The logic of embodiment in *Capital,* the relation between the system of exchange and particular bodies or objects within that system does not consist of a relation between essence and appearance. What does it mean for Marx to be at once a materialist and an anti-essentialist? The answer lies in a reconsideration of sensationalism and fetishism. Before the relations between sensationalism and Marx's discussion of commodity fetishism can be analyzed, however, it is necessary to follow his argument into the factory.

On the Threshold of the Hidden Abode of Production

In order to set the scene for his account of the factory, Marx structures *Capital* as the revelation of a secret. As he moves through the opening chapters, outlining the logic of value and exchange, the question that remains unanswered is how the exchange of one commodity for another leads to the accumulation of capital. Marx's story reaches a moment of climactic suspense when he turns from the marketplace to the factory, from the sphere of exchange to the sphere of production. The drama of this transition is punctuated by his use of a fictional scenario, which lends a melodramatic sensationalism to what has thus far been a narrative about abstract entities. He has explained how commodities are exchanged with one another, and he has established that labor-power is a special commodity, for which the worker receives wages equivalent to the cost of the labor required to reproduce himself (and his family). But, behind the scenes of this apparently fair exchange, there is another story to be told:

> Let us therefore, in company with the owner of money and the owner of labour-power, leave this noisy sphere, where everything takes place on the surface and in full view of everyone, and follow them into the hidden abode of production, on whose threshold there hangs the notice "No admittance except on business." Here we shall see, not only how capital produces, but how capital is itself produced. The secret of profit-making must at last be laid bare. (I, 280)

Marx's revelation of "the secret of profit-making" is figured as a journey behind closed doors into the hidden abode of production. The sphere of exchange is characterized as an arena in which things are deceptively open and visible. It is a place in which "all eyes are allowed entry" ["aller Augen zugängliche"] as opposed to the more exclusive realm of the factory. The implication is that understanding the secret of capitalism requires a movement from one place to another, but also from that which is immediately visible to that which may not be accessible to the senses. The passage can be read both literally and figuratively. Moving literally from the marketplace to the factory, Marx reveals the secret horror of the working conditions that prevail in the factory as the capitalist tries to extract as much surplus value as possible from the worker, by extending the working day and increasing productivity, increasing absolute surplus value and relative surplus value, respectively. Read figuratively, the passage announces Marx's subsequent discussion of the concept of surplus value, the "secret of profit-making" whose place in the exchange between the owner of money and the owner of labor-power is not immediately apparent in their exchange of labor for wages. The revelation of the "secret" involves both the literal journey into a "hidden" place, and the figurative move from the material to the conceptual.

When Marx wants to reveal exploitation, his text becomes both more figurative and more concrete, dramatizing the implications of the argument thus far in the form of a theatrical tableau in which capitalist and laborer confront one another. As the scene shifts from the marketplace to the factory, the identities of the "owner of money" and the "owner of labor-power" change in a way that is *visible:*

> When we leave the sphere of simple circulation or the exchange of commodities, which provides the "free-trader *vulgaris*" with his views, his concepts and the standard by which he judges the society of capital and wage-labour, a certain change takes place, or so it appears, in the physiognomy of our *dramatis personae*. He who was previously the money-owner now strides out in front as a capitalist; the possessor of labour-power follows as his worker. The one smirks self-importantly and is intent on business; the other is timid and holds back, like someone who has brought his own hide to market and now has nothing else to expect but—a tanning. (I, 280)

The change in *dramatis personae* from the "owner of money" and the "owner of labour-power" in the sphere of exchange to the "capitalist" and the "worker" in the sphere of production is a substitution of terms that reveals the exploitation behind the apparently free and equal contractual exchange by which the worker sells his labor-power. Marx's substitution of persons for more abstract terms suggests that one of the ways that exploitation is rendered invisible is through the work of discursive abstraction. By treating the worker as simply the owner of a commodity that is a necessary raw material for production, the capitalist can ignore his human agency and his body, which are subjected to untold horrors in the factory. Marx's drama personifies this abstract relation. But the change that Marx describes is qualified by the phrase "or so it appears" ("so scheint es"), suggesting that the outward change of physiognomy is a metaphorical rather than a literal transformation. The qualification suggests that Marx's revelation of the secret of surplus value will make it possible to see the apparently neutral exchange between capitalist and laborer as though it were the scene of a beating. The vividness of his description of the worker bringing his hide to market represents the power not of literal vision but of metaphor or language.

The interplay of the literal and the figurative in this passage reveals Marx's complex use of sensationalism. The substitution of persons for discursive abstractions is actually the production of personas. The relation between the terms "owner of money-power" and "capitalist" is not the relation of false to true, or abstract to concrete, but the relation between two different signs, each of which constructs reality. Thus, the choice of one term over the other is dictated by strategy. And Marx does not choose one strategy over the other, for there may be reason to prefer the abstract and less sensational language of terms like "owner of labour-power" over the more loaded terms "capitalist" and "worker," if they allow us to see the structural operations of capitalism. Even as he deploys the strategy of sensationalism, Marx is careful to show that his strategy is a strategy, rather than a revelation of real or natural essences. These passages suggest how we might think of the literalization of capital's structures as a process of figuration.

In the Factory: Bodies or Theories?

Once inside the factory, Marx not only explains exploitation in terms of the concept of surplus value but seeks to make this abstract notion come alive by offering a concrete empirical account of the effect of industrial production on the worker's body. These two projects are not, strictly speaking, equivalent; as long as workers do not receive the profits generated by their surplus labor, they are still being exploited regardless of the quality of their working conditions or the physical demands of the labor process. However, in chronicling the horrendous working conditions within the factory, Marx uses a narrative strategy that is quite literally sensational in order to reveal the physical pain that underlies profit making.

Central to the sensational power of Marx's depiction of the factory is the assumption that humans and objects are different kinds of entities. The ills of capitalism can thus be attributed to the violation of this natural distinction; the factory system turns the body into a lifeless machine and animates machines, which become grotesquely human. The rhetoric of the sensation novel and the gothic novel is present in Marx's melodramatic description of capital as an "animated monster that begins to work as if its body were by love possessed" (I, 302).[10] The life that exists in the worker's body is transferred to the production process, creating the illusion that capital itself has a body and is capable of reproducing itself independently of human labor. In the symbiotic relation between the worker and the other raw materials required to produce commodities, the flesh, blood, nerves, and muscles of the worker give life to the system of production but leave the body itself dead with fatigue and sensory deprivation. In Marx's ghastly horror story, "Capital is dead labour, which, vampire-like, lives only by sucking living labour, and lives the more, the more labour it sucks" (I, 342). He refers to the "werewolf-like hunger for surplus labour" and to "capital's monstrous outrages, unsurpassed, according to an English bourgeois economist, by the cruelties of the Spaniards to the American red-skins" (I, 353). Using the language of sensational fiction, Marx personifies capitalism in order to suggest that it has the power to consume human life and that its lifelike power is ultimately stolen from the worker.

Marx's gothic and sensational imagery is accompanied by what might seem to be less metaphorical accounts of factory conditions, most notably in the chapters on the working day and on machinery and large-scale industry. Quoting extensively from parliamentary reports filed by the inspectors of factories and the Children's Employment Commission, he draws on the empirical authority of statistics, tables, and a vast accumulation of individual case histories. Yet, these materials have their own sensational force, and Marx's appropriation of them constitutes another step in the process of constructing an affectively powerful representation of the laboring body. Particularly striking is the focus on the labor of women and children, whose exploitation seems more reprehensible because their bodies are more fragile. For example, Marx quotes the *Daily Telegraph* description of how "children of nine and ten years are dragged from their squalid beds at two, three, or four o'clock in the morning and compelled to work for a bare subsistence until ten, eleven, or twelve at night, their limbs wearing away, their frames dwindling, their faces whitening, and their humanity absolutely sinking into a stone-like torpor, utterly horrible to contemplate" (I, 353). The emphasis on the beholder's horror at the spectacle of the children's bodily decay suggests that what is at stake here is not simply their experience of suffering but the threat their loss of humanity poses to conceptions of personhood.

Factory production threatens not only conceptions of humanness but conceptions of gender. In another anecdote, the death of a female milliner draws its lurid appeal from the discrepancy between her working conditions and the frivolity of the women for whom she produces her goods:

> It was necessary, in the twinkling of an eye, to conjure up magnificent dresses for the noble ladies invited to the ball in honour of the newly imported Princess of Wales. Mary Anne Walkley had worked uninterruptedly for 26½ hours, with sixty other girls, thirty in each room. The rooms provided only ⅓ of the necessary quantity of air, measured in cubic feet. At night the girls slept in pairs in the stifling holes into which a bedroom was divided by wooden partitions. . . . Mary Anne Walkley fell ill on the Friday and died on the Sunday, without, to the astonishment of Madame Elise, having finished off the bit of finery she was working on. (I, 364–365)

Marx refers to the newspaper headline reporting this "Death from simple over-work" as "sensational" but his account suggests that such occurrences are to be expected given the nature of working conditions. The sensational has become the commonplace, although Marx's bitter tone suggests his outrage that the working conditions he describes should be accepted at a "highly respectable dressmaking establishment." He is indignant about the use of child labor in silk mills, where silk is spun "for 10 hours a day out of the blood of little children who had to be put on stools to perform their work. . . . The children were quite simply slaughtered for the sake of their delicate fingers, just as horned cattle are slaughtered in southern Russia for their hides and their fat" (I, 406). The appeal to the reader's sentiment through the mention of "delicate fingers" makes the prospect of humans being slaughtered like animals all the more appalling. Yet some of this sentiment was generated in the interest of protective legislation that would preserve traditional family structures and gender roles by keeping the workplace the domain of men. The entry of women into the work force, made possible by the introduction of machinery that required less physical strength to operate, was problematic because it threatened gender differences. "These females employed with the men, hardly distinguished from them in their dress, and begrimed with dirt and smoke, are exposed to the deterioration of character, arising from their loss of self-respect, which can hardly fail to follow from their unfeminine occupation" (I, 368, quoted from *Children's Employment Commission, Fourth Report,* 1865). The need to rescue women from poor working conditions emerges as much from an ideology of femininity as from a concern about the labor process itself.[11]

Had Marx considered more explicitly the role of gender ideology in the representation of labor he might have been less inclined to distinguish between people and things. His attempt to preserve this distinction sustains, for example, his relative silence about the conditions of reproduction that enable the worker to bring his labor-power to the workplace. The role of the home and the family in enabling production is given short shrift in his masculinist emphasis on the world of the production. The domestic sphere remains invisible in his account of the structures of industrial capitalism, only referred to in the abstract as the domain in which the amount of socially necessary labor required to reproduce the worker's means of subsistence would be determined. But the distinction between persons and objects or products is more difficult to maintain in the sphere of reproduction, since there the "object" being produced is in fact a person. Marx's model of labor as a relation between a person and an object does not account for parenting, where affective, as well as physical, labor is invested between subject and object or producer and produced. The gendered division of labor is assumed in *Capital* and the invisible structure of psychic violence chronicled, for example, in the Victorian novel, cannot easily be assimilated to the model of visible physical oppression that he chronicles in the factory.[12] The material form that exploitation takes is conceived of in terms of the body's experience, not in terms of intersubjective or affective relations.

Despite its dependence on the distinction between people and machines, Marx's account of the labor process sometimes verges in the direction of challenging that distinction by focusing on the fact that people are embodied creatures. For example, the blacksmith "can strike so many blows per day, walk so many steps, breathe so many breaths, produce so much work, and live an average, say, of fifty years; he is made to strike so many more blows, to walk so many more steps, to breathe so many more breaths per day, and to increase altogether a fourth of his life. He meets the effort; the result is, that producing for a limited time a fourth more work, he dies at 37 for 50" (I, 366–367). Like a tool or a piece of machinery, the body can only perform the same operation for a fixed number of times before being used up. In this sense, humans are like machines, possessing physical limitations that materially determine the shape of their lives. As the capitalist system comes alive with the energy of the worker's labor-power, the worker himself is like an object whose resources can be exhausted just as a machine gets worn out.

In fact, Marx's analysis of capitalism, far from being dependent on essentialist or humanist distinctions between persons, animals, and machines, can also be said to denaturalize such distinctions by emphasizing the interpenetration of the material and the human. The interactions between humans and objects, between constant and variable capital, and between worker and commodity produce a transmutation by which the objects come alive and the worker is increasingly threatened with death. When a commodity is created, labor is embodied in it, leaving the worker's body and occupying a new material object. In this sense, the object does have a kind of life because it carries with it the history of its making and is socially constructed by human relations. Similarly, Marx's stress on the interdependence of human beings within the social relations produced by capitalism militates against the individualism and voluntarism of a bourgeois ideology that insists on the distinctness of humans and objects. One of the positive effects of the factory system is that it produces the cooperation between workers that might ultimately lead to social transformation. The individual's participation in a collective effort can constitute a new social identity rather than threatening that identity. The interdependence of humans and machines cannot so easily be distinguished from the interdependence of humans.[13]

Whereas the chapter on the working day focuses on the quantity of work, the chapter on machinery focuses on its quality, emphasizing the dreary reduction of the worker to a cog in the machine, the "living mechanism of manufacture." "The worker who performs the same simple operation for the whole of his life converts his body into the automatic, one-sided implement of that operation" (I, 448). "[Manufacture] converts the worker into a crippled monstrosity by furthering his particular skill as in a forcing house, through the suppression of a whole world of productive drives and inclinations, just as in the states of La Plata they butcher a whole beast for the sake of his tallow" (I, 481). The worker in a system of factory production becomes a machine or an animal, but in any case not human, as the sensational potential of human life is reduced to single monotonous gestures.

Not only does the worker become a monstrosity, but the machine itself becomes a gigantic organism:

> An organized system of machines to which motion is communicated by the transmitting mechanism from an automatic centre is the most developed form of production by machinery. Here we have, in place of the isolated machine, a mechanical monster whose body fills whole factories, whose demonic power, at first hidden by the slow and measured motions of its gigantic members, finally

bursts forth in the fast and feverish whirl of its countless working organs. (I, 503)

Described as a monstrous body, the machine becomes a metaphor for capitalism, which takes over the agency of the worker and controls him, rather than being controlled by him. The reversal of relations between subjects and objects, or persons and things, that characterizes the relation between capital and labor is represented in microcosm by the image of the machine as a living, and hence monstrous, being and the worker's body as a mechanical, alienated, and inhuman tool. The "factory exhausts the nervous system to the uttermost; at the same time, it does away with the many-sided play of the muscles, and confiscates every atom of freedom, both in bodily and in intellectual activity" (I, 548). Linking physical lack of freedom to a psychological or existential lack of freedom, Marx depicts the working class's exploitation in terms of the body's restriction.

Marx's readers often fail to notice that the worker's body is a metaphor or a sensational figure in his account of factory labor. Marx gives the abstract social relations of capitalism a sensational force by representing the physical suffering of the human body. As the counterpart to his theoretical enterprise of positing the concept of surplus value, the long chapters on the working day and on machinery and large-scale industry are the story of the body's fate under capitalism. The extraction of surplus value takes the form of the consumption and depletion of the worker's physical resources, and Marx chronicles the body's pain and deprivation in order to reveal the harsh realities of capitalism that are obscured by the apparent ease with which profits are generated in the marketplace. Ultimately, however, the connection between the capitalist mode of production and the body's suffering is contingent, rather than natural or necessary. To forget this fact when reading Marx's empirical accounts of working conditions under industrial capitalism is to fetishize or naturalize the worker's body as the visible site of exploitation.

Because the suffering body of the worker *embodies* capitalist exploitation, however, it is easy to collapse the distinction between them. The importance and complexity of the logic of embodiment in Marx's thinking is evident in Elaine Scarry's eloquent, but ultimately problematic, reading of *Capital*. Scarry places Marx's analysis of the production of commodities within the more general context of a theory about the relation between humans and the objects or artifacts they produce. She argues that an artifact or made object is an extension of the worker's body, not something wholly other to it. Capitalism severs this connection between producers and their products; the worker loses control over the commodity into which his body has been extended and does not derive from his creation the benefit of disembodiment or the remaking of the body that it can bestow. As the link between producers and products becomes increasingly attenuated, not only do products serve primarily as exchange values that generate profit rather than as use values, but the worker cannot even see himself as the creator of products. When Marx personifies capitalism and machinery, he is not just indicating that the relation between persons and things has become perversely inverted. Capital, commodities, and machinery are in a sense not just metaphorically, but literally, alive because there is a human dimension to the work process and the profit-making system of exchange.

For Scarry, the political import of Marx's argument derives from his representation of class difference as a function of the distinction between embodiment and disembodiment. In her parable of capitalism, the worker experiences unrelieved sensation and embodiment, while the capitalist is disembodied because protected by the artifacts the worker's labor has generated:

> In the midst of a vast industrial plain stood an artifact, a commodity, a pile of luminous coal so glittering with reflected sunlight that it seemed to belong to the world of heat, yet so deep and dark in its purple and blue that its blackness seemed not just its color but the very thing that it once must have been, something far removed from the sunlit surface of the plain. Two men crossed the plain, approached the commodity, and stood on either side of it. The one extended his arm and touched the artifact and, as he did so, his body grew larger and more vivid until all attention to his personhood or personality or spirit was made impossible by the compelling vibrancy of his knees, back, hands, neck, belly, lungs: even the interior of his body stood revealed in small cuts and larger wounds. Simultaneously, the other extended his arm and touched the artifact and as he did so, his body began to evaporate, grow airy: he was spiritualized, and disappeared. A name was given to each of the two: in his bodily magnification, the first was called by the name "worker"; in his bodily evaporation, the second was called by the name "capitalist." [14]

For Scarry, the ills of capitalism are immediately discernible in the body's sensations. Political and economic injustice or the distinction between classes can be measured in terms of an inequality in embodiedness. Although her argument eloquently captures the relation between bodies and commodities in Marx's thinking, she also illuminates, by taking for granted, the relation between the body's sensations and the meaning of those sensations, or between differences of embodiment and differences of class. There is a crucial difference between reading her parable as a story about how social differences are grounded in the body, and reading it as a story about how bodily experience is constructed by social relations. On the first reading, the apparently indubitable nature of bodily sensations, especially painful ones, makes social divisions equally indubitable or sensible. On the second reading, bodily sensations are not indubitable physical facts but cultural products that affect people differently depending on their class positioning. For Scarry, and for the Marx Scarry discovers, the relation between bodily sensation and class is literal, rather than the social body of capitalism being metaphorically represented in the image of the too-embodied worker and the disembodied capitalist.

Scarry's account of Marx captures the powerful political force of sensationalist representations that link social and economic exploitation with bodily pain. Like Marx, Scarry engages in a politics of redescription, attempting through her language to render the body's sensations visible and tangible in order to provoke an awareness of the realities of war, torture, and capitalism as activities that destroy the body. Both writers turn to the body because it makes the effects of social processes manifest and because it is sensational or visible in a way that abstract systems are not.

What the strategy of sensationalism does not account for is the possible disarticulation of bodily sensation and exploitation. In other words, what if exploitation does not manifest itself as physical pain and cannot be sensationalized by an appeal to the body?[15] Attention to the body alone leaves out those forms of exploitation or domination where the violence is invisible, and potentially leaves out social agents other than the worker, such as wives and children, who are also "behind the scenes" of capitalism. A historical account of the process of embodiment is necessary in order to specify whose body is being represented and what conditions produce exploitation in the form of physical pain or too much embodiment. In the nineteenth century, specific historical conditions made it possible for the male body in the factory to be the visible site of exploitation under capitalism. Naturalizing the link between bodily pain and exploitation potentially fails to account for historical conditions in which exploitation does not take the form of physical suffering. For example, within twentieth-century postindustrial modes of production, working conditions have improved to the point where factory labor is no longer as physically demanding as it once was. Shifts from manufacturing economies to service economies also decorporealize labor. These changes in the body's experience of capitalism do not, however, mean that exploitation has disappeared. The extraction of surplus value can continue even when the reform of labor practices prevents particularly egregious or obvious forms of physical abuse. Furthermore, attention to bodily suffering as a means of gauging the effects of capitalism cannot account for the forms of invisible psychic pain that the sensation novel, for example, discovers in the middle-class woman's domestic circumstances. It may be necessary to chronicle not just physical suffering but affective suffering in order to render visible the intersections between class relations and gender relations.

Scarry's attempt to put the body into discourse is problematic in so far as it collapses the difference between language and the body. Her vivid accounts of the body's sensations are moving and persuasive *representations* of the body, whose meanings are not self-evident. Under capitalism, for example, the body's pain is a symptom, not the problem itself. Scarry's politics of sensationalism consists in the hope that a sensational description of the body will be moving enough to force readers to give up the destruction of the body that takes place most vividly during war, but also during the labor process. Yet, not only might representations of dying bodies not work to counteract violence, but the explanation of why violence occurs might require something other than a description of bodily sensations. Marx's account of the worker in the factory cannot simply take the form of a description of bodily sensations; what finally matters are the meanings that are attached to those sensations. *Capital* seeks to show not simply bodily pain, but that which produces it—the extraction of surplus value. Its sensational discourse about the worker's body is accompanied by a theoretical discourse that explains physical suffering in terms of an analysis of value.

It is also significant that Scarry has little to say about Marx's account of exchange; she describes commodities only as use values and exchange as the means by which their use can be extended to a larger social network. Underlying her model is the utopian prospect of an organic interrelation between man and objects in which exchange would simply facilitate those relations. Such a model cannot account for the symbolic use of objects, the terms for which are provided by Marx's notion of exchange value as a means by which one object can represent or signify another. It is this dimension of exchange that is at stake in Marx's analysis of commodity fetishism, which Scarry also does not mention. The fetishized commodity raises the possibility that objects are not simply use values that extend the body or enable its disembodiment but also the locus of fantasies and affective investments that give them nonmaterial or symbolic uses. If the worker's body and its physical pain should not be naturalized or fetishized as the source of the truth about capitalism, then Marx's discussion of commodity fetishism can be read as a general theory about the meaning, not just of commodities, but of objects.

The Commodity Fetish

Marx's often cited remarks on commodity fetishism in the first chapter of *Capital* deserve their fame, but his argument can lose its force and subtlety when read out of context. The discussion of commodity fetishism explains why, despite their glaring obviousness to some observers, the reality of the worker's body and physical labor and the secret of surplus value often go unrecognized. In arguing that the commodity becomes fetishized within the capitalist mode of production, Marx is first of all proposing that it obscures the factory, "the hidden abode of production," and that it thus renders invisible what might otherwise be visible. At the same time, however, (and this dimension of Marx's argument is often neglected or overlooked by his readers), the commodity also renders the invisible visible in so far as it is the tangible material product of the otherwise abstract social relations that govern the labor process in the factory.

To put it in somewhat different terms, the commodity represents the return of the repressed relation between capital and labor, even as it enables the continued repression of the worker's labor. The psychoanalytic language is appropriate because Marx's commodity fetish operates by the same double logic as Freud's sexual fetish. Just as the sexual fetish both is and is not the penis, the commodity fetish is the surrogate object that stands in for the absent or invisible worker's body and that represses that body's absence.[16] Although understanding the commodity to be the embodiment of the worker's labor might be one way of explaining what it "really" is, Marx must also explain why that which is in fact a mere object is invested with tremendous symbolic significance. When the commodity is fetishized, the meaning and affect that should be attached to human bodies and social relations are transferred or displaced onto objects. Fetishism is thus another way of talking about the politics of affect or sensationalism. Like sensationalism, fetishism often carries a negative connotation, but I want to suggest that, just as sensationalism's capacity to make abstractions concrete can have both progressive and conservative effects, fetishism is not inherently suspect.

The fetishized commodity, like the bodies of the sensation novel's thrilling women, exerts its fascination because it is both sensational in the sense of being tangible and sensational in the sense of being mysterious or shocking. It has this power because it is the material embodiment of social processes. When the commodity "reflects the social characteristics of men's own labour as objective characteristics of the products of labour themselves, as the socio-natural properties of these things," an intangible process is reified as a material object (I, 164–165). The relation between producers and their products becomes inverted, and "the definite social relation between men themselves . . . assumes . . . the fantastic form of a relation between things" (I, 165). The fetishized commodity is both too material and strangely immaterial, creating the illusion of tangibility and taking on a ghostly life of its own as it appropriates the powers of the labor that produced it. Marx depicts this sensational power through the figure of the monstrously anthropomorphized table: "It not only stands with its feet on the ground, but, in relation to all other commodities, it stands on its head, and evolves out of its wooden brain grotesque ideas, far more wonderful than if it were to begin dancing of its own free will" (I, 163–165). Cut off from the process of its production, it appears to have demonic powers of its own.

Marx's "demystification" of commodity fetishism might seem to consist of pointing out that, because the commodity is merely an object, its sensational power is an illusion. It is more accurate, however, to say that Marx insists that the source of this power is not a natural or physical property of the commodity; it is because the commodity embodies labor that it has a sensational aura. The relation of embodiment that connects the process that produces objects and the objects themselves is difficult to grasp because it deconstructs both empiricist and idealist epistemologies. Marx's use of phrases such as "congealed labor" and "crystallized labor" to describe the commodity points to its double status as material object and sign, simultaneously concrete and abstract. As the tangible evidence of the system of production and exchange, the commodity is not simply a material object but a social object. Like those poststructuralist theorists who argue that the body or sexuality are constructed rather than natural, Marx insists that the commodity be understood as a social construct. Those social processes cannot be read independently of their material instantiation in the commodity or body, however, and the commodity is thus something more than the arbitrary sign of a referent that could be located elsewhere. This crucial point in Marx's argument is overlooked if we consider the factory to be the "real" location of the labor process that the commodity hides or obscures. The solution to the fetishization of the commodity cannot be the fetishization of the worker's body or physical pain as the "real" site of capitalism. Part of Marx's argument in the commodity fetishism section consists in warning against fetishism in general, not just the fetishism of commodities, where fetishism means the naturalization of the social processes embodied in material objects. In order to fully understand the relations between, on the one hand, the factory and the worker's body and, on the other hand, the marketplace and the commodity that obscure them, it is necessary to understand abstract concepts such as the theory of surplus value. One cannot simply replace a false material object, the commodity, with a "real" material object, the worker's body.

In describing commodity fetishism as a secret or mystery, Marx is not, therefore, as some readers have mistakenly suggested, constructing a theory of ideology as false consciousness. To lift the veil of the commodity and discover its origin in social relations is not to strip the commodity of its magical power and return it to the mundane status of being merely an object. Marx deconstructs the commodity, but he can't make it go away. He is interested in commodity fetishism because it is not simply a mistake to endow an object with sensational power; under capitalism objects replace people and become their signs, and their investment with a power beyond their object status gives them a symbolic value. The fetish is important because it is a cultural sign, rendering that which is intangible, tangible.

In order to make the reader feel or sense exploitation, Marx tells the commodity's story from the vantage of the factory rather than the marketplace. His attention to the sensational details of the worker's plight is one narrative strategy for exposing or demystifying the secret of the production of value. When he shifts his focus to the sphere of production, however, the world of exchange and consumption still remains in place. Although commodities are "false bodies," they are also real objects that "bear traces" of the origins of production. Commodity fetishism cannot be "corrected" simply by perceiving commodities differently; what produces fetishism is in part the material distance between the spheres of production and consumption, and the difficulty that this separation creates for the process of perceiving or understanding the system of capitalism in its totality. A narrative about the factory does not stand in relation to a narrative about the commodity as truth to falsehood or realism to sensationalism.[17]

It is a mistake to assume that Marx is arguing that fetishism and commodification are inherently bad or specific to the capitalist mode of production. Although the particular forms that these processes take under capitalism may be problematic, fetishism itself, as one form of a more general process by which objects are invested with symbolic meanings, is not inherently suspect. The wholesale dismissal of fetishism is similar to the argument that, in critiquing capitalism, Marx is critiquing exchange value and recommending a system of exchange in which objects are returned to their status as use values. It is also a mistake to accuse Marx of having a nostalgia for use value, or of suggesting that exchange value is a secondary and derivative form of value that must be stripped away in order for objects to be under the control of their producers. In any social structure in which objects are exchanged, those objects have an exchange value; the elimination of capitalist exploitation does not require the elimination of exchange or exchange value. Marx is simply pointing out that the exchange value of commodities is not an inherent or natural property. To this end, he must defetishize or desensationalize the commodity and explain how its power to generate profit is not a visible or tangible property. He accomplishes this project in part by telling a story about the realm of production and explaining how it is linked to and gives rise to the realm of consumption. But the discussion of commodity fetishism suggests the alternative possibility of examining capitalism from the vantage of consumption. *Capital* itself is devoted to the world of production more than to the world of consumption, but it does not preclude the usefulness of narratives about the latter; in fact, the story of consumer culture is arguably now indispensable to the project of explaining developments in capitalism since Marx's time.

It is all the more necessary to consider commodity fetishism as one form of a more general process by which objects are invested with cultural meanings in light of the connotations of the word "fetish." One of the reasons why it is so easy to dismiss fetishism is because of the colonialist ideology out of which it emerges. The use of the term "fetish" originates in the colonial encounter between European merchants and traders and West African tribes. Borrowed as it is from a Eurocentric discourse used to dismiss African and other non-Western religious practices as primitive, the term suggests Marx's affiliation with enlightenment rationality and a "scientific" explanation of the value of objects.[18] The distinction between the apparently arbitrary value of the fetish and the economic value of the commodity is used to consolidate the ideology of a market economy. The concept of the fetish is thus part of a system of discursive oppositions designed to legitimate the capitalist political economy that Marx is critiquing. To use the term "fetishism" pejoratively is implicitly to accept the distinction between "primitive" and "civilized" that underlies the distinction between irrational and rational investments in objects.

In fact, recent work in anthropology suggests that commodification and exchange are not specific to capitalist economies and juxtaposes other cultures with Western European societies in order to examine the peculiarities of what Arjun Appadurai calls "the social life of things." [19] Fetishism can then be taken seriously as a form of symbolic practice, rather than as the "irrational" or "primitive" belief that objects are invested with value by gods or by chance. By the same token, to use the term "fetishism" to describe cultural practices under capitalism would not imply that such practices are a regressive return to mysticism. Understood not as an error but as how objects are affectively invested with meaning, commodity fetishism can serve as a conceptual category within an investigation of consumer culture. As a "social hieroglyph," the commodity is both a material entity and a socially constructed object, the tangible or sensational evidence of systems of production and consumption in which not just use values but symbolic ones are exchanged.

It is important to locate Marx's discourse within the context of European colonialism because that history is intimately linked to the rise of industrial capitalism. Marx's use of terms such as "fetish" and "hieroglyph" are signs of how capitalism is defined by its difference from cultures that he implicitly constructs as primitive or mysterious. Although apparently less derogatory, comparisons that take the form of nostalgia for a pre-capitalist era in which, in the absence of commodification and market exchange, social relations were more authentic are equally suspect. If exchange and commodification are general features of any social system, it is then necessary to examine the specific forms they take under capitalism without dismissing them in advance. Commodity exchange should not be assumed to be less "pure" than uncommodified forms of exchange, such as gift exchange or symbolic exchange. The commodification of social relations or objects that might previously not have entered into a market economy is certainly a phenomenon whose history is worth tracing, especially if its political effects are not a priori certain. For example, a study of the relation between market economies and affective economies might be a valuable way to understand capitalism. Marxist notions of "alienation" suggest that industrialization produces the waning of affective relations between employer and employees, which then leads to a corresponding intensification of affective relations within the family. Furthermore, the linking of social status with consumptive power is an important cultural development within capitalism. The social or affective significance of the commodity is thus not false; it is a social construct that merits explanation. Marx's discussion of commodity fetishism is one of the few sections in *Capital,* a work primarily concerned with production and commodity exchange, that acknowledges the importance of consumption, symbolic exchange, and affective economies.

Understanding Marx's notion of fetishism in a more general sense is particularly useful for forms of capitalism other than nineteenth-century industrial production where the factory may not be the most sensational locus of exploitation in the social system. Although Marx's appeal to the worker's body may be both historically accurate and rhetorically forceful, it is important to remember that it depends on the metaphorical equation made between physical exploitation and structural exploitation. Surplus value can be extracted from the worker regardless of whether he is suffering physically. With the development of service and information industries, labor has become less strenuous, although it may still take its toll on the body in the form of stress and monotony. In such cases, the presence of exploitation cannot be registered in terms of visible suffering, and a "sensational" account of labor practices would not be possible or politically useful.[20] In the twentieth century, consumer culture is just as important to understand as production if what sustains the exploitative relations between capital and labor is the construction of consumptive desires and pleasures. It is important that the suffering worker's body not be fetishized as the only site from which to experience the realities of capitalism; exploitation is not a "socio-natural" property of the body itself, but the result of the system of social relations that allows surplus value to become the property of the capitalist.

There is no single site from which the critic of capitalism can analyze the relations that connect the commodity, the worker in the factory, and the sensation novel's primary subject, the middle-class woman. Despite its insistent focus on the factory, *Capital* emphasizes this fact by constructing categories such as "abstract labor" and "surplus value," which do not refer directly to tangible entities, but explain the processes of exchange, circulation, and profit-making. Although it seems as natural as the body and affect itself, the sensational story of the worker's body in the factory is, like them, constructed. It is sensational in a figurative rather than literal sense, representing in affectively powerful form the systemic relations of capitalism. *Capital* uses sensationalism, not realism, to bring exploitation to affective life and to reach the sympathetic reader's body. Marx tries to make the impersonal system of capitalism as tangible as the fatigue produced in the factories and to show how capitalism feels to the human being as physical body. In order to sensationalize exploitation, he must have recourse to material entities such as commodities and workers, which embody capitalist social structures. These objects are to be read as signs, the visible and tangible inscriptions of social processes that are also named by more abstract terms, such as "exploitation" or "the production of surplus value." The choice of the factory is a strategic one, however, not a necessary one, and its usefulness depends on the extent to which exploitation takes the form of tangible suffering within the workplace. The twentieth-century critic of multinational and transnational capitalism may have to look elsewhere for sensational exploitation.

Capital reveals that although fetishism in the sense of the choice of a symptom may be necessary, fetishism in the sense of naturalizing the sensationalized site is not. Rather than tracing the secret of the commodity to its origin in the worker's labor, Marx suggests that capitalism creates a system of material objects that embody social relations and that generate enormous affective power because they function as sensational signs. The "secret" of the commodity cannot necessarily be dispelled by the revelation of the immediate sight of injured and oppressed working bodies. It may be available only through more magical signifiers such as commodities, which bear the traces of labor, or such as the mystery women of the sensation novel who, like the commodity, are both material bodies and embodiments of social processes.

EPILOGUE

Understanding *Capital*'s account of the relation between the commodity and the worker in the factory or between the marketplace and the workplace makes it possible to reconsider the significance of the sensation novel. Confronted with the mysteries of capitalism, Marx investigates the allure of the commodity and the secret of exploitation. The solution to *Capital*'s mystery is not a thing or person, however, but a structure of relations that can be explained by the unsensational concept of the production of surplus value. In revealing the worker's labor in the factory, Marx sensationalizes or makes tangible exploitation. But the secret story of capitalism need not be told through representations of the factory because the production of surplus value cannot literally be seen or felt. It resides in the relational structure connecting (or separating) the workplace, the marketplace, and, moreover, the home. Thus, we cannot privilege stories about the worker over stories about the middle-class woman as more fundamental to an analysis of capitalism. We must avoid the economism implicit in the claim that the real story behind the sensation novel is the story of the relation between capital and labor and that stories about affect sensationally mystify or disguise the truth.

Among the limitations of Marx's focus on the factory and the worker's body is its failure to explain the intersection of class relations and gender relations. Marx has little to say in *Capital* about the home or the family, except as they serve as the site for the reproduction of a labor force that is for the most part either ungendered or implicitly male. Whether working- or middle-class, however, the family is the locus for gendered relations of power that are no less significant than the relations between capital and labor. Because they take the form of affective bonds that appear natural and outside the sphere of commodified exchange, these relations of power are often largely invisible. And in addition to what actually takes place within the confines of the home, the ideology of middle-class domesticity plays an important role in establishing the separation of private and public spheres that sustains the relations between men that *Capital* chronicles. Lacking an account of that process, *Capital* reproduces a separation of feminine and masculine spheres that contributes to the exploitation it documents.

The emotional drama of the middle-class woman is a story that the sensation novel, rather than *Capital,* reveals as it depicts the affective and unwaged labor that indirectly sustains the workplace. The sensation novel's suffering middle-class woman, no less than Marx's alienated and exploited laborer, furnishes the subject for a narrative about the distress caused by nineteenth-century capitalism. Indeed, representations of the middle-class woman are particularly important for revealing the less tangible effects of capitalist social structures. *Capital's* narrative might seem more urgent than the sensation novel's because unless one looks for emotional or psychic rather than physical pain, suffering may be far less visible in the factory than it is in the home. The representation of affective or psychic pain challenges assumptions about whether the severity of suffering can be measured in terms of the distinction between physical and nonphysical forms of pain. Attention to the sensation novel's politics of affect opens up the problem of the discrepancy between everyday experience or sensation and processes of exploitation.

It is this problem that Marx's account of commodity fetishism addresses. In addition to occupying a position structurally similar to the worker's in *Capital,* as someone whose exploitation is hidden, the middle-class woman also functions much as the commodity does in Marx's analysis, as that which seems to draw attention away from exploitation and the factory. Marx's account of the sensational commodity's mysterious power also explains the sensation novel's representations of beautiful and mysterious women. Like the commodity, the female body serves in capitalist culture as a lure, simultaneously fetishized as the locus of pleasure and voyeuristically investigated for its secrets. Appearing to be naturally invested with power, both embody the power of social structures that give their material substance meaning and value. As both Marx's discussion and the sensation novel reveal, the affective pleasures provided by the fetishized commodity and the sensationalized woman serve important social functions. However, they are often dismissed as trivial, decadent, and evil, not only by social discourses that are suspicious of both commodification and femininity, but by the theoretical paradigms that explain those discourses. Both women and commodities are represented as the seductive objects that hide other, more important sites for social explanation. Ideologies of gender difference help to sustain distinctions between consumption and production, the home and the workplace, the superficial and the real, and pleasure and pain. *Capital*'s masculinist bias in favor of the factory, production, and the worker is challenged by contemporary cultural theory that articulates the political significance of the home, consumption, and personal affective life. Attention to gender has legitimated the study of the forms of pleasure that capitalism produces. Furthermore, the politics of affect at stake in the home reveal that pain and pleasure may be difficult to distinguish. For the middle-class woman, for example, domination can take the gentle forms of the provision of food and shelter, and the experience of love and romance. To explore the politics of affect is to reckon with fantasy, pleasure, and femininity as part of the political domain.

If *Capital* should not be read as privileging the sensational story of the worker over the sensational story of the commodity, then its economic narrative should not be privileged as the real story obscured or mystified by the affective pleasures and problems of the sensation novel. The pleasures generated by sensational representations of the female body in advertising, pornography, and other form of mass culture are as much a part of the smooth operation of capital as the suffering worker in the factory or the emotionally distressed woman on the psychiatrist's couch. These sensational pleasures cannot be replaced by the "truth" or "realism" of the factory. To assess the politics of sensationalism or affect, we cannot simply appeal to a de-sensationalized narrative or substitute realism and documentary for sensationalism and melodrama. Realism as a counterdiscourse won't solve the problem because, as *Capital* itself reveals, it is necessary to explain the structural relations that connect and separate domains such as the marketplace, the factory, and the home, and to explain why the factory remains hidden in the consumer-culture marketplace. Moreover, *Capital* challenges the distinction between realism and sensationalism, strategically using melodramatic language to describe working conditions. Furthermore, a realism based on the politics of sensation may not work in an age when there is no missing body that can be made to reappear. The melodrama of the sensation novel is no less revealing than the story that *Capital* tells, for in each case the body can speak only a portion of the story of its relations to the social structure.

If the representation of the commodity or the middle-class woman, no less than the representation of the worker, sensationalizes social relations, then it is not necessary to choose the most exploited person or the site of greatest suffering to reveal the social structure. Part of my agenda in juxta-posing *Capital* and the sensation novel has been to disrupt that impulse within contemporary cultural studies, which continues to be motivated by the quest for secret repositories of suffering. Marx's factory worker has his contemporary counterpart in the figure of the Third World woman, the in-visible subject who must be represented in order to draw attention to ex-ploitation that is structured around racial, national, and gender hierarchies, not just class divisions. Gayatri Spivak suggests that the strategy of correcting Western ignorance by seeking out the oppressed Third World woman can be the product of a nostalgic desire for an impossible authenticity.[1] Such quests produce a "foreshortened mode of production narrative," which col-lapses an analysis of the international division of labor and the investigating intellectual's subject-position into a sentimental portrait of the suffering ob-ject of oppression. The subaltern does not speak even when she appears to, because she is a Western construction produced as an object of knowledge in a gesture that repeats the gestures of imperialism rather than correcting them. The male laborer plays a role in Marx's *Capital* similar to that of the subaltern woman in Spivak's discourse, at once the forgotten or erased agent of history, but as such only one subject-position in a complex network of relations that constitutes the capitalist mode of production. Like Spivak, Marx is both seeking to combat that erasure by making those forgotten agents reappear, and at the same time explaining the structuring relations that keep those bodies out of sight. Capitalist exploitation cannot be ad-dressed or analyzed simply by making the worker or the subaltern woman speak.

Cultural criticism must reckon, on the one hand then, with the need to sensationalize otherwise abstract social processes and, on the other, with the need to avoid "fetishizing" representations of individual objects or per-sons that embody social relations. Critiques of commodity fetishism aside, Marxist cultural criticism has often demonstrated the power of sensational-ism, perhaps best exemplified by Walter Benjamin's use of the arcades of Paris and the poems of Charles Baudelaire to tell the story of nineteenth-century capitalism. His influence can be found in Fredric Jameson's account of how walking through Los Angeles's Bonaventura Hotel constitutes an em-blem of the cultural logic of late capitalism or postmodernism, and Michael Taussig's readings of how the symptoms of capitalism are manifest in the experience of nervousness.[2] Similarly, feminists have read the hysteric or the emotionally distressed and repressed woman as a figure for or symptom of the oppression of women more generally. In tracing the cultural work of sensationalism, I do not mean to suggest that bodily sensations, visions, and feelings are not linked to systemic suffering, or that the representation of sensational suffering is not an effective or appropriate strategy for calling attention to structural violence. However, in juxtaposing the sensation novel and *Capital,* I do mean to question the privileging of one sensational site or symptom over another, and more particularly, to examine the effects of focusing on one gender to the exclusion of the other. Because of the gendered separation of the public and private spheres, an isolated analysis of the worker in the factory or the middle-class woman in the home keeps the other half invisible.

My investigation of the sensation novel does not aim simply to represent the experiences and subjects neglected by *Capital* or explanatory paradigms that fail to consider gender. The sensationalized women of the Victorian novel reveal that exploitation may not be experienced in any direct or obvious way. The pleasures provided by the beautiful woman and the commodity include the aura of mystery created by their invisible connections to other social sites. Sensationalism is the strategy of a culture in which it is increasingly difficult to grasp the social structure from the experiences provided by any one location or perspective. In the absence of such perceptions, the affective pleasures provided by the female body in particular have served as a guarantee that sensations are real and reliable. Gender is central to a history of sensationalism that can explain why sensationalism has been both dismissed and desired and what objects and people have been sensationalized. The sensation novel demonstrates the seductions of the figure of woman in mass culture, which feeds the desire for tangibility by providing beautiful female bodies. The sensational visibility of women in mass culture suggests that feminist cultural analysis must contend not just with women's absence or lack of power in the political arena but with their presence.

The political effects of the middle-class woman's expression of feeling are neither obvious nor automatically liberatory. The sensation novel's heroines need not be suffering or oppressed, however, in order to be culturally significant. If anything the reverse is true; what is interesting about the figure of the middle-class woman in the sensation novel is that she is alternately the source of pain and pleasure, alternately privileged and oppressed, in ways that challenge the binary oppositions between those categories. In addition to illuminating the cultural work that substitutes affective expression for political action, the sensational female figures reveal the more general significance of affect and sensationalism as aspects of political life and everyday experience. Although *Capital* demonstrates that sensationalism exists in political discourse and not just in mass culture or women's culture, for the most part, in order to investigate the politics of affect, one must turn to the feminine domains of the home and the family, where emotional life has been confined by middle-class cultures and ideologies. The role of affective economies cannot be dismissed as trivial, as it might be if one were to substitute *Capital* for the sensation novel in order to understand the nineteenth century. To dismiss the politics of affect or the middle-class woman in the name of more urgent political issues, more "real" forms of violence, or more oppressed subjects is to reestablish a narrow definition of politics that the category of affect challenges. Whether privileged or victimized, whether conservative or resistant, the sensationalized woman serves as an example, sometimes in spite of herself, of the political powers of affect.

NOTES

Introduction

1   See Nancy Armstrong, *Desire and Domestic Fiction: A Political History of the Novel* (New York: Oxford University Press, 1987).

2   Darrell Yates Rist, "AIDS as Apocalypse: The Deadly Costs of an Obsession," *Nation,* 13 February 1989; "Exchange: Gay Politics and AIDS," *Nation,* 20 March 1989; and the letters column in the 1 May 1989 issue of the *Nation.*

3   For an analysis of how the link between homosexuality and AIDS has been used to generate a moral panic, see Simon Watney, *Policing Desire: Pornography, AIDS, and the Media,* 2d ed. (Minneapolis: University of Minnesota Press, 1989).

4   Throughout this book, I intentionally and strategically use the terms "mass culture" and "popular culture" interchangeably because I take them to be evaluative rather than descriptive. Critics who think the mass production of culture under capitalism replaces or eradicates an earlier folk culture or a genuine popular culture tend to use the term "mass culture." Those who argue that capitalism merely transforms or produces new versions of popular culture continue to use the term "popular culture." The use of the term "mass culture" can also imply that the culture industry, interested only in profits and power, imposes dominant ideology on passive and deluded consumers. The term "popular culture" can suggest that the existence of a culture industry does not preclude the possibility that audiences can receive and appropriate popular culture for their own purposes. In other words, "mass culture" often implies a critical or negative perspective about mass-produced culture, whereas "popular culture" can imply a position that allows for mass-produced culture that is progressive, resistant, or transformative. These positions need not be mutually exclusive, and I continue to use the term "mass culture" in order to indicate that the existence of a culture industry does not preclude the positive effects indicated by the term "popular." For a discussion of these issues, see Andrew Ross, *No Respect: Intellectuals and Popular Culture* (New York: Routledge, 1989).

One. Marketing Affect

1   See Michel Foucault, *The History of Sexuality, Volume 1: An Introduction,* trans. Robert Hurley (New York: Vintage, 1980).

2   "Belles Lettres," *Westminister Review* 87 (July 1866): 10; [H. L. Mansel], "Sensation Novels," *Quarterly Review* 113 (April 1863): 482.

3   "The Popular Novels of the Year," *Fraser's* 68 (August 1863): 253.

4   Wilkie Collins, "The Unknown Public," in *My Miscellanies* (London: Samson and Low, 1863), 1:170.

5   [Margaret Oliphant], "Sensation Novels," *Blackwood's* 91 (May 1862): 567.

6   For an account of this process, see Terry Lovell, *Consuming Fiction* (London: Verso, 1987). For a survey of Victorian criticism that reflects the tensions between the novel's status as popular entertainment and its role as high art and as a vehicle for moral education, see Edwin M. Eigner and George J. Worth, eds., *Victorian Criticism of the Novel* (Cambridge: Cambridge University Press, 1985).

7   See, for example, Winifred Hughes, *The Maniac in the Cellar: Sensation Novels of the 1860s* (Princeton: Princeton University Press, 1980). Hughes's description of the sensation novel is enormously useful, and much of my discussion of the Victorian critics is indebted to her research. I have no intention of attempting to duplicate or "correct" her work; rather I am questioning the form of scholarship that would attempt to account for the sensation novel as a discrete genre or in terms of a literary history understood independently of cultural or social history. For background on the sensation novel and the Victorian critical responses, see also Sally Mitchell, *The Fallen Angel: Chastity, Class, and Women's Reading, 1835–1880* (Bowling Green, Ohio: Bowling Green University Press, 1981), and Elizabeth Helsinger, Robin Lauterbach Sheets, and William Veeder, *The Woman Question: Society and Literature in Britain and America, 1837–83,* 3 vol. (New York: Garland Publishing, 1983), 3:122–263.

8   For discussions of Victorian theatrical melodrama, an important influence on the sensation novel and other popular novel genres, see Michael R. Booth, *Victorian Spectacular Theatre, 1850–1910* (Boston: Routledge and Kegan Paul, 1981); Frank Rahill, *The World of Melodrama* (University Park: Pennsylvania State University Press, 1967); and M. Willson Disher, *Melodrama: Plots That Thrilled* (New York: Macmillan, 1954).

9   "The Popular Novels of the Year," 263.

10   For descriptions of the Victorian publishing industry, see Walter C. Phillips, *Dickens, Reade, and Collins: Sensation Novelists* (New York: Columbia University Press, 1919), especially chapter 2, "The Background of Sensationalism"; Richard D. Altick, *The English Common Reader: A Social History of the Mass Reading Public, 1800–1900* (Chicago: University of Chicago Press, 1957); J. A. Sutherland, *Victorian Novelists and Their Publishers* (Chicago: University of Chicago Press, 1976); Guinevere L. Griest, *Mudie's Circulating Library and the Victorian Novel* (Bloomington: Indiana University Press, 1970); Margaret Dalziel, *Popular Fiction 100 Years Ago* (London: Cohen & West, 1957); and John Feather, *A History of British Publishing* (London: Croom Helm, 1988). These books are largely descriptive rather than analytical, and thus tend to take for granted the distinc-

tion between high and mass culture, rather than exploring the history of its construction. They often, for example, fail to distinguish between middle-class and working-class popular literature, or entirely neglect the latter. They do, however, suggest that a constant tension between aesthetic and commercial demands affects the production, consumption, and critical reception of the novel, and furthermore that, despite the Victorian critics' reservations, there is an ongoing market for sensationalist literature. The history of the novel has been distorted by critics, working within traditional models, who have sought to create a respectable place for it in the canon of English literature by looking for great novels and great novelists. Although these histories of the publishing industry are useful, an account of the history of the novel as a popular, mass-produced, and commodified form remains to be written. For Marxist work that takes this approach, see Raymond Williams, *The Long Revolution* (London: Chatto and Windus, 1961), and N. N. Feltes, *Modes of Production of Victorian Novels* (Chicago: University of Chicago Press, 1986). Feltes's book uses an Althusserian framework to examine the effects of different publishing methods, such as serialization, triple-decker volume publication, and single-volume publication, on the form and content of nineteenth-century novels.

11   "Sensation Novelists: Miss Braddon," *North British Review* 43 (September 1865): 180.

12   "Belles Lettres," 271.

13   [Margaret Oliphant], "Novels," *Blackwood's* 102 (September 1867): 260, 275.

14   Collins, "The Unknown Public," 170–171.

15   On consumer culture, see Rosalind H. Williams, *Dream Worlds: Mass Consumption in Late Nineteenth-Century France* (Berkeley and Los Angeles: University of California Press, 1982); Rachel Bowlby, *Just Looking: Consumer Culture in Dreiser, Gissing and Zola* (New York: Methuen, 1985); and Thomas Richards, *The Commodity Culture of Victorian England* (Stanford: Stanford University Press, 1990).

16   [Mansel], "Sensation Novels," 483.

17   Mansel describes this policy as follows: "A real competition between old favourites and new would have a good effect, not in destroying, which is not to be wished, but in weeding the luxuriant produce of the present day.... There would be an increased struggle for existence, under the pressure of which the weaker writers would give way, and the stronger would be improved by the stimulus of effective competition" ("Sensation Novels," 513). When the rhetoric of evolutionary biology is used to describe the mechanisms of literary evaluation, the result is a process that sounds like free-enterprise capitalism.

18   [Margaret Oliphant], "Novels," *Blackwood's* 94 (August 1865): 168.

19   [Mansel], "Sensation Novels," 482.

20   Ibid.

21   "Sensation Novelists: Miss Braddon," 203.

22   [Mansel], "Sensation Novels," 502.

23   Ibid., 485.

24   "Sensation Novelists: Miss Braddon," 202.

25   [Oliphant], "Sensation Novels," 568.

26   George Henry Lewes, "Farewell Causerie," *Fortnightly Review* 6 (1 December, 1866): 894.

27   "The Popular Novels of the Year," 257.

28   D. A. Miller, "*Cage aux folles:* Sensation and Gender in Wilkie Collins's *The Woman in White,*" *Representations* 14 (Spring 1986): 110.

29   [Oliphant], "Novels," *Blackwood's* 102, 259.

Two. Theorizing Affect

1   Louis Althusser, "Ideology and Ideological State Apparatuses," in *Lenin and Philosophy and Other Essays,* trans. Ben Brewster (New York: Monthly Review Press, 1971), 162.

2   Tony Bennett, "Introduction: Popular Culture and 'The Turn to Gramsci,' " in *Popular Culture and Social Relations,* ed. Tony Bennett, Colin Mercer, and Janet Woollacott (Milton Keynes: Open University Press, 1986), xiii. For other accounts of the concept of hegemony and its usefulness for the study of popular culture, see Stuart Hall, "On Postmodernism and Articulation: An Interview with Stuart Hall," *Journal of Communication Inquiry,* 10, no. 2 (Summer 1986): 45–60; Dick Hebdige, *Subculture: The Meaning of Style* (New York: Methuen, 1979); and Stuart Hall and Tony Jefferson, eds., *Resistance through Rituals: Youth Subcultures in Post-War Britain* (London: Unwin Hyman, 1976).

3   See, for example, Max Horkheimer and Theodor Adorno, "The Culture Industry: Enlightenment as Mass Deception," in *Dialectic of Enlightenment,* trans. John Cumming (New York: Continuum, 1972), 120–167.

4   Fredric Jameson, "Reification and Utopia in Mass Culture," *Social Text* 1, no.1 (Winter 1979): 144.

5   Two recent volumes of essays that announce their state-of-the-art relation to mass-culture studies confront the problem of specifying how mass culture might be subversive, given that this assumption is necessary in order to justify its importance. See Tania Modleski, ed., *Studies in Entertainment: Critical Approaches to Mass Culture* (Bloomington: Indiana University Press, 1986); and Colin MacCabe, ed., *High Theory/ Low Culture: Analysing Popular Television and Film* (New York: St. Martin's Press, 1986). Modleski, however, faults earlier analyses for seizing on audience reception as the locus of the utopian and describes the book as inspired by a chastened recognition that the links between mass culture and capitalism need to be acknowledged anew: "There seemed, then, to be a need for a book which would adopt a more critical view of mass cultural production and mass cultural artifacts, one in particular that would concentrate on texts without, however, disregarding contexts" (Modleski, "Introduction," in *Studies in Entertainment,* xiii).

6   Fredric Jameson, *The Political Unconscious* (Ithaca: Cornell University Press, 1981), 287.

7   Jameson, "Reification and Utopia in Mass Culture," 141.

8   See Foucault, *The History of Sexuality, Volume 1.*

9   Neil Hertz, "Medusa's Head: Male Hysteria under Political Pressure," in *The End*

of the Line: Essays on Psychoanalysis and the Sublime (New York: Columbia University Press, 1985), 206.

10   Janice Radway, *Reading the Romance: Women, Patriarchy, and Popular Literature* (Chapel Hill: University of North Carolina Press, 1984), 218, 222. Another study of Harlequin romances, soap operas, and Gothic romances, influenced by Jameson's work, is Tania Modleski, *Loving with a Vengeance: Mass-Produced Fantasies for Women* (New York: Methuen, 1982).

11   Radway, *Reading the Romance,* 112–113.

12   Ibid., 222.

13   See Jane Tompkins, *Sensational Designs: The Cultural Work of American Fiction, 1790–1860* (New York: Oxford University Press, 1985).

14   Elaine Showalter, *A Literature of Their Own* (Princeton: Princeton University Press, 1977), 160. The title of the chapter on the sensation novel—"Subverting the Feminine Novel: Sensationalism and Feminine Protest"—is revealing of Showalter's critical strategy.

15   See Michel Foucault, *Discipline and Punish: The Birth of the Prison,* trans. Alan Sheridan (New York: Vintage, 1977).

16   Judith Newton, "Historicisms New and Old: 'Charles Dickens' Meets Marxism, Feminism, and West Coast Foucault," *Feminist Studies* 16, no. 3 (Fall 1990): 449–470.

17   I see this as a problem with some of the essays in the collection edited by Irene Diamond and Lee Quinby, *Feminism and Foucault: Reflections on Resistance* (Boston: Northeastern University Press, 1988). The editors, for example, begin the introduction by emphasizing how Foucault enables feminists to provide "new views of empowerment and resistance" (ix). If this is so, feminists must also contend with how Foucault, by expanding definitions of the political, makes it necessary to explore new methods of power and domination.

18   See Lora Romero, "Bio-Political Resistance in Domestic Ideology and *Uncle Tom's Cabin," American Literary History* 1, no. 4 (Winter 1989): 715–734. Romero points out that even Foucauldian critics sometimes seem to forget this point when, collapsing the distinction between punishment and discipline, they imply that because resistance cannot consist in "radical alterity," it cannot exist at all. The misreading of Foucault by some feminists, then, is understandable given the misreading of Foucault by some of his own admirers.

19   See, for example, Armstrong, *Desire and Domestic Fiction,* for a Foucauldian analysis of how the rise to power of the middle-classes depends on the construction of the middle-class woman in relation to domestic ideology. Far from being the suffering or hidden victim of patriarchal domination, the Victorian middle-class woman, according to Armstrong, had considerable cultural and discursive power.

20   See Jacqueline Rose, *Sexuality in the Field of Vision* (London: Verso, 1986).

Three. Detective in the House

1   For the most comprehensive description of the genre, see Hughes, *The Maniac in the Cellar.* Other discussions include Patrick Brantlinger, "What is Sensational

about the 'Sensation Novel'?" *Nineteenth-Century Fiction* 37, no. 1 (June 1982): 1–28; Martha Vicinus, " 'Helpless and Unfriended': Nineteenth-Century Domestic Melodrama," *New Literary History* 13, no. 1 (Autumn 1981): 127–143; Showalter, *A Literature of Their Own,* 153–181; Jonathan Loesberg, "The Ideology of Narrative Form in Sensation Fiction," *Representations* 13 (Winter 1986): 115–138.

2   Henry James, "Miss Braddon," in *Notes and Reviews* (Cambridge, Mass.: Dunster House, 1921), 110.

3   Mary Elizabeth Braddon, *Lady Audley's Secret* (New York: Dover, 1974), 94. All further references in the text are to this edition.

4   See Jeanne Fahnestock, "Bigamy: The Rise and Fall of a Convention," *Nineteenth-Century Fiction* 36, no. 1 (June 1981): 47–71. In 1857, divorce laws were liberalized somewhat, creating a great deal of public interest in the issue. Fahnestock explains, "These more liberal divorce laws weakened the sanctified, indissoluble state of marriage, and the absence of its former permanence left something of a vacuum, a need for a new definition or basis for marriage" (66). Novels about bigamy present second marriages as both attractive and threatening, thus making it possible to explore ambivalence about divorce.

5   "Our Female Sensation Novelists," *The Living Age* 78 (22 August 1863): 353–354.

6   "Sensation Novelists: Miss Braddon," 186–187.

7   Showalter, *A Literature of Their Own,* 158–159.

8   Ibid., 160.

9   Ibid., 167.

10   For Marxist approaches to the novel that stress its capacity to reveal social contradictions, see Pierre Macherey, *A Theory of Literary Production,* trans. Geoffrey Wall (London: Routledge and Kegan Paul, 1978); Terry Eagleton, *Criticism and Ideology* (London: Verso, 1976); and Jameson, *The Political Unconscious.*

11   D. A. Miller, *The Novel and the Police* (Berkeley and Los Angeles: University of California Press, 1988), 69.

12   See Jacques Donzelot, *The Policing of Families,* trans. Robert Hurley (New York: Random House, 1979), for a discussion of how the institution of psychoanalysis acts as a masked form of social control and discipline. The detective, when investigating the family, performs a similar function.

13   There are, for example, no models of the nuclear family in the novel because mothers are conspicuously absent. Robert Audley, Alicia Audley, George and Clara Talboys, and Helen Maldon have all lost their mothers in early childhood. This fact calls into question the ideal of family life and also allows the novel to reveal more clearly the relations that really seem to matter in the family—those between fathers (all of whom wield their patriarchal authority firmly) and their children.

14   Charles Dickens, *Bleak House* (Harmondsworth: Penguin, 1971), 466.

15   Ibid., 812.

16   The problem, as Dominick LaCapra puts it in a critique of Miller's reading, is to see "how symptomatic, critical, and possibly transformative forces interact in relating a text to its various contexts (or subtexts)." Defending a poststructuralist criticism, and drawing on theorists such as Bakhtin and Derrida, LaCapra argues

that narrative or literary representations always contain contestatory moments. See his "Ideology and Critique in *Bleak House*," *Representations* 6 (Spring 1984): 117.

17   Eve Kosofsky Sedgwick, *Between Men: English Literature and Male Homosocial Desire* (New York: Columbia University Press, 1985), 22, 25. Sedgwick is interested in the mutual interaction of questions of class and sexuality in the portrayal of homosexuality in the novel. She has also argued for the centrality of homosexuality in the gothic novel (in a review of *The Literature of Terror*, by David Punter, in *Studies in Romanticism* 21 [Summer 1982]: 243–253), a claim that, given the ties between the sensation novel and the gothic, suggests that the sensation novel might figure importantly in a general theory of the role of homosexuality in nineteenth-century culture.

18   Sigmund Freud, "Medusa's Head," in *Sexuality and the Psychology of Love*, ed. Philip Rieff (New York: Collier, 1963), 212. In the same piece, Freud connects homosexuality and images of the Medusa's head: "Since the Greeks were in the main strongly homosexual, it was inevitable that we should find among them a representation of woman as a being who frightens and repels because she is castrated" (213). I am arguing that Robert Audley's homoerotic tendencies make him a particularly appropriate agent of patriarchal values, which are sustained by projecting responsibility for conflict onto women.

19   Clara's vestigial function in the plot is demonstrated by the adaptations of the novel for the stage, in which her character is left out entirely. See, for example, Brian J. Burton, *Lady Audley's Secret or Death in Lime Tree Walk* (Birmingham: C. Combridge, 1966), based on the several Victorian dramatizations of the novel that appeared in the 1860s. A narrative that focuses on Lady Audley, as the plays do, doesn't need Clara; she is crucial, however, if one reads for Robert Audley's psychological drama and his relation to Lady Audley and her secret.

20   Jameson, "Reification and Utopia in Mass Culture," 148, 147. For Foucault on power and resistance, see *The History of Sexuality, Volume 1,* 92–96. For example, "where there is power, there is resistance, and yet, or rather consequently, this resistance is never in a position of exteriority in relation to power" (95).

21   Dickens, *Bleak House,* 340.

22   Ibid., 503.

23   For a discussion of the relations between the novel (and Dickens's work in particular) and the developing institutions of advertising and consumer culture, see Jennifer Wicke, *Advertising Fictions* (New York: Columbia University Press, 1988).

24   Dickens, *Bleak House,* 340.

Four. Ghostlier Determinations

1   Wilkie Collins, *The Woman in White* (Harmondsworth: Penguin, 1974), 33. All further citations will be included in the text and refer to this edition.

2   Wilkie Collins, *The Woman in White,* ed. Harvey Peter Sucksmith (London: Oxford University Press, 1975), xxx.

3   See D. A. Miller, "From *roman policier* to *roman-police:* Wilkie Collins's *The Moonstone,*" *Novel* 13, no. 2 (Winter 1980): 153–170, for a discussion of how detection or surveillance operates through the form of multiple narration rather than through the overt intervention or representation of the police or even, finally, a detective. He argues that the novel aims to align ordinary experience with detection. For another important discussion of Collins and the social functions of the sensation novel, see Jenny Bourne Taylor, *In the Secret Theatre of Home: Wilkie Collins, Sensation Narrative, and Nineteenth-Century Psychology* (New York: Routledge, 1988).

4   Miller, "*Cage aux folles,*" 109. Although I agree with much of what Miller says, especially his argument that the sensation novel has to be read in terms of its production of bodily sensation, my reading departs from his in so far as he sees the somatic experience of sensation as a threat to be defended against, whereas I argue that it serves as a welcome screen and conduit for Walter Hartright's accession to power. Rather than having to secure himself against the feminizing, and hence debilitating, effects of sensation, Walter is able to acquire power because of his sensitivity to affect. I also argue that the somatic nature of sensation has to be read in relation to its projection onto a narrative and thus do not separate textual sensation and bodily sensation as readily as Miller does.

5   Perhaps the most conclusive instance of this phenomenon is one critic's discovery that, despite Collins's elaborate plotting, the scheme to substitute Laura for Anne was in fact technically impossible according to the dates established in the narrative. Collins corrected this error in subsequent editions, but the critic admits that the irrelevance of the supposedly all-important facts to the reader's enjoyment of the novel is testimony to the author's power: "A plot that is worked out of impossibilities, like that of robbing the almanack of a fortnight, may be treated as a jest; but we vote three cheers for the author who is able to practise such a jest with impunity. He will not have a reader the less, and all who read will be deceived and delighted" ("Appendix A," in *The Woman in White,* ed. Sucksmith, 586). That Collins could make such an error suggests that the affect produced by his mystery is more important than the solution to it.

6   My understanding of Freud's notion of deferred action is derived from his case study of the Wolfman. Of the retroactive projection of meaning onto a primal event, which may itself only be a construction of the imagination, he says, for example: "Scenes from early infancy, such as are brought up by an exhaustive analysis of neuroses . . . are not reproductions of real occurrences, to which it is possible to ascribe influence over the course of the patient's later life and over the formation of his symptoms. [The interpretation] considers them rather as products of the imagination, which find their instigation in mature life, which are intended to serve as some kind of symbolic representation of real wishes and interests, and which owe their origin to a regressive tendency, to an aversion from problems of the present" (Sigmund Freud, "From the History of an Infantile Neurosis (1918)," in *Three Case Histories,* ed. Philip Rieff [New York: Collier, 1963], 236–237).

7   Freud describes fetishism as the cathexis on an object that substitutes for the

penis the mother lacks. The fetish object both represents the threat of castration and provides reassurance against it: "He [the fetishist] retains this belief [that the mother has a penis] but he also gives it up; during the conflict between the deadweight of the unwelcome perception and the force of the opposite wish, a compromise is constructed such as is only possible in the realm of unconscious modes of thought—by the primary processes. . . . It [the fetish] remains a token of triumph over the threat of castration and a safeguard against it; it also saves the fetishist from being a homosexual by endowing women with the attribute which makes them acceptable as sexual objects" (Sigmund Freud, "Fetishism [1927]," in *Sexuality and the Psychology of Love*, ed. Rieff, 216).

Walter reassures himself against the threat posed by the woman in white (and the threat of feminization posed by his susceptibility to sensation) by finding pleasure in Laura's image. However, I don't want to read this moment simply as the sign of Walter's mastery of the shock he receives from Anne Catherick, as though that were the primal moment whose threat requires some form of reassurance. The earlier moment is no more primary than this one.

8   Neil Hertz, "Freud and the Sandman," in *The End of the Line*, 97–121.

9   Sigmund Freud, "The 'Uncanny,'" in *Standard Edition of the Complete Psychological Works of Sigmund Freud*, ed. James Strachey (London: Hogarth Press, 1953–1974), 17:237.

10   Jacques Derrida, "My Chances/*Mes Chances:* A Rendezvous with Some Epicurean Stereophonies," *Taking Chances: Derrida, Psychoanalysis, and Literature*, ed. Joseph Smith and William Kerrigan (Baltimore: The Johns Hopkins University Press, 1984), 4.

11   Karl Marx, *Capital, Volume I*, trans. Ben Fowkes (New York: Vintage, 1977), 164–165.

12   Ibid., 165.

13   Ibid., 167.

14   I am indebted to Sabrina Barton for this observation.

Five. Crying for Power

1   Raymond Chandler, *The Lady in the Lake* (New York: Vintage Books, 1976). The epigraph to this chapter is quoted from pages 89 and 90 of this edition.

2   For descriptions of the stage productions of the novel, see Sally Mitchell's introduction to *East Lynne* (New Brunswick: Rutgers University Press, 1984), vii–xviii. By March of 1863, there were three stage versions playing in New York, and "at least nine different adaptations by unknown authors were presented between 1866 and 1899." Mitchell also notes that the play finally ceased production when stock companies in rural areas were displaced by movie theaters, a fact suggesting that changes in popular consumption are governed as much by material transformations as by ideological transitions.

In the 1916 film version of *East Lynne*, Isabel was played by Theda Bara, and in the 1925 version, she was played by Alma Rubens. Both actresses were known for their portrayals of femmes fatales. Theda Bara also played the role of Lady Audley in the 1915 film version of *Lady Audley's Secret.* For an analysis of the novel, play, and film versions of *East Lynne,* see E. Ann Kaplan, *Motherhood and Representation: The Mother in Popular Culture and Melodrama* (London and New York: Routledge, 1992).

3   See, for example, Christine Gledhill, ed., *Home Is Where the Heart Is: Studies in Melodrama and the Woman's Film* (London: British Film Institute, 1987); Christina Crosby, *The Ends of History: Victorians and "The Woman Question"* (New York and London: Routledge, 1991), especially chapter 3, "History and the Melodramatic Fix"; Judith Walkowitz, "The Maiden Tribute of Modern Babylon," manuscript.

4   My analysis thus differs, for example, from that of Elaine Showalter, who reads the second half of the novel as the story of Isabel's punishment for her "surrender to impulsive passion": "the magnitude of her disciplines seems necessary as a deterrent, so tempting is her flight. . . . The urgency of Mrs. Wood's message suggests that she felt herself to be speaking to a large and desperate audience. When women found it nearly impossible to obtain a divorce and had no means of support outside marriage, fantasies of pure escape had a great deal of appeal" (*A Literature of Their Own,* 172–173). Showalter fails to consider how fantasies of suffering might also be appealing to a female audience.

5   Cited in Steve Neale, "Melodrama and Tears," *Screen* 27, no. 6 (November–December 1986): 6.

6   Franco Moretti, "Kindergarten," in *Signs Taken for Wonders* (London: Verso, 1983), 162.

7   Mrs. Henry Wood, *East Lynne* (New Brunswick: Rutgers University Press, 1984), 141. All further citations are included in the text and refer to this edition.

8   Peter Brooks has suggested that the silenced or repressed feeling or sentiment is an important mechanism for generating melodramatic pathos. I would further add that this mechanism has a particular charge for women, who are typically represented in nineteenth-century culture as suffering mutely. See Peter Brooks, *The Melodramatic Imagination: Balzac, Henry James, Melodrama, and the Mode of Excess* (New Haven: Yale University Press, 1976), especially chapter 3, "The Text of Muteness."

9   Moretti, "Kindergarten," 160, 162.

10   Hertz, "Medusa's Head," in *The End of the Line,* 206.

11   For an account of this process, see Armstrong, *Desire and Domestic Fiction.*

12   Christian Viviani, "Who Is Without Sin?: The Maternal Melodrama in American Film, 1930–39," *Wide Angle* 4, no. 2 (1980):7.

13   Mary Ann Doane, *The Desire to Desire: The Woman's Film of the 1940s* (Bloomington: Indiana University Press, 1987), 71. For the most comprehensive account of the history and theory of the genre, including a discussion of *East Lynne,* see Kaplan's *Motherhood and Representation.*

Much of my thinking about maternal melodrama has been informed by feminist discussions of Hollywood cinema. Despite the differences in period, many of the structures that Doane, Viviani, Kaplan, and others identify in the women's films of the 1930s, 1940s, and 1950s are to be found in *East Lynne.* One of the significant differences is the emphasis in the twentieth-century films on the conflicts between professional life and mothering, evident, for example, in *Mildred Pierce* or *Imitation of Life,* a structure that does the work of returning women to the home by reminding them that the price they pay for working is the loss of their children or the production of bad children. Yet, the basic mechanism that interests me, the production of irresolvable conflicts in women's affective lives, is evident in both nineteenth-century and twentieth-century narratives, as is the conflict between sexual and maternal desire. At issue in the claim that the nineteenth- and twentieth-century forms are similar is the relation between historical and psychoanalytic discourse. The use of psychoanalysis tends to imply that the maternal melodrama reveals fundamental psychic structures, but the similarity can also be attributed to melodrama's participation in the ongoing construction and maintenance of the affective economies necessary to the nuclear family under capitalism.

14   As Mary Ann Doane suggests, "Everyone has a mother, and furthermore, all mothers are essentially the same, each possessing the undeniable quality of motherliness. In Western culture, there is something *obvious* about the maternal which has no counterpart in the paternal" (*The Desire to Desire,* 70).

15   "Because the daughter's pre-oedipal ties to her mother persist throughout the oedipal period, her external and internal object worlds become triadic. This is to say that although her genital and erotic desires are focused on her father, she continues to maintain an intense emotional commitment to her mother and all that is female. . . . This finally produces in women a continuing wish to regress into infancy to reconstruct the lost intensity of the original mother-daughter bond. . . . Girls . . . feel themselves to be continuous with and related to the external object world and thus possess quite permeable ego-boundaries. As a result, they tend to experience an ongoing need for nurturance and attachment well into their adult lives. . . . If this need is not adequately addressed by a relationship with an adult male, Chodorow reasons, a woman may turn to mothering as a way of establishing that necessary relationality. By identifying with the child she mothers, she imaginatively regresses to that state where all her needs were anticipated and satisfied without any exertion on her part" (Radway, *Reading the Romance,* 136–137).

16   Jane Gallop, "Reading the Mother Tongue: Psychoanalytic Feminist Criticism," *Critical Inquiry* 13, no. 2 (Winter 1987): 314–329. Gallop discusses Chodorow's place in the collection called *The (M)other Tongue;* she argues that the attempt to valorize the mother in order to redress emphasis on the father risks forgetting how language necessarily introduces difference into any structure or positing of structure, whether pre-Oedipal or Oedipal. See also, Rose, *Sexuality in the Field of Vision.*

17   See, for example, Julia Kristeva, "L'abjet d'amour," *Tel quel* 91 (Spring 1982): 17–32. See also *Powers of Horror: An Essay on Abjection,* trans. Leon S. Roudiez (New York: Columbia University Press, 1982), and *Tales of Love* trans. Leon S. Roudiez (New York: Columbia University Press, 1987).

18   See, for example, Jean Laplanche, *Life and Death in Psychoanalysis,* trans. Jeffrey Mehlman (Baltimore: The Johns Hopkins University Press, 1976), and Samuel Weber, *The Legend of Freud* (Minneapolis: University of Minnesota Press, 1982).

19   See Jessica Benjamin, *The Bonds of Love: Psychoanalysis, Feminism, and the Problem of Domination* (New York: Pantheon, 1988).

20   An example would be Adrienne Rich's influential essay, "Compulsory Heterosexuality and Lesbian Existence," in *Powers of Desire: The Politics of Sexuality,* ed. Ann Snitow, Christine Stansell, and Sharon Thompson (New York: Monthly Review Press, 1983), 177–205.

21   Braddon, *Lady Audley's Secret,* 232.

22   For discussions of the complex relations between middle-class feminism, abolitionism, and ideologies of domesticity in nineteenth-century American culture, see Karen Sanchez-Eppler, "The Intersecting Rhetorics of Feminism and Abolition," *Representations* 24 (Fall 1988): 28–59; and Romero, "Bio-Political Resistance in Domestic Ideology and *Uncle Tom's Cabin,*" 715–734.

23   Harriet Beecher Stowe, *Uncle Tom's Cabin or, Life Among the Lowly* (Harmondsworth: Penguin, 1981), 623–624.

24   See Tompkins, *Sensational Designs: The Cultural Work of American Fiction, 1790–1860.*

25   Ibid., 146.

26   For positive assessments of the use of sentimentality by African-American women writers, see Hazel Carby's discussion of Frances Harper's *Iola Leroy* in *Reconstructing Womanhood: The Emergence of the Afro-American Woman Novelist* (New York: Oxford University Press, 1987), 62–94, and Wahneema Lubiano, "Taking Seriously the Writing and the Tears: *The Color Purple* and Genre Appropriation" (Paper presented at the Institute on Culture and Society, Summer 1989).

27   Hortense Spillers suggests the outlines of such a project in "Mama's Baby, Papa's Maybe: An American Grammar Book," *Diacritics* 17, no. 2 (Summer 1987): 75–81. She discusses, for example, the strategic representation of the African-American mother as a threat to the "normalcy" of the African-American family found in texts such as the Moynihan Report. A discourse about maternity that emphasizes the problem of excessive mothering has particularly insidious effects in the context of discussions of the African-American family, enabling the scapegoating of mothers for the effects of racist social structures.

28   Toni Morrison, "The Site of Memory," in *Out There: Marginalization and Contemporary Culture,* ed. Russell Ferguson, Martha Gever, Trinh T. Minh-ha, and Cornel West (Cambridge: MIT Press, 1991), 299–305. For a discussion of *Beloved*'s relation to slave narrative, and its engagement with the differences between Euro-American audiences and African-American audiences, see Avery Gordon, *Ghostly Memories* (Minneapolis: University of Minnesota Press, forthcoming).

29   See Douglas Crimp, "Mourning and Militancy," *October* 51 (Winter 1989): 3–18.

Six. The Inside Story

1   See, for example, Thomas P. Wolfe, "The Inward Vocation: An Essay on George Eliot's *Daniel Deronda,*" in *Literary Monographs* 8 (Madison: University of Wis-

consin Press, 1976), 1–46. Wolfe analyzes "egoism/altruism" pairings in *Daniel Deronda* and other novels, suggesting that Eliot projects her desire for rebellion onto her egoists, such as Gwendolen, and her desire for submission onto her altruists, such as Daniel. Although his analysis is useful for understanding the interdependence of these pairs of characters, Wolfe neglects the gender relations that make Gwendolen's "egoism" a very minor form of rebellion from within a social position that limits her personal agency. And Daniel's final submission to Judaism can be seen as relatively small price to pay for what in fact is his accession to patriarchal power; in bowing to the Father he becomes a father. Rebellion and submission are thus not so neatly divided between characters, and, social context, as well as psychoanalytic structures and ethical categories, must be taken into account to explain Eliot's intersubjective pairings.

2   George Eliot, *Daniel Deronda,* ed. Barbara Hardy (Harmondsworth: Penguin, 1967), 669. All further references will be cited by page number in the text and refer to this edition.

3   "Silly Novels by Lady Novelists," *Essays Of George Eliot,* ed. Thomas Pinney (London: Routledge and Kegan Paul, 1965).

4   See Jameson, "Reification and Utopia in Mass Culture," 130–148. For a discussion of modernist constructions of mass culture as feminine and thus trivial, see Andreas Huyssen, "Mass Culture as Woman: Modernism's Other," in *Studies in Entertainment,* ed. Modleski, 188–207.

5   Suzanne Graver, *George Eliot and Community* (Berkeley and Los Angeles: University of California Press, 1984), 3. Graver finds Marx, as a thinker who "puts political revolution before a revolution in sensibility," irrelevant to her project of placing Eliot within the tradition of nineteenth-century social theorists who favor the latter kind of revolution. My own interest lies in examining the relation between these two theories of social change, rather than taking their difference for granted, in order to explain why and how Eliot belongs in one camp rather than the other.

6   Eagleton, *Criticism and Ideology,* 121. For discussions of Eliot's ethical project and the politics of sympathy, see Daniel Cottom, *Social Figures: George Eliot, Social History, and Literary Representation* (Minneapolis: University of Minnesota Press, 1987); and Forrest T. Pyle, *The Ideology of the Imagination* (Stanford: Stanford University Press, forthcoming).

7   Eliot added this passage to the original manuscript at a later date, which suggests that she self-consciously attempted to locate the Grandcourts' marriage within a larger social and historical context. See the introduction to George Eliot, *Daniel Deronda,* ed. Graham Handley (Oxford: Clarendon Press, 1984), xx.

8   Implicit in my description of Grandcourt's power over Gwendolen is the model of modern power outlined in the later works of Michel Foucault, a power that consists in discipline and surveillance rather than punishment, and in the regulation rather than repression of affect and sexuality. See especially *Discipline and Punish* and *The History of Sexuality, Volume 1.* Like Foucault, Grandcourt understands that power is productive rather than negative; just as the production of sexuality as a form of transgression provides an alibi for the establishment of

institutions of social control, so too does Grandcourt's ability to produce resistance or rebellion in Gwendolen provide him with a rationale for regulating her behavior. Furthermore, Grandcourt's management of Gwendolen's behavior constitutes an exemplary instance of power as surveillance, most notably encapsulated in Foucault's discussion of Bentham's panopticon. Like the prisoners in the panopticon, Gwendolen's behavior is reguated by her own sense that she is being observed, not by her direct perception of that observation. Although Foucault does not explicitly discuss the institution of bourgeois marriage as an instance of a strategy for domination that operates without direct force, feminists have found his work useful for describing how power operates within the private and domestic spheres, as well as in accounting for the discursive construction of those spheres.

9   See Rosalind Coward, *Patriarchal Precedents: Sexuality and Social Relations* (London: Routledge and Kegan Paul, 1983), especially chapter 5, "The Concept of the Family in Marxist Theory," and Michele Barrett, *Women's Oppression Today: Problems in Marxist Feminist Analysis* (London: Verso, 1980), especially chapter 6.

10   Frederick Engels, *The Origin of the Family, Private Property, and the State,* ed. Eleanor Burke (New York: International Publishers, 1972), 128.

11   In a discussion of ownership and property in the Victorian novel, Jeff Nunokawa has described Grandcourt's endless appropriation of Gwendolen's psyche as a process by which the novel attempts to produce an instance of absolute possession or ownership. Nunokawa's focus on Victorian conceptions of property illuminates the peculiar character of the Grandcourts' marriage in ways that are congruent with my own analysis, but somewhat different in emphasis. See "The Afterlife of Property in Victorian Fiction" (Diss., Cornell University, 1989), especially chapter 3, "*Daniel Deronda* and the Afterlife of Ownership."

12   "The seller of labour-power, like the seller of any other commodity, realizes its exchange-value and alienates its use-value. He cannot take the one without giving the other. . . . The owner of the money has paid the value of a day's labour-power; he therefore has the use of it for a day, a day's labour belongs to him. On the one hand the daily sustenance of labour-power costs only half a day's labour, while on the other hand the same labour-power can remain effective, can work during a whole day, and consequently the value which its use during one day creates is double what the capitalist pays for that use; this circumstance is a piece of good luck for the buyer, but by no means an injustice towards the seller" (Marx, *Capital, Volume I*, 301).

13   Walter Benn Michaels, "The Phenomenology of Contract," *Raritan* 4, no. 2 (Fall 1984): 47–66.

14   Ibid., 64.

15   See Thomas Weiskel, *The Romantic Sublime: Studies in the Structure and Psychology of Transcendence* (Baltimore: The Johns Hopkins University Press, 1976), 93.

16   "Both the authors of the literature of the sublime and their interpreters [have] an investment in moving from the murkier regions of the pre-Oedipal or maternal into the clearer light of what Weiskel reads as a 'secondary oedipal system' and

what I would call 'the sublime of conflict and structure,' where the positions of Father, Mother, and Child are more firmly triangulated—at considerable cost, but in a reassuring fashion" (Neil Hertz, *The End of the Line,* p. 230).

17   To borrow from contemporary popular psychology, Daniel might be diagnosed as co-dependent, displacing his own anxieties and acquiring power through his concern for other people's problems. Most often used to describe women, the discourse of co-dependency, like other discourses about affect, problematically locates a social problem as an emotional and personal one, failing, for example, to account for the socialization of women as caretakers. Although it might be more respectable, Eliot's discourse is equally problematic, and the link between the two kinds of texts is useful for identifying the ambiguous nature of sympathy as a form of power. See, for example, Robin Norwood, *Women Who Love Too Much* (New York: Pocket Books, 1985).

18   Leo Bersani, "Representation and Its Discontents," in *Allegory and Representation: Selected Papers from the English Institute, 1979–80,* ed. Stephen J. Greenblatt (Baltimore: The Johns Hopkins University Press, 1981), 150. Bersani's discussion of the relations between sympathy, masochism, and sexuality draws on Laplanche's *Life and Death in Psychoanalysis,* which outlines a model of primary masochism and its pleasures. For an application of this work to Wordsworth's portraits of suffering women, see Adela Pinch, "Female Chatter: Meter, Masochism, and the *Lyrical Ballads,*" *ELH* 51 (Winter 1988): 835–852, and "Conventions of Feeling" (Diss., Cornell University, 1990).

19   "The problem, in other words, can be 'solved' only by the invention of a *displaced* totality outside the sterile detotalisation of post–Reform Bill England—a totality which is then, as it were, instantly exported, as Deronda leaves to discover his destiny in the Middle East. The difficult then is to bring this factitious totality into regenerative relation with bourgeois England—a difficulty 'solved' by Deronda's redemptive influence on the broken, dispirited victim of that society, Gwendolen Harleth. But in attempting this solution the novel splits into self-contradiction—splits, indeed, down the middle. For Daniel can only fulfill his destiny by withdrawing from Gwendolen to the Middle East, abandoning her to a nebulous Arnoldian trust in some ideal goodness. The formal dislocations of *Daniel Deronda* are the product of its attempt to overcome the ideological contradictions from which it emerges; it is in the silence between its 'Gwendolen' and 'Daniel' episodes that the truth of those contradictions speaks most eloquently" (Eagleton, *Criticism and Ideology,* 122). Eagleton is correct about the split in the novel's plots, but fails to specify that the political issues raised by Gwendolen's situation concern more that just the structure of government in "post–Reform Bill England." What is at stake is not just the distinction between utopian and real-world politics, but the definition of what is political.

20   Hertz, *The End of the Line,* 230.

21   See Sedgwick, *Between Men,* for an account of how homoerotic bonds operate as the repressed content of patriarchal relations and how women serve as the vehicle for relations between men.

22   See Benedict Anderson, *Imagined Communities: Reflections on the Origin and Spread of Nationalism* (London: Verso, 1983).

23   See Edward W. Said, "Zionism from the Standpoint of Its Victims," *Social Text* 1, no. 1 (Winter 1979): 7–58, for a discussion of the links between Zionism and European imperialism as formulated in the nineteenth century. He uses *Daniel Deronda* as an instance of how Zionism, drawing on the rhetoric of imperialism, is described as an enlightened, progressive political force that will colonize the barbaric natives. Such a connection suggests that Zionism, rather than being a utopian politics in the novel, is simply an extension of English capitalism. By identifying himself with such a cause, Daniel joins the conservative forces that produce the social structures responsible for Gwendolen's difficulties.

24   "[The sublime] is the very moment in which the mind turns within and performs its identification with reason" (Weiskel, *The Romantic Sublime,* 93–94).

Seven. The Mystery of the Commodity

1   Karl Marx, *The German Ideology,* in *The Marx-Engels Reader,* ed. Richard C. Tucker (New York: W. W. Norton, 1978), 154.

2   Althusser, "Ideology and Ideological State Apparatuses," 162.

3   See Elaine Scarry, *The Body in Pain: The Making and Unmaking of the World* (New York: Oxford University Press, 1985), especially chapter 2, "The Structure of War: The Juxtaposition of Injured Bodies and Unanchored Issues."

4   My thinking about the politics of affect in representations of war is indebted to Patrick Hagopian's work on the social memory of the Vietnam War, part of which was presented in a paper titled "Memory and Filiation: A Cultural Study of the California Vietnam Veterans Memorial" at the Institute on Culture and Society, 17 June 1991.

5   Jan Zita Grover, "Visible Lesions: Images of People with Aids," *Afterimage* 17, no. 1 (Summer 1989): 10–16. For other discussions of the cultural representation of AIDS, see Douglas Crimp, *AIDS: Cultural Analysis/Cultural Activism* (Cambridge: MIT Press, 1987), and Simon Watney, *Policing Desire: Pornography, AIDS, and the Media.*

6   For other discussions of the literary and rhetorical qualities of *Capital,* see Richard Terdiman, *Discourse/Counter-Discourse: The Theory and Practice of Symbolic Resistance in Nineteenth-Century France* (Ithaca: Cornell University Press, 1985); Robert Paul Wolff, *Moneybags Must Be So Lucky: On the Literary Structure of Capital* (Amherst: University of Massachusetts Press, 1988); Tom Keenan, "The Point Is to (Ex)change It: A Reading of a Few Pages in *Capital,*" in *Fetishism as Cultural Discourse: Gender, Commodity, and Vision,* ed. Emily Apter and William Pietz (Ithaca: Cornell University Press, forthcoming).

7   Marx, *Capital, Volume I,* 125. All further citations will be noted by volume and page number and refer to this text.

8   Karl Marx, *Capital, Vol. III* (New York: International Publishers, 1967), 48. All further citations will be noted by volume and page number and refer to this text.

9   A number of poststructuralist thinkers have noted the similarity between Marx's theory of value and Saussure's theory of the sign. Just as the signifier is arbitrary with the respect to the signified, so money is the arbitrary sign of value, rather

than having an intrinisic value or meaning. See, for example, Jean Baudrillard, *For a Critique of the Political Economy of the Sign* (St. Louis: Telos Press, 1981); Jean-Joseph Goux, *Symbolic Economies: After Marx and Freud* (Ithaca: Cornell University Press, 1990); and Gayatri Chakravorty Spivak, "Speculations on Reading Marx: After Reading Derrida," in *Post-structuralism and the Question of History,* ed. Derek Attridge, Geoff Bennington, and Robert Young (Cambridge: Cambridge University Press, 1987).

10   For a discussion of the relation between Shelley's *Frankenstein* and the rise of industrial capitalism, see Moretti, "Dialectic of Fear," in his *Signs Taken for Wonders,* 83–108.

11   For a discussion of the relations between gender and class in the development of industrial capitalism and the formation of a working class, see Joan Scott, *Gender and the Politics of History* (New York: Columbia University Press, 1988), especially "Women in *The Making of the English Working Class*" and "A Statistical Representation of Work: *La statistique de l'industrie à Paris, 1847–1848.*" The latter chapter discusses the need to examine the ideologies that govern the production of statistical documentation of labor practices. For a discussion of how representations of labor construct and are constructed by ideologies of gender and femininity, see Nancy Armstrong and Leonard Tennenhouse, "Gender and the Work of Words," *Cultural Critique* 13 (Fall 1989), 229–278.

12   For a discussion of how Marx's category of the "economic" presumes the gendered division between the market place and the home, see Linda Nicholson, "Feminism and Marx: Integrating Kinship with the Economic," *Feminism as Critique* (Minneapolis: University of Minnesota Press, 1987), 16–30.

13   *Capital* might thus be said to offer up a precursor to Donna Haraway's image of the cyborg, her figure for the deconstruction of the boundaries between technology and nature, persons and machines, and minds and bodies. Just as Haraway glimpses socialist-feminist possibilities in the development of cyborg technology, so too does Marx at moments suggest the utopian potential of industrialization, which both enslaves and frees the body. See Donna Haraway, "A Manifesto for Cyborgs: Science, Technology, and Socialist Feminism in the 1980s," in *Coming to Terms: Feminism, Theory, and Politics,* ed. Elizabeth Weed (New York: Routledge, 1989), 175–204.

14   Elaine Scarry, *The Body in Pain: The Making and Unmaking of the World* (New York: Oxford University Press, 1985), 275.

15   For a discussion of the problem of Scarry's absolute distinction between making and unmaking, and culture and power, see Mark Seltzer, "Statistical Persons," *Diacritics* 17, no. 3 (Fall 1987): 87–89. For Seltzer, Scarry fails to consider forms of power that operate on the body, not by inducing bodily pain, but by avoiding physical confrontation.

16   See Nancy Armstrong, "The Pornographic Effect: A Response," *The American Journal of Semiotics* (forthcoming). For other accounts of the connections between Marx's and Freud's theories of fetishism, see Slavoj Zizek, *The Sublime Object of Ideology* (London: Verso, 1989); and Emily Apter, *Feminizing the Fetish: Psychoanalysis and Narrative Obsession in Turn-of-the-Century France* (Ithaca: Cornell University Press, 1991).

17   For a similar argument, see Stuart Hall, "On Ideology—Marxism without Guarantees," *Journal of Communication Inquiry* 10, no. 2 (Summer 1986): 28–44.

18   For an historical account of the "invention" of the term "fetish," see William Pietz, "The Problem of the Fetish," published in three parts in *Res* 9 (Spring 1985): 5–17; *Res* 13 (Spring 1987): 23–45; and *Res* 16 (Autumn 1988): 105–23.

19   See Arjun Appadurai, *The Social Life of Things* (Cambridge: Cambridge University Press, 1986); and Michael Taussig, *The Devil and Commodity Fetishism in South America* (Chapel Hill: University of North Carolina Press, 1980).

20   Gayatri Spivak, however, argues that accounts of postmodern capitalism that emphasize the disappearance of physical or factory labor too readily dismiss Marx's relevance. She suggests that the factory has not disappeared; rather, the international division of labor has rendered it increasingly invisible to First World consumers because manufacturing has been relocated to the export processing zones of Third World nations where labor is cheap. See "Scattered Speculations on the Question of Value," in *In Other Worlds* (New York: Methuen, 1987), 154–175.

Epilogue

1   Spivak, "Scattered Speculations on the Question of Value," and "Can the Subaltern Speak?" in *Marxism and the Interpretation of Culture,* ed. Cary Nelson and Lawrence Grossberg (Urbana: University of Illinois Press, 1987), 271–313.

2   See Walter Benjamin, "Paris, Capital of the Nineteenth Century," in *Reflections,* ed. Peter Demetz, trans. Edmund Jephcott (New York: Harcourt, Brace, Jovanovich, 1978), and *Charles Baudelaire: A Lyric Poet in the Era of High Capitalism* (London: New Left Books, 1973); Fredric Jameson, "Postmodernism, or the Cultural Logic of Late Capitalism," *New Left Review* 146 (July/August 1984): 53–94; and Michael Taussig, *The Nervous System* (New York: Routledge, 1992).

Index